THE HISTORY OF THE COPTIC CHURCH
AFTER CHALCEDON

THE HISTORY OF THE COPTIC CHURCH
AFTER CHALCEDON

By

H.G. BISHOP YOUANIS

THE HISTORY OF THE COPTIC CHURCH
AFTER CHALCEDON

COPYRIGHT © 2018
St Shenouda Press

All rights reserved. Except for brief quotations in critical publications or reviews, no part of this book may be reproduced in any manner without prior written permission from the publisher.

ST SHENOUDA PRESS
8419 Putty Rd,
Putty, NSW, 2330
Sydney, Australia

www.stshenoudapress.com

ISBN 13: 978-0-6482814-1-2

All scripture quotations, unless otherwise indicated, are taken from the New King James Version®. Copyright © 1982 by Thomas Nelson, Inc. Used by permission. All rights reserved.

CONTENTS

PUBLISHER'S INTRODUCTION 7

THE WESTERN AND EASTERN CHURCH 9

THE ARAB CONQUEST OF EGYPT 31

The Islamic legislation and Dhimmis 46

THE COPTIC CHURCH UNDER
MUSLIM RULERS (642-868) 65

Important personalities of the time 78
The Plight of the Coptic Language 93
The Arab invasion of Egypt 96
Important Personalities of the Time 104
The Hermit Saints, Wilderness and Monasteries 114
Scholars and Biographers 114

THE TULUNIDS AND
THE IKHSHIDID (868-969) 117

The Reign of the Tulunids and
the Ikhshidids (868-969) 135
Important Personalities of the Time 144

THE FATIMID RULE (972-1171) 153

Important Personalities
of the Fatimid Era 186

THE CRUSADERS (1096-1292) 289

The Popes During the Ayyubid Era 297
Famous Copts During the Ayyubid Era 311

PUBLISHER'S INTRODUCTION

"I write so that you may know how you ought to conduct yourself in the house of God, which is the church of the living God, the pillar and ground of the truth."
1 Timothy 3:15

The Coptic Church indeed has a glorious history. One of the five major patriarchates along with Rome, Constantinople, Jerusalem and Antioch, the Copts have arguably been the theological leaders of the Church since the Council of Nicaea. True to her belief that Christ's Incarnation has made everything a potential means of sanctification, the Coptic Church through her famous School of Alexandria did not neglect the secular sciences either.

Persecuted by the Byzantines and then by the Arabs, the Church entered into survival mode. In her quest for survival, the Church became weakened internally also.

Yet the theological reality of the Church as the Body of Christ and the sole Ark of Salvation remained, even as some of its members succumbed to human weakness. Even in the darkest chapters of the Church's history, holy men of God were still growing in their relationship with Christ through their participation in the life of the Church.

These holy people came from all walks of life including clergy, monks, martyrs, laymen and women. Despite tough times in the Church, many of the laypeople glorified God not only in their theological studies, but also in their secular endeavours, such as engineering, science and technology, literature and medicine.

This book is an essential read for anyone interested in the history of the Church, particularly in the often neglected medieval era. Studying the history of our Church enlightens us as to where we have come from and illuminates our path ahead for the future.

THE WESTERN AND EASTERN CHURCH

The Council of Chalcedon had serious repercussions, resulting in a major division within the Church of Christ. The Byzantine Church in the West accused the Oriental Church in the East of being Monophysite, while the Oriental Church accused the Byzantine Church of being Diophysite. The Copts led the way among the Oriental churches, identifying themselves as Miaphysite Orthodox rather than Monophysite. Besides being a theological issue, this was also a manifestation Egyptian nationalism reacting against a growing Byzantine imperialism. This imperialism reached its zenith during the reign of Justinian (527-565).

We are not intending to focus our discussion on the theological component of this debate, as it is irrelevant to our current study in ecclesiastical history.

The West labelled the Alexandrian Church as Eutychian, indicating a belief in one composite nature of Christ (Monophysitism), that is, one nature which is a mixture of Christ's divinity and humanity. In reality, the Coptic Church (Miaphysite) believes that Jesus Christ is perfect in humanity and perfect in divinity and these two natures are united into one without mingling, nor confusion, nor alteration. The early Church Fathers defended this belief using the Holy Scriptures, the First Council of Nicaea (325 AD) and the teachings of Saint Cyril the Great at the First Council of Ephesus (431 AD).

There were multiple factors contributing towards the Churches of Rome and Constantinople adopting this shameful stance towards the Oriental Churches. The Alexandrian Fathers played a leading role in the first three Ecumenical Councils. It suffices to read the historian Lane-Poole in his book 'Lectures on the Eastern Churches', who says, "Then the Alexandrian Patriarch became the judge of Christianity across the universe." The History of the First Ecumenical Council in Nicaea mentions that King Constantine the Great stood in the middle of the Council, which consisted of 318 bishops from all over the Christian world to greet Athanasius the Deacon, who later became the Archbishop of Alexandria. King Constantine said to Athanasius, "You are the hero of the Church of God." Then the Fourth Council was held at Ephesus in 449 AD, under the chairmanship of Archbishop Dioscorus, and it was dominated by the Church of Alexandria. Consequently, Rome and Constantinople were both deeply disturbed. The West described this Second Council of Ephesus as a Council of Robbers, reflecting their anger against the Alexandrian Church and its fathers. Marcian and the Western Churches unified their efforts to gather about six hundred bishops to attend the Council of Chalcedon. At this later Council, they overruled the decisions of the Second Ephesus Council,

MIAPHYSITE

The Coptic Orthodox Church was accused of being 'Monophysite' in the Council of Chalcedon. The term monophysite comes from two Greek words meaning "single nature". Monophysitism merged Christ's humanity into His divinity so that effectively it meant that in Christ there was one composite nature. This is NOT what the Coptic Orthodox believes. We believe that "Christ's divinity parted not from His humanity, not for a single moment nor a twinkling of an eye" and we recite this statement in every liturgy. As a result, we are Miaphysite and not Monophysite. Miaphysitism ("one nature") means the Lord Jesus Christ is perfectly human and perfectly divine and these two natures are united together without mingling, nor confusion, nor alteration into one nature.

The Byzantine Orthodox Churches who were accused of believing in two natures (Diophysitism) were wrongly understood to be denying the unity between the two natures of Christ. In the recent dialogue, the two churches confessed their belief in the union of the two natures according to the formula of St. Cyril of Alexandria Miaphysis, tou theo tou logo se sarkomeeni, which means one nature for the incarnated Logos of God.

stating bluntly the global supremacy of the Roman See over the rest of Christian Sees.

The governing authority in Constantinople attempted to impose the teachings of Chalcedon on the Eastern Churches. But the Eastern Churches, led by the Alexandrian Church, stood strong against those heretics, despite their ranks. The Eastern Christians, preferred martyrdom to complacency in their faith. Countries like Egypt, Palestine, Iraq, Armenia, Persia and Syria passed through serious turmoil.

On 7th of February 452 AD, Marcian issued a decree to excommunicate any clergyman or dignitaries that would discuss this doctrinal issue publicly. Marcian additionally stirred severe persecution against the Orthodox believers. Many bishops, priests, monks and believers were martyred for refusing to submit to the decrees of the Council of Chalcedon. Yet, some bishops submitted to those decrees, in order to satisfy the king. Such bishops were the cause for shedding much righteous blood, especially in Egypt and Palestine.

The event of Chalcedon, namely the defeat of the Alexandrian Church and its humiliation in the defrocking and exile of Archbishop Dioscorus of Alexandria, was not the end of the conflict - it was only the beginning. An imperial messenger arrived to Alexandria bearing a decree to depose Archbishop Dioscorus, appointing in his place an Alexandrian priest Proterius (452-457 AD). The decree was executed by force. The messenger from Marcian also delivered a message threatening severe punishment for any person who dared to object. The Copts did not accept this decree and went out demonstrating throughout Alexandria. A new era of persecution had begun. It is believed that the martyrs were numbered in the thousands. Someone stated the number to be 24,000, mostly bishops, priests and monks.

Among the martyrs was Saint Tkoy from Upper Egypt. He lived in Alexandria, and the Governor attempted to force him to sign the Chalcedonian decree but he firmly refused. One of the soldiers kicked Tkoy, who fell and died instantly, for he was an elder. Other bishops who refused to sign were exiled.

Marcian died in February 457 AD and was succeeded by Leo I (457-474 AD). The Alexandrians captured the opportunity to ordain a successor for Archbishop Dioscorus, who had deceased on the 4th September 454 AD. Archbishop Timothy II (the 26th Patriarch) was enthroned on the 16th of March 457 AD. This led to the split of the Alexandrian bishopric into two chains of archbishops, the Melkites and the Copts. The Melkites were of Greek origin, usually ordained in Constantinople and endorse the Council of Chalcedon, whereas the Copts do not. The Copts were patriotic and rejected both Roman and the Greek authority. After the enthronement of Pope Timothy II, he held a Council at Alexandria where he condemned the Council of Chalcedon. Accordingly, he was arrested by the Governor of Alexandria and was exiled to Abu Sir. As a consequence, the number of killings noticeably grew.

The civilian authority did not pay any attention to this

split within the Alexandrian Church that resulted from introducing a new Patriarch who was a supporter of Chalcedon Council. During these times, the Governor of Alexandria was occupied with fighting both in North Africa and in Upper Egypt (against the Blemyes). The Alexandrians seized this opportunity and attacked Pretorius and dragged him through the streets of Alexandria. They burnt his body as a sign of revenge. This incident happened on the 28th March 457 AD. This prompted Pope Leo's decree to exile Pope Timothy II to Gangra in Paphlagonia where Pope Dioscorus had been exiled. Pope Timothy II had devoted his efforts in writing against the Nestorians, Chalcedonians and Eutychians.

After the exile of Archbishop Timothy, the Chalcedonians ordained an intruding Patriarch, Timothy Salophaciolus, by the decree of Emperor Zeno. The Alexandrians boycotted him, and instead resorted to monasteries for worship. In the meantime, they did not cease to appeal requesting the re-instatement of Pope Timothy from his exile. Emperor Zeno was deposed by Basiliscus who became the new emperor. In 476 AD, Basiliscus decreed the re-instatement of Pope Timothy. It seems that Basiliscus' motive for this decree was to gain the support of the Alexandrians. Pope Timothy arrived at Constantinople and received an adoring reception by the believers and was hosted at the royal palace. Many visited him for blessings and in the hope of healing. From Constantinople, Pope Timothy went to Ephesus then to Alexandria. At Alexandria he was given a fervent reception by the congregation, clergy, monks and nuns. Everyone was cheering saying, "Blessed is He who comes in Name of the Lord." Pope Timothy entered the Cathedral after the intruding pope left it. With the permission of the Emperor, Pope Timothy transferred the body of Pope Dioscorus in a silver casket to Alexandria, where a great memorial service was held. The body was then placed in the Papal burial place.

In 476 AD, Pope Timothy II asked Emperor Basiliscus to issue a decree denouncing Pope Leo's Tome, as well as the extra doctrinal clauses that were added by the Council of Chalcedon. Basiliscus accepted this request and held a Council at Constantinople, attended by five hundred bishops, under the leadership of the Alexandrian Pope Timothy and Peter II of Antioch. This Council condemned the decisions of the Council of Chalcedon and Leo's Tome. Paul, a monk from Alexandria, wrote down the decision of this Council. The decision emphasised the necessity of adopting three Ecumenical Councils, Constantinople 381 AD, Ephesus the First 431, and Ephesus the Second 449 AD. The decision also commanded the burning of Leo's Tome wherever it existed. The decision was endorsed by Pope Timothy the Alexandrian, Peter of Antioch, Paul the Ephesian, Bishops of Asia Minor, Anastasius of Jerusalem, bishops of Jerusalem and many other totalling about seven hundred bishops. Bishop Acacius, the Patriarch of Constantinople, was hesitant to sign.

King Zeno and Orthodoxy

Acacias the Patriarch of Constantinople was concerned about the victory achieved by the Orthodox under the leadership of Pope Timothy. Acacias convoked the clergy and monks of Constantinople. Basiliscus had to reverse his previous decree, for the political atmosphere was not in his favour; Zeno had prepared a great army to fight him in order to restore his throne. Zeno was successful in reclaiming his throne, expelling Basiliscus in September 476 AD. Zeno also issued a decree to abolish that of Basiliscus and to exile both Paul the Ephesian and Peter the Bishop of Antioch. He also sent to Pope Timothy of Alexandria to threaten him. Pope Timothy passed away in 477 AD. The Orthodox people enthroned Pope Peter III as his successor, known as Peter the Mongus (477-490 AD – 27th Patriarch). Peter III was a disciple of Pope Dioscorus and had been his Archdeacon. Immediately upon his enthronement, Peter III held a synod where he disavowed the Council of Chalcedon and Leo's Tome. Zeno threatened him. Peter III was forced into hiding in the believers' houses around Alexandria. In the meantime, the King re-instated the Chalcedonian Patriarch Timothy Salophaciolus, but he passed away in 482 AD. The Copts begged to the King to maintain Peter Mongus as their sole Pope, but the king rejected their petition. Another Chalcedonian Patriarch was enthroned, John Talaia, who was fully endorsed by Rome. He was neither on good terms with the palace nor with the Church of Constantinople. He ended up fleeing to Rome. In the meantime, Acacius the Patriarch of Constantinople (471-489 AD) and Peter III (Peter Mongus) became acquainted. Zeno was losing hope in winning the Alexandrian Orthodox to his side.

Henoticon

A new way to achieve ecclesiastical peace was was proposed, known as Henoticon. The term Henoticon means 'the act of union' or 'the creed of union.' Both Emperor Zeno and Acacius the Patriarch of Constantinople had Chalcedonian inclinations. Basiliscus' decree, albeit short-lived, proved the strength of the Orthodox and the need to establish peace with them. Acacius was the one who formulated the Henoticon. Both he and the emperor aimed at restoring the Church to the united Christian belief pre-Chalcedon. In 482 AD, he was able to convince the Emperor Zeno of this new strategy of his. The Henoticon admitted the decrees of the first three Ecumenical Councils and banned Nestorius, Eutyches and their followers. However, the Henoticon did not touch on the core of the issue - Monophysitism.

The decree was a message from the Emperor Zeno to the bishops, clergy, monks and believers in Alexandria, Egypt, Libya and five western cities.

The Henoticon may be summarised in the following quotation:

> *"It is only our perfect faith that protects us from everything. The sons of God, the abbots and monks, pleaded in tears for the union of the blessed churches. The churches were separated by the act of evil a while ago. Many believers died without receiving the sacrament of Baptism. Others died without the Eucharist. Many died and shed their blood, which enriched our the air and soil of our land. Hence we decided, we and the*

> *Orthodox Church all over the universe, with the archbishops, that we do not know any other faith but that instituted by our saintly fathers who gathered at Ephesus and we anathematise Nestorius and his followers. We also anathematise Eutyches. We accept the twelve chapters written by Pope Cyril, the blessed Alexandrian Pope. We believe that the Only Son of God and Lord Jesus Christ, Who descended and truly Incarnated of the Holy Spirit and of Mary the Mother of God, is of one divine nature with the Father and took our human nature in one nature not two. The tortures that He endured in the body befell the only begotten son of God... We are not introducing a new faith or belief. We are merely demonstrating the necessity to anathematise all opposing beliefs, whether resultant from the Council of Chalcedon or other Councils. Beliefs like those of Nestorius or Eutyches are purely a figment of their imagination."*

From the above, we can conclude that the Henoticon was a big step towards our Orthodox way of thinking. The immediate result was closeness between the Churches of Alexandria and Constantinople. The Roman Church, however, was not particularly welcoming to the Henoticon.

In 482 AD some Alexandrian scholars approached Zeno, to petition him in relation to their Patriarch Pope Peter III (Mongus). They narrated before Zeno the consequences that befell the believers because of the Council of Chalcedon. The King was convinced that the Patriarch should be reinstated but under two conditions: (1) the endorsement of the Henoticon and (2) the re-union with other bishops endorsing the Henoticon.

Reaction in Alexandria

Pope Peter discovered that the Henoticon was not opposed to the Orthodox faith. For the Henoticon accepted the faith and the decrees of the first Ecumenical Councils, the anathemas imposed by Cyril the Great the 12th Patriarch, and condemned Nestorius and Eutyches. Pope Peter accepted the Henoticon and promised the acceptance of those who accept it.

Some clergymen took a hard line and maintained their reservations towards the Henoticon. Their main objection was the absence of a direct anathema to the additional clauses introduced in the Council of Chalcedon. They even attacked Patriarch Peter for its acceptance. In response, Pope Peter anathematised Leo's Tome and the Council of Chalcedon to avoid controversy.

Reaction in Rome

In 484 AD, Felix, Bishop of Rome, held a council to anathematise Acacius, despite the imprisonment of his representatives at Constantinople at the command of Zeno. At Constantinople, mentioning the name of Bishop of Rome was banned. The split between Constantinople and Rome was great and was historically known within the Catholic Church as the Schism of Acacius. This schism lasted for 35 years.

Successors of Zeno

Acacias died in 489 AD, and Peter Mongus died in 490 AD, and King Zeno in 491 AD. Despite their death, the Henoticon was endorsed by the new Emperor Anastasius I (491-518 AD). Bishops of Constantinople had to sign the Henoticon at the time of their ordination. This policy remained in effect until the death of Anastasius. It was in this period when Saint Severus of Antioch (512-518 AD) rose to prominence as a great defender of the Miaphysites in his theological sermons.

The pendulum swung in the opposite direction when Emperor Justin I (518-527 AD) was enthroned, aided by his cousin, Justinian. Both were Chalcedonians. Severus of Antioch was deposed and fled to Egypt. Unity between the Churches of Constantinople and Rome was restored with the efforts of Hormisdas, Bishop of Rome. Hormisdas sent representatives to the Palace of Constantinople with another statement of faith, cursing Nestorius, Eutyches, Dioscorus, Acacius, and all their followers.

Justinian

Justinian was enthroned (527-565 AD). As a successor of Roman Caesars, he felt a duty to restore the Roman Empire, as an Empire with one faith, one belief and one church. He was determined to achieve the union of the church as an essential step to control it. He was a Chalcedonian, and showed favouritism towards the Chalcedonians. In the meantime, he backed off any confrontation with the non-

Chalcedonians. His wife, Empress Theodora, practiced Orthodoxy secretly. She strongly defended the Orthodox believers but was wise in her support to avoid the anger of the Emperor. She was a strong religious woman, and her influence impacted the development of the State's religious policies. Due to her efforts, Justinian allowed the Orthodox bishops to return to their sees and dioceses. He also required them to dialogue and debate with their opponents. Thus, Severus of Antioch was able to return to Constantinople in 533 AD, leading a strong group for that purpose. He remained there for a year.

In 544 AD, Justinian issued a creed condemning the baptism of Nestorians, a creed known as Tria Kephaiaia. The three referenced in this creed were, Theodore of Mopsuestia, Theodoret of Cyrus and Ibas of Edessa. The Eastern Churches welcomed this condemnation but the Western Churches were hesitant. The issue settled with the death of Justinian. He was succeeded by Justin II (565-578 AD), who issued another Henoticon in 571 AD.

Circumstances in Egypt

Egypt had a deteriorated administrative system. The religious conflict was probably a fundamental reason for this deterioration. The State's forces supported the Melkites, while the Copts were relying on their own capabilities. This period had seen a growing sense of national patriotism. The barbarians were 'flying' at the Egyptian borders like harmful crows. Hence, Justinian divided Egypt into two administrative divisions, Alexandria and Lower Egypt under a prefect, and Upper Egypt under another prefect. Justinian aimed at the alleviation of burdens on a sole-governor. But this process of division was the seed for further deterioration and administrative failure.

Justinian also initiated a policy that had a terrible effect on Copts and the political future of Egypt. When he enthroned Appolinarius on the Alexandrian See in 541 AD, he, Justinian, allocated Appolinarius considerable military capacity in order to support his religious policy. This enabled the Melkite Patriarch to directly impose and collect taxes for the maintenance of churches. This was a serious precedent for the successive patriarchs. They provided their followers with means to annoy their religious enemies and to renew the religious persecution, but this time, Christians fought against Christians. The catastrophe began by the intruding Bishop Appolinarius, and the result was a horrifying public slaughter.

However, Justinian may be commemorated by his keen interest in abolishing Paganism. He sent missions to Nubia. Justinian also closed the pagan Temple of Isis at Philla and the Temple of Amus at the Oasis of Siwah. These temples were replaced with Christian churches. Additionally, he built the Monastery of Saint Catherine at the Mount of Sinai. This Monastery was known previously as the Monastery of Conversion (the conversion of bread and wine into His Body and Blood.)

Monotheletism

The remaining years of Byzantine rule were characterised by sadness and misery. Constantinople was the controlling authority and greedily abused Egypt's resources. There was also the competition between the two prefects in Egypt that led to disturbance and uncertainty in governmental affairs. Thus, Egypt was exposed to divisions from the inside and the threat of invasion from the outside. Gangs appeared within cities, robbing some cities like Abu Sir (a city close to Alexandria). Each of the prefects was preoccupied with the deposition of the other prefect, in order to overtake power in the other city. The throne of Emperor Phocas (602-610 AD) was unstable. He was defeated by an invader: Emperor Hercules, who was a Byzantine leader of armies in African countries. Hercules crossed the Mediterranean and overtook the throne in 610 AD.

The Persian army, under leadership of Chasroes Parirz, invaded the Asian nations of Syria and Palestine. At the time of the enthronement of Hercules (610-641 AD), the Persian army was in close proximity to the city of Antioch. In 613 AD, he entered Damascus. In 614 AD, Jerusalem fell to him. He carried away the Holy Cross and the tools used for torturing Jesus Christ. In 619 AD a Persian army division was directed towards Egypt and it remained occupied by the Persians for about ten years.

The Roman Empire

The status of the Roman Empire was saddening. Hercules

was considering fleeing to Carthage, North Africa. The Byzantine Patriarch Sergios offered the funds of the church to undertake a mission to retrieve the Holy Cross. Hercules planned to press the Persians near Constantinople in order to oblige them to withdraw from Egypt. The withdrawal took place in 627 AD. Hercules was able to retrieve the Holy Cross and placed it in the Holy Sepulchre in Jerusalem.

Egypt came under Byzantine government one more time. Hercules did not learn his lesson. He implemented the policies of Justinian and appointed a Melkite Patriarch, who became a Prefect for all of Egypt. The prefect was given wide authorities: religious, military, financial, administrative and judicial. Hercules attempted to attract the Orthodox to his side, without jeopardising his relationship with Western Chalcedonians. He rephrased a new theological belief, to replace the partially successful Henoticon. Hercules united with Sergios, the Patriarch of Constantinople (610-638 AD). In 622 AD, he proclaimed the new theological belief known as Monotheletism, meaning "One Will" of Christ. It was hoped that would this replace the assumed monophysitism in Syria and Egypt.

The Monotheletism focused on the singleness of both Divine Willing and the Human Will, both being identical, compatible, and unchangeable. Hercules hoped that the Orthodox would accept this new belief, and that this belief did not contradict that of the Chalcedonians.

Some church leaders, from both sides, initially accepted this belief. Among those were Athanasius, Patriarch of Antioch

(621-629 AD) and Honorius, Bishop of Rome (625-638 AD). That acceptance continued among Lebanese Maronites but was strongly objected to by Western bishops.

In 638 AD, Hercules printed his Creed, known as Ecthesis, and was determined to force all parties to accept it. The greatest resistance to this Decree was among the Copts of Alexandria. The Copts rejected any Chalcedonian decree or resolution. They did not wish to be distanced from the belief of Athanasius and Cyril. Also, the Copts were extremely patriotic. They were very adamant not to change their long-standing traditions.

Egypt was of special status to the Empire. It was a prime wheat store. Hence, Hercules was determined to impose his belief by each and every possible means. The first step in his plan was to appoint Cyrus, Bishop of Phasis (around the Black Sea), as a Melkite Patriarch for Alexandria and the Prefect for Egypt, on the condition that he, Cyrus, neither oppress the Copts nor oblige them to accept either Chalcedonianism or Monotheletism. (Cyrus is known in Arabic references as Al-Mokawkas). He arrived to Alexandria in 631 AD. He introduced a harsh plan, and within ten years, he became one of the most hated tyrants in history of Egypt.

The popularity of Hercules declined after the once-extraordinary status that he attained when he retrieved the Holy Cross. He persecuted the Copts, the bishops and nationalists. The Book of 'The History of the Patriarchs' records that in the tenth century tremendous hardships and burdens befell the Orthodox believers by Cyrus.

Consequently, many had gone astray, many were tortured, many were bribed, and many were misled. Among those were Cyrus, Bishop of Nikus, Victor, Bishop of Fayoum and many others, who betrayed the Orthodox faith. Those that betrayed the faith were not obedient to the command of the blessed Pope Benjamin.

Pope Benjamin I (38th Patriarch, 633-662 AD) fled to a minor monastery in Upper Egypt. He disappeared until the time of the Arab Conquest. Among those who suffered during the same period, was Mina, brother of Pope Benjamin, as described in 'The History of the Patriarchs', "The blessed Mina, brother of Pope Benjamin, was arrested and tortured, by all cruelty, until his death by being thrown in the sea."

The mere visits of Al-Mokawkas both to Upper and Lower Egypt caused enormous horror. Usage of whips for tortures was the norm. Confiscation of ecclesiastical assets was all too common. Monasteries were not any safer than churches. Monks either fled or were arrested and tortured to death. Bishop Samuel the Confessor of Qalamon, Fayoum, was dragged by chains, as if he were a criminal. After excessive tortures, his followers could secretly brought him back, in a near-death condition.

The Copts

The Copts were greatly humiliated. The Coptic Orthodox Church bore the brunt of this blasphemous Melkite. The Church powerfully sustained these burdens, and remained united and alive, despite the weakness of some of its sons and their diversion off the right path. The Copts held massive hatred toward Byzantine persecution. They reflected their hatred in their Coptic literature and Coptic arts. The gap had widened between the Coptic Church and the Byzantine Church. The disagreement surpassed all reasonable limits.

The shining stars of this period included, Saint Pisentius, Bishop of Qift, Bishop Youanes of Borolos, and Bishop Daniel, of Shehit. The Arab Conquest began, indicating the commencement of a new era for the ancient Alexandrian Church.

Persian Invasion of Egypt

We ought to briefly discuss the Persian occupation that lasted for ten years (617-627 AD), where they destroyed and demolished numerous churches and monasteries.

The hatred between the Romans and the Persians was long-standing. Each party aimed at possessions of the other party. The Persians took the opportunity of the weakness of the Byzantine Empire. After the Persians conquered the Levant, they went towards Egypt. Other previous Persian invaders, Cambeez, and Alexander the Great, followed the same route that was followed by the Arabs later on. All marched from El-Arish, parallel to Mediterranean Coast, to Farama, then to Memphis, Rasheed, Nikus then to Alexandria.

Alexandria was strongly fortified. The Persians failed to invade it in year 500 AD. However this time, Alexandria was weak. It contained several races, like Romans, Syrians and Jewish, beside its patriotic Copts. Several students and refugees also inhabited Alexandria, and all had no common strong link between them.

Sources mentioned that the betrayer who facilitated the conquest of Alexandria was not a Copt, but a student seeking education. He came from a place in northeast Arabia, and we do not know his religion, whether Christian, Jew or pagan. We do not know a motive for this betrayal other than the fact that his country of origin was under the Persian control.

Severus, the author of 'The History of the Patriarchs', states that the Persians extended their barracks around Alexandria. They vented their anger on nearby monasteries, confiscating their assets and possessions. It was said that the number of nearby monasteries approached 600. The monks did not take protective measures against a possible Persian invasion. Monks were killed by the sword and churches were also demolished. Upon entering Alexandria, the Persians killed numerous of its inhabitants. Some were taken as captives to Persia. Among the rescued was Pope Andronikus (616-623 AD), although it was said he was well treated at the hands of his captors. His life ended in sadness at what had befallen the Copts and Egypt.

While Alexandria was on the verge of falling to the Persians, its Prefect and John, the Melkite Patriarch fled to Constantinople on a ship.

After the fall of Alexandria, the Persians marched to the

south, parallel to the Nile, heading toward Upper Egypt. The Persian leader had the very same strategy towards all Copts: killing and destruction! When the Persian army reached Nikus; an enemy reported that some monks were in hiding in a nearby mountain. The army leader surrounded the mountain and killed all monks therein.

The Persians reached the furthest point in Upper Egypt. They spread death and destruction wherever they went. They carried out enormous disasters. We have a manuscript citing a prophecy by Bishop Shenouda the Archimandrite about the Persian invasion to Egypt, and the destruction they would cause. It is to be noted that Saint Shenouda the Archimandrite died about 166 years before the invasion. Also **Saint Pisentius**, Bishop of Qift mentioned the invasion of the Persians and the fate of Copts under this invasion.

Hercules did not send an army to expel the Persians, but led a fierce attack in 627 AD, leading to the retreat of the Persians and their withdrawal from Egypt.

THE ARAB CONQUEST OF EGYPT

Egypt Before the Arab Conquest

Egypt was administered by the Justinian system, administratively, military and civilian. Emperor Justinian organised the Byzantine army into a decentralised system, to eliminate the possibility off an army leader splitting off and seeking the independency of Egypt from Constantinople. Additionally, Justinian divided Egypt into five divisions, each governed by a prefect appointed by the Emperor. The prefects were selected among the local citizens to ensure their religious loyalty to Constantinople. These prefects held both civilian and military authority. Yet, there was no common administrative union between these divisions, due to the weak authority shown by the Byzantine Prefect of Alexandria.

During the sixth and seven centuries, Egypt was no longer a Byzantine region, as the Byzantine influence was very weak over Egypt. The relationship between Egypt and Byzantium was purely a financial one, where Egypt, annually, used to send its portion of wheat and seeds to Constantinople. That was the sole concern of Constantinople. Imposed taxes were a cause for complaint, not to mention the aggressive methods used to collect these taxes.

The Arab Conquest

The arrival of Arabs to Egypt was of utmost importance; it re-arranged the history of the Middle East. Arabs, in particular, knew the entire region including Egypt before the inception of Islam, as Arab dealers used to pass through Egypt via the Red Sea and the Eastern deserts.

Amro Ibn-el-Ass himself, who led the attack on Egypt, was said to have had some dealings with many Arab countries and around the Nile valley. It is probable that he visited Alexandria where he witnessed its elegance and wealth. After conquering the Levant in the Battle of Yarmuk in 636 AD, and the surrender of Jerusalem in 638 AD, Amro was adamant to request permission from Omar Ibn el-Khattab to conquer Egypt, the most prized Byzantine region. He was also aware that the Persians had conquered Egypt twice, and that the Arabs defeated the Persians at el-Qadeseya in 636 AD.

The Arab Conquest of Egypt 33

After some hesitation, Ibn el-Khattab permitted Ibn-el-Ass to conquer Egypt. Yet again Ibn el-Khattab considered postponing the conquest as he had concerns about the potential consequences. Ibn el-Khattab wrote to Ibn-el-Ass asking him to retreat if he had not passed the Egyptian borders. The army consisted of 4000 militants.

Ibn-el-Ass followed the very path followed by earlier invaders. The path, along the northern border of the Peninsula of Sinai, was parallel to the Mediterranean Sea, from Arish to Farama. The Farama, known as Pelsium, of the Eastern shore of Port Said, was the northern opening of Egypt. It contained numerous monuments for churches and monasteries. Farama fell to the Arabs after a one-month siege in 640 AD. A month later, Belbeis fell too, after a massive battle that costed the Byzantine a thousand deaths and three thousand captives, and many from the Arab side as well.

The Arabs progressed to the Babylon fortifications at the head of the Delta, overlooking the northern and the southern parts of Egypt. These barracks were built by Emperor Trajan and was known as the Palace of Wax. Few remnants can still be seen next to the Hanging Church, Old Cairo. The Arabs surrounded the barracks for quite some time. Military supplements, led by el-Zobeir Ibn el-Awam, arrived to the Arabs at the barracks. The Arabs were able to conquer the village of Omm Denein (Tindonias) north of the barracks. Nowadays, this is known as the el-Azbakeya, more specifically, the area of Awlad Anan (Sons of Anan). It was replaced by the Mosque of el-Fatah, immediately adjacent to

Ramsis Square in the centre of Cairo. The Byzantine soldiers retreated to the area of Ain Shams. Other supplementary forces arrived to Memphis (near to what is known currently as el-Badrashein). The Arabs then conquered el-Fayoum. All these cities were conquered during 640 AD.

El-Mokawkas offered negotiations and the surrender of the barracks. According to Alfred J. Butler,[1] El-Mokawkas was also known as Keros, who was neither a Copt nor a patriot. El-Mokawkas submitted his offer, through a messenger from Ibn el-Ass, on the 6th of April 631 AD. The Coptic Church was celebrating Good Friday on that day. The Arabs surrounded the barracks for over seven months. The reply of Ibn-el-Ass was,

> "You have one of the following three options. Firstly, to convert to Islam and become our brothers, and 'you have what we have and we have what you have', secondly, if you reject the conversion, you must pay the jizyah, or thirdly, fight us till God judge between us."

The Romans refused to submit to the Arabs. They were determined to continue fighting. El-Mokawkas wrote these conditions to Hercules. Hercules replied to El-Mokawkas and to the Roman leader blaming them for their retreat before the Arabs. During that time, el-Zobeir Ibn el-Awam was able to escalate the siege, and ordered his soldiers to pray loudly when they hear him pray.

This took place during the night. The Romans thought that

---

[1] An articulate scholar who wrote a book entitled 'The Arab Conquest'.

the Arabs conquered the barracks successfully, so they fled the place. El-Zobeir then proceeded to the barracks and opened it. Those inside the barracks requested reconciliation with the Arabs. The Copts posed the following conditions in order to accept the reconciliation:

1- Each Copt that decides to remain a Copt is to pay two denarii annually, exempting elders, women, children and the needy.

2- Muslims are not to attack churches and not to interfere with the affairs of the Copts.

After the surrender of the Babylon barracks, Amro Ibn el-Ass progressed to Alexandria. The Romans were ready for a decisive battle with the Arabs. Hercules intended to supervise this battle personally, but he died untimely. His death greatly undermined the morale of the Romans. Amro Ibn el-Ass surrounded Alexandria for fourteen months. The Byzantine Empire was full of civilian troubles due to death of Hercules, and the greed of many to acquire the throne. The sole objective of the Byzantines was to terminate the confrontation with the Arabs through a treaty in order to attend to their domestic problems. Kyros went to Babylon requesting reconciliation and was successful in reaching a second treaty known as the 'Treaty of Alexandria' or the 'Treaty of Babylon.' This Treaty considered Copts as dhimmis. Following the Treaty of Alexandria, the influence of the Arabs extended gradually over every region within Egypt. Then Amro Ibn el-Ass progressed to Pentapolis[2] and,

---

[2] Also known as the Five Western Cities - trans.

he imposed jizyah. He also sent troops to Nubia under the leadership of Amro Abdallah Ibn Saad Ibn Abi-Sarah in 642 AD.

At that time, Nubia was an independent kingdom, and it was too strong for the Arabs. Amro Ibn el-Ass ordered Amro Abdallah Ibn Saad Ibn Abi-Sarah to retreat immediately. In 651 AD, Amro Abdallah Ibn Saad Ibn Abi-Sarah re-attempted the attack on Nubia. After a fierce battle, a political and financial treaty was reached between Egypt and the Nubian Christian Kingdom.

JIZYAH

A poll tax, or capitation tax, was imposed on all able-bodied non-Muslim subjects of the Islamic state. It was required of Dhimmis, who were Christians, Jews, and other monotheistic non-Muslims with a protected status. They were barred from enlisting in Islamic armies, and their poll tax was supposed to pay for Muslims to take their place in fighting the battles of Islam. The jizyah was totally independent of the Kharaj, which was levied on land rather than individuals. The jizyah, fixed in the seventh century by Caliph 'Umar ibn al-Khattat, originally amounted to forty-eight dirhems for the rich, twenty-four for the middle class, and twelve for the poor. This estimate, however, was subject to greater increase by the imams, who did not hesitate to multiply it under later Caliphs.

The Romans attempted to liberate Alexandria by sending a huge fleet in 645 AD. The Byzantines were able to retrieve Alexandria. They crept forward to further regions in Lower Egypt. These events took place during the governorship of Osman Ibn Effan, who sent Amro Ibn-el-Ass when the situation became critical. Amro Ibn-el-Ass was successful in his mission; he defeated the Byzantines and killed their leader, thus, ending the Roman era in Egypt. Ultimately, the Arabs became fully established in Egypt.

Reasons for the victory of Arabs

The victory of the Arabs over the Romans is astonishing, considering their number and their power. How could Amro Ibn-el-Ass with four thousand soldiers conquer Egypt and how did it surrender? We may briefly summarise the reasons in the following points:

Religious reasons, as per the Byzantine Empire's aforesaid attempt to subject the Copts to their belief. They used all possible means to achieve this using oppression and persecution. Many were martyred while defending their belief. The oppression and persecution lasted for 190 years, i.e. between the Council of Chalcedon till the Arab Conquest. The religious enthusiasm among the Muslim fighters also cannot be overlooked. This particular factor remained constant since the era of the Prophet when he controlled the Arabian Peninsula through his attempts to reach treaties and contracts with the Christian tribes. In 630 AD, the Prophet wrote to the Christians of Nagran (Yemen) asking them to enter a treaty with him. The Nagran tribe sent a messenger to negotiate with Mohammed in an attempt to obtain the best conditions. The messenger made it very clear that the Nagran Tribe would maintain their Christian faith at any cost. Upon their arrival, the Nagranic messengers met Mohammed, who instantly invited them to adopt Islam. Ibn Khaldon mentions another incident. When Omar Ibn el-Khattab became a Caliph, he gave a sermon calling the Muslims to conquer Iraq, saying, "Expand on the earth that Allah promised you would inherit." A common condition in all treaties between Muslims and any oppressed nation was: adopt Islam or pay the jizyah or die by the sword. Economic factors, for the Arabs, coming as they did from an area bereft of resources, made them quite desperate to enjoy the riches of conquered nations. The military factor contributing to the Arab Conquest was the fact that the Roman army was of low in determination and morale.

The Stance of the Copts towards the Invaders

It is almost certain that the Copts were passive towards the invaders, meaning they neither cooperated with them nor opposed them. A question remains: who assisted the Arabs through the conquest? According to Severus Ibn el-Moqafaa, Emperor Hercules had a dream that a circumcised nation would overthrow him and prevail over the whole earth. Hercules thought initially that this nation was the Jewish nation. He ordered that all Jewish and Samaritans, all over the Empire, be baptised. These actions made the Jewish people offer assistance to the Arabs. They provided the Arabs with all needed information. They assisted the

Arabs in Syria and in Egypt.³ Butler further explains, that:

"There was no single Copt engaged in the battle. It is wrong to assume that the Copts were able to meet or fight or negotiate with the Arabs."[4]

The Copts did not regard the Arabs as liberators to their country. The Copts were completely ignorant of the Arabs' intentions. The Copts were not aware that the Arabs would impose Islam on them. The Copts were very strenuous in rejecting Chalcedonian beliefs and even faced the Emperor to defend their faith. Had the Copts known that the Arabs would impose a new religion on them; they would not have possibly accepted a new religion. The Arabs spoke neither Greek nor Coptic. Relatively, the Arabs showed more mercy in their battles than shown by the Persians. Yet the Arabs still often behaved barbarically in battle. The Arabs could not win the sympathy of the majority of the people.

Bishop John of Nikus mentions examples of deeds committed by the Arabs in his Chronology, the only contemporary source of the Arab Conquest. He tells us that Omar ordered the arrest of Roman judges, putting their hands and feet in fetters and wooden sticks. He seized taxes from peasants by force. Additionally, Omar committed violent deeds. Bishop John also ascribes the Arabs' enthusiasm to Islam saying,

> "When Muslims entered cities, they are accompanied by the converted Christians (Christian converted to Islam) to

[3] The History of the Patriarchs

[4] History of Arab Conquest.

> *overtake the assets of the escaped Christians. They called the servants of God 'the enemies of God.'"*

We could conclude that Christians did not regard the Arabs as liberators but as invaders. Severus Ibn el-Moqafaa in his Chronology, says,

> *"Three years into the government of Amro, the Muslims possessed Alexandria, destroyed its fences, and burnt numerous churches. They burnt the Church of St Mark, where the relics of St Mark was kept, and also burnt what was around that Church."*

We ought, out of truthfulness, to mention that these deeds were not the common attitude throughout the early stages of the Arab conquest. Professor Grohmann discovered two papyri dated 642 AD, written in Greek language, with an Arabic attachment. The first papyrus is a receipt issued by a Prince of Soldiers, named Prince Abdallah, declaring that he received sixty-five na3gas to feed the soldiers. John the Deacon registered the receipt on the thirtieth of Barmuda of 642 AD. The back of the receipt reads:

> *"A statement of delivering the na3gas to the soldiers and others who had came to this country, in return for an exemption from the first-due jizyah."*

The second papyrus reads as following:

> *"In the Name of God. I, Prince Abdallah, write to you, all dealers of city of Psoftus. I ask you to sell to Amro Ibn Aslaa,*

to the team of Qoota, wheat worth three golden dirhams, to each two ba3roor and to each soldier a three-course meal for lunch."

Professor Grohmann comments on both papyri saying,

"This kind of good treatment was rarely manifested by a superior nation to an oppressed nation."

In his book 'Omar El-Farouq', Dr. Mohamed Hussein Pasha says,

"There is no doubt that the Copts did not support the Romans in fighting the Arabs. They, additionally, undoubtedly did not cooperate with the Arabs, aside from perhaps a few isolated individuals. They were only the anxious audience of a battle between two other nations. There is not single ancient text that indicates that Copts offered any assistance to the army of Omro during their siege of Babylon, which was the first stage of the Arab conquest."

Destruction of the Library of Alexandria

The leadership of Amro Ibn el-Ass is closely connected to the burning the Library of Alexandria, according to instructions he received from the Caliph Omar Ibn el-Khattab. The sources mention that Amro sent to Omar Ibn el-Khattab for his insight, and Omar Ibn el-Khattab replied saying, *"if the contents of the library are in agreement with the Quran, then we do not need it, for we have the Quran. If in disagreement, we should not keep it, and it must be burnt."*

When Amro received this reply, he ordered the burning of the books and all contents of the Library. The books and contents were distributed throughout the baths of Alexandria to be used as an energy source for heating. The burning took six months. However, there are many who oppose this version of the story.

The Persian traveller Abdel Latif el-Baghdadi, who received his education at Baghdad, was the first to give the above version of the story. He came to Egypt where he studied at el-Azhar then he went to Damascus to meet Salah El Din El Ayyoubi. When he went back to his home city Baghdad, he wrote his memoirs entitled 'Akhbar Misr'. He died in 1231 AD.

Abu el-Farag el-Araby also states that the story of Library of Alexandria, by Amro Ibn el-Ass, was well spread in his days. He adds, "There was the Library that Amro burnt by the instructions of Omar Ibn el-Khattab."[5] However, those who had written before these examples did not refer to this story. John of Nikus omitted such a story. Those opposing the credibility of the story identify many reasons to discredit the story. Scholars have not finally decided on the burning of the Library. We ought to mention three ecclesiastical scholars, Sozomen, Theodoret and Rufinus who agreed that

[5] Summary of Nations' History, written in 1200 AD. He died in 1286 AD.

the Library still existed during the fourth and fifth centuries. Saint Cyril Maqar, Patriarch of Catholic Copts, who was the President of Egyptian Scientific Forum, in a research he conducted about the Therapium of Alexandria, supported with ancient evidences, that:

> "The Therapium that endorsed the great Library of Alexandria was not burnt by orders of Juvianos in 364 AD, or destroyed by the order of Theophilus in 391 AD. But rather it remained alive, along with other libraries, in the fifth century until the conclusion of the sixth century."

The Arabs were reputed for the burning of Persian books, according to Ibn Khaldon. This probably reinforces the opinion that the great Library had also been burnt by Amro Ibn el-Ass as per instructions of Omar Ibn el-Khattab.

The Return of Pope Benjamin

Pope Benjamin (38th Patriarch) fled from El-Mokawkas, the Melkite Patriarch. After the defeat of the Romans and the departure of their army, the Copts felt more secure. They sensed religious freedom. When Amro found out about the disappearance of the Coptic Pope Benjamin, he wrote to him, assuring him that where the Coptic Pope is, peace and safety would be also. He asked him to return, to run the affairs of his people in peace. It is said that a Copt named Sinutius (Shenouda), who was among the Roman leaders, promoted this cause. It is also said that Amro, while returning from Alexandria, was greeted by monks of Wadi el-Natroun.

When Pope Benjamin received the decree, he returned to Alexandria in a victorious reception. The Alexandrians celebrated their Pope's joyful return after 13 years' exile. Ten years of this absence was prior to the Arab Conquest. Pope Benjamin had a respectable and glorious appearance. He spoke wisely and charismatically. The Pope's personality captured Amro Ibn el-Ass, who commented after their encounter, "in all places we possess, I have not seen one like this man." Amro looked at the pope and said, "Manage and attend to all your churches and all your people. If you pray for me to expand my possession westwardly to Pentapolis, I will grant you, upon my victorious return, all what you ask." Pope Benjamin wished Amro the best wishes and left the place in honour.

Upon the return of Pope Benjamin, many Chalcedonian followers returned to the Coptic faith. Severus, Ibn el-Moqafaa says in this regard:

> "The spiritual father Pope Benjamin radiated peace among his people and his followers. All Egypt rejoiced his return. He attracted many who had been misled by King Hercules. He called his people to a life of honesty and safety, in all his sermons and teachings. He also invited the schismatic bishops to re-join the Orthodox Church. Many came back with tears while many died far from the church's bosom."

Alfred J. Butler expands on Patriarch Benjamin,

> "The return of Benjamin had the utmost effect on the Copts. The Copts needed him the most at that particular point in

time. They needed that charismatic wise personality to guide and manage their affairs."

Pope Benjamin was successful in regathering his people. He then attended to the needs of the monasteries and the need to restore the demolished ones. The Persians and Chalcedonians had destroyed many of the monasteries of Wadi el-Natroun. He visited the Monastery of Abu Maqar (St Macarius) and built a new church, where he saw Jesus Christ Himself consecrating its Altar alongside an apparition of Saint Abu Maqar.

How many Copts lived at the time of Arab Conquest?

Early Christian and Muslim historians agreed that the number of Copts, who were enlisted to pay a 2 denarii jizyah, were six million. Other taxes were imposed, called kharaj, a kind of land tax. The total jizyah and kharaj collected amounted to 12 million. Jizyah was imposed on males aged between 15 to 60 years. Women, elders and children were exempted, along with the disabled, the poor and the monks. Those eligible to pay the jizyah composed one quarter of the population. When we consider the number of Copts exempted from paying jizyah, combined with those who were subjected to paying jizyah, what would the number

KHARAJ

A tax imposed on property and districts rather than on individual persons. The exact meaning of the word is "land yield," signifying the harvest produced by a given territory.

of the Copts be then? We believe that the number cannot be less than twenty-five million. The English historian Stanley Lane-Poole says, "Ibn Adbel Hakam estimates the number of payers of jizyah between six to eight million people. If so, the number of Coptic population would be around the thirty million."[6]

THE ISLAMIC LEGISLATION AND DHIMMIS

The Arabs were not familiar with administrative matters due to their tribal environment. The Quranic contents in relation to managing the dhimmis, made it more difficult for Arabs to manage and control the Copts. Some rulers acted according to circumstances ignoring the teachings of the Quran, and some rulers interpreted these teachings according to their personal wishes and preferences. So the Quranic teachings were seriously and continually challenged from the early stages of Arab conquest. The gap widened between teachings and application. We ought to discuss the Islamic legislation concerning the employment of Copts in Islamic administration, Coptic attire, and the establishment of churches. This discussion should explain the sphere within which the Copts lived.

The Dhimmis in the Quran

The Quran mentions the dhimmis more than once. Sooret[7]

---

[6] Stanley Lane-Poole, History of Medieval Egypt, p. 19

[7] Soora or Sooret is an Arabic word meaning Chapter.

The Arab Conquest of Egypt

Al Omran 27 reads, "The believers [Muslims] should not take guidance from among the infidels [non-Muslims], at the expense of the believers. He who does this is not from God."

Sooret El-Maeda 50 reads,

> "O you the believers [Muslims], do not take Jews or Nazarites, as leaders. He who is administered by them is one of them. For God does not guide unjust people."

In the Soora of Repentance 7, we read,

> "And if they appear to you, you ought not to esteem them, for they please you with their mouths, while their hearts are rejecting, and they are mostly impious."

Dr Turton says:

> "It is historically agreed on, that a prophetic saying mentions that no two religions can co-exist within nations of Arabs. This made Omar Ibn el-Khattab expel all Jews and Nazarites from the Arabian Peninsula, for it was considered the Home of Islam. El-Hijazz was completely void of them. The same concept did not lead to the expulsion of the dhimmis from Yemen. We see conflicting application of this concept. During the life of Mohammed, there was a Nazarite named Mawheb, who lived in Mecca itself. While Omar Ibn el-Khattab during his Caliphate, banned non-Muslims from entering Medina, he only accepted one person named Abu Lo-lo-a, for he was a skilful workman. It was the need for

some Nazarites that mandated Muslim rulers to let them enter the sanctioned cities. Thus did Osman Ibn Afan and Moawyeha Ibn Abi Sefian when he sent his son Yazid on a pilgrimage, accompanying with him a Nazarite physician, Abu el Hakam. Also the Caliph Abdel Malek Ibn Marawan sent a Roman engineer to Mecca to undertake certain technical work following the floods that threatened the Kaaba. The El-Waleed Ibn Abdel Malek Ibn Marawan sends eighty workers, Roman and Copts, to restore the Mosque of Mohammed. Many dhimmi workers had participated in building of mosques."[8]

Dhimmis and Era of Omar Ibn el-Khattab

The dhimmis were subject to decrees imposed by Omar Ibn el-Khattab. The Qalqashandi (1355-1418 AD) mentioned this in his book 'Morning of Dawn'. Often Muslim rulers adopted these creeds. These creeds were rendered in a letter issued to the people of Syria. They sent the letter to Omar Ibn el-Khattab for his endorsement. The following is the text of the letter, as cited by Qalqashandi,

"When you approached us, we asked your peace, on ourselves, offspring, assets, and people. We imposed on ourselves for in return that we do not to restore any ruined monastery or church, and we do not disallow our churches to host any Muslim for three nights, and we do not hide in our houses or churches to spy, and we do not conceal corruption of Muslims, we don't teach our children the

---

[8] Turton, "The People of Dhimmis in Islam," pp. 203-204

> ## DHIMMIS
>
> *During the time of the Islamic conquest of Egypt, the Muslims established a special category of non-Muslims who were willing to submit to the Muslim rule. They became distinguished as Ahl al-Dhimmah, or Dhimmis, with the right of protection from foreign inroads by the Muslim military power, security of personal property, and with a limited freedom to practice their religion.*
>
> ***First****, Dhimmis were required to disarm completely and to submit to Muslim rule. Any person found to be armed was either killed or enslaved.* ***Second****, Dhimmis were allowed to practice their own faith within churches or synagogues established prior to the advent of Islam, but building of new religious houses was prohibited.* ***Third****, the Dhimmis were liable to pay a tribute known as Jizyah fixed by the Muslim authority on all able-bodied men, thus excluding women and children. On the social front, the Coptic Dhimmis were required to wear a vestment distinctive from that of the Muslims. They were also required to ride only donkeys and to desist from the use of horses and they were supposed to rise in the presence of Muslims.*

Quran, we do not show infidelity or call anyone to infidelity, we don't forbid our people to adopt Islam if they wish, and we shall honour the Muslims and erect their gatherings and assemblies, we do not resemble Muslims in their appearance, not wearing head cover or shoes or hair form. We don't talk their talks, and don't adopt their names, we do not ride horses or carry swords, we don't carry or keep weapons, and we don't use seal in Arabic, and we don't sell spirits, and girdle our bodies, we don't show crosses on our churches, we don't resemble any Muslim path or marketplace, we don't ring churches' bells freely but softly, we don't read loudly in churches, or in the presence of Muslims, we bury our deceased different from Muslims, we don't bury our deceased near their houses, we don't have slaves against the wish of Muslims and we don't look at them in their houses."

Abdel Rahman Ibn Ghanam says,

> "We, Omar Ibn el-Khattab, received the letter, he added to it, 'we don't beat or hit any Muslim', as a final condition for peace. If we break any of these conditions, we will no longer be considered dhimmis (a protected status) and will deserve all hardships imposed."

The Qalqashandi summed up these creeds in the following points;

> "Jizyah and hospitality, submissiveness to rulers, mount donkeys with both feet on one side, to let the Muslims be leaders, to wear distinguished colour from the Muslims, their buildings to never exceed those of Muslims in height, and not to build churches in places initiated by Muslims."

The era of Omar Ibn el-Khattab is still controversial. There is no doubt that several rulers followed the same trend towards Copts during their reign.

Omar Ibn el-Khattab induced the jizyah on the Copts. El-Maqrizi mentions that Omar Ibn el-Khattab wrote to Amro Ibn el-Ass ordering him "to seal the necks of dhimmi with lead (wearing a lead necklace), to show their girdles, mount their donkeys laterally, only males to pay the jizyah, exempting women and infants, and do not let them resemble Muslims in appearance."

Copts and Financial System

The Islamic caliphate was occupied with collecting taxes. The correspondence between Omar Ibn el-Khattab and Amro Ibn el-Ass reveals that Omar Ibn el-Khattab wanted to collect an equal portion to that collected by Romans in Egypt. It is attributed to Amro Ibn el-Ass that he said to the Copts "He who conceals a treasure from me will be killed." Ibn el-Hakam also says that Amro killed a wealthy man from Upper Egypt named Peter, which led the Copts to reveal their treasures.[9]

Was that a form of seizure for Amro's own benefit or was that to increase the value of jizyah and to contribute towards the nation's budget? It is hard to extract the facts from the available sources. Yet it is clear that Copts bore the brunt of imposed taxes, similar to their suffering under the Romans. The need for taxes was increasing to cover the needs of beneficiaries, rulers and governors and workers. Dr Kashef adds, "the main interest for Arabs was the jizyah. It was the reason for conversion of many Copts, to escape the financial burden, thus reducing the income of the government / nation. Accordingly, rulers doubled the jizyah on those remaining Copts."[10] It was said that the Copts had to pay jizyah on their

---

[9] Ibn el-Hakam, Egypt: Conquest and News.

[10] Dr. Sayeda Kashef, Egypt during the era of rulers, p. 122-123

deceased. The more the financial burden increased on Copts, the more Copts convert to Islam to alleviate their financial suffering. Abdel-Aziz Ibn Marawan (685-705 AD) imposed jizyah on monks too, ordering a census for all monasteries all over Egypt. He decreed one dirham on each monk. Additionally, he decreed that no one becomes a monk after the census. That was the first time the monks had to pay jizyah.

During the era of El-Waleed Ibn Abdel Malek and the era of his brother Abdalla Ibn Abdel Malek (705-709 AD) the financial burden increased exceedingly, and more Copts converted. During these eras, a passive resistance movement against the Arabic financial policy began by those who refused to convert. The movement involved their escape to different areas from which they were originally enlisted. The ruler was severe in destroying that movement. The ruler ordered the sealing / stamping of strangers in every name and sent them to various areas. This movement of escape continued during the era of Qora Ibn Shareek who succeeded Abdalla Ibn Abdel Malek (709-714 AD); the movement took another shape where numerous entire families relocated from one place to another to avoid the taxes. Osama Ibn Zeid el-Tanoukhi was in charge of collection of kharaj, during the rulership of Soliman Ibn Abdel Malek (715-717 AD). He was very strict in ordering his subordinates not to show mercy during the collection of kharaj and jizyah, a conduct which led many to seek Islam merely to get rid of financial burden. Osama also ordered that no Christian be hosted in churches or hotels or any other form of accommodation. He also conducted a second census on monks, reviving the ongoing instruction for monasteries not to ordain new monks. He ordered each monk to be stamped on the left hand with a metal chain, written on it the name of the monastery, and the date of becoming a monk. If any monk were to be found without that ring, he would be subject to harsh punishment.[11]

Some rulers also collected jizyah from recent converts. It is without doubt that Copts adopted Islam principally and only to escape the financial penalty, not out of admiration of the new religion. It was decreed once, during the third period of the rulership of el-Waleed, that the caliph at the time issued a decree to exempt all converts from jizyah. Twenty-four thousands Copts converted immediately. A similar incident took place under the rulership of el-Abbassi Abu el-Abbass.[12]

Ahl-el-Dhemma and Official Posts

During the caliphate of Omar Ibn el-Khattab, no Copt held any official government employment. Omar Ibn el-Khattab was very strict in implementing the commands of the Quran. Sheikh Ibn el-Naqash, the Emam[13] of mosque of Ibn Tolon, dated the 9th century, cites a few examples of Omar Ibn el-Khattab's attitude to this matter, saying,

> *Abu Moussa el-Asharry said to the caliph, "I hired a Nazarite person," Omar Ibn el-Khattab replied, "What have you done, man? Allah will punish you. Don't you understand the saying of Allah, 'O You believers; do not hire Jews or Nazarites, for he who hires them is from them, for Allah does not guide the*

---

[11] Dr. Sayeda Kashef, Egypt during the era of rulers, pp. 123-128

[12] Dr. Sayeda Kashef, Egypt during the era of rulers, p. 129

[13] Emam is another Arabic for sheikh – Trans.

unjust people."[14] *The man replied, "O the Prince of Believers, I hired them, and put aside his belief."* Omar Ibn el-Khattab replied, saying, *"This is not an acceptable excuse. I will never honour those who are humiliated by Allah. I will never raise any whom Allah abandons, I will never approach any who Allah forsakes."*

One of Omar's leaders wrote to Omar Ibn el-Khattab, enquiring about hiring the infidels to official posts, saying,

> *"The treasures are full, for money flowed in abundance. Only they can perform these accounting tasks, so advise the correct path of action."*

Omar Ibn el-Khattab replied,

> *"Do not participate with the infidels in your deeds. Do not give them what Allah forbade. Do not put your treasures in their hands. Do not forget these principles which must be followed by every man."*

The Caliph also wrote to one of his leaders, saying,

> *"He who hires a Nazarite scribe has to have no mercy and not to hold kind feelings towards him, or consult or seek advice, for both the Prophet and the Caliph commands no utilisation of Ahl-el-dhemma."*

Omar Ibn el-Khattab also received a letter from Moawyeha Ibn Abi Sefian asking,

---

[14] El-Maeda 50

> "O Prince of Believers, I am hiring a Nazarite, without whom, I am unable to collect kharaj. I am after your advice in this regard."

Omar Ibn el-Khattab replied saying,

> "I pray for Allah to protect me from such evil. I read your letter regarding the Nazarite, and know that that Nazarite had died. Peace."

The opinion of Sheikh el-Naqash was not less striking than that of Omar Ibn el-Khattab, 230 years later. The sheikh was once asked,

> "What is the opinion of Muslim scholars, who are leaders of nations, in regard to employing the dhimmis as scribes for the princes, or in administrative roles, or to collect kharaj? Is it legitimate or illegitimate?"

Ibn el-Naqash replied, saying,

> "It is illegitimate to hire dhimmis. This is the opinion of all Muslim scholars. At a minimum, they are dissatisfied with such an arrangement. For they stated 'we do not have a covenant with the prophet'. This is applies to the Copts of Egypt who believe they are not in covenant with Muslims. The cited verses only relate to feelings of friendship towards Nazarites. But when it comes to hiring the Nazarites, I say, only hire he whom you can trust. After all, Allah the mighty solved that problem decisively when he said, 'he who hires them is from them.'"

The Umeyad Caliph Omar Abdel Aziz hated when the dhimmi has the upper hand, thus having power or authority over Muslims. He forbade this. The Caliph sent to all governors, saying,

> "Allah honoured and glorified the Muslim nation with Islam. Allah too commanded the humiliation of those who don't adopt Islam. Allah made you the best nation in the universe. Hence, do not let dhimmis run affairs of Muslims, where they may multiply and enlarge in success, and they might humiliate those who are honoured and glorified by Allah."

Accordingly, Omar Abdel Aziz isolated the Coptic labourers replacing them with Muslims. He was very strict in implementing this rule. He once wrote,

> "He who wants to establish a kingdom in his country, he should adopt the religion of Mohammad. He who does not, should leave it."[15]

Dhimmis and Attire

Omar enforced restrictions related to attire. The scholars then interpreted what he had said,

> "Abu Yousif, the judge of Baghdad in his book on Kharaj

---

[15] El-Kanadi, Governorship & Judges: Ibn Abdel Hakam, the Biography of Omar Abdel Aziz, the Complete History for Ibn el-Atheer, Severus Ibn el-Moqafaa, The History of the Patriarchs, p. 326.

says, 'we have to stamp their necks with seals as Osman Ibn Haneef did when he was asked to break their necks. No one should be allowed to appear like a Muslim, both in attire and in appearance. They must have girdles tied around their waists, their head cover be stripy, their shoe sole be twisted, and they must not proceed in the path of a Muslim, their women should mount on animals, they are forbidden to build churches. Hence, order your workers to hire dhimmis in this given description. That was Omar Ibn el-Khattab' policy, who ordered his workers as such, so a Muslim could be easily identified from among the others."

Dhimmis and Compensation for their Murdered

This is a controversial issue among scholars. It has been said that Mohammad and Omar Ibn el-Khattab legalised the blood of any Muslim who kills a Nazarite intentionally. It is known about Mohammad that he said that whoever kills a dhimmi will never enter the paradise. However, Ali Ibn Abi Taleb said,

"A believer should not be killed in return of an infidel."

His stance stemmed from his opposition to killing a Muslim who kills a dhimmi.

It is also said that both Abu Bakr and Omar and Osman demanded a ransom in exchange for the killing of a dhimmi that was equal to the sum in the case of a Muslim being killed. However, Malek Ibn Anas says that the ransom for a dhimmi is half that of a Muslim, whether the killing was accidental or intentional. It has been also said that the ransom for a killed dhimmi during the era of Mohammad was half that of a Muslim. When a Muslim man is killed in lands of dhimmis, the dhimmis had to pay the ransom if the murderer is unknown or could not be arrested.[16]

Islam and Apostasy

Muslim scholars agree that death is the penalty for apostasy. There is an established saying that "He who changes his religion is to be killed." Some insist that the apostates should be killed, without regard to any circumstances. Others believe that the converted person should be allowed repentance, if these attempts succeed, then they should not be killed. This applied to dhimmis who might have converted to Islam, but considered returning to their religion of origin. Although scholars agreed on the death penalty, yet they are not in agreement on the time that should lapse between their conversion to the execution of death penalty. Some say that the converted must be killed immediately. Others say that the converted should be allowed three days for repentance. Omar Ibn el-Khattab was once asked about a man who converted to Islam, then left Islam for a while, then returned to Islam, would his Islam be accepted? He replied,

> *"Accept his Islam, offer him Islam, if he accepts it, accept him. If he does not accept it, slaughter his neck."*

---

[16] Ahl el-Dhimma in Islam, pp. 207-210

Omar Abdel Aziz, said regarding a Jew who converted to Islam then renounced it,

"*If he adopts Islam, let him free. If he does not, kill him.*"[17]

Islam and the Testimony of the Dhimmi

Muslim scholars mostly agree that a testimony of a dhimmi against a Muslim cannot be accepted under any circumstances. It is said that Omar Ibn Abdel Aziz was the first to adopt this concept. Other sources display a strictness in application. Abu Hanifa, Malek and el-Shafie reject the testimony of dhimmi, so in the case of a terminally-ill Muslim person, or one who is travelling and therefore needed to appoint an agent to act on his behalf, if he appointed a dhimmi, the testimony of this dhimmi must be rejected.[18]

Moderate Islamic views Regarding Ahl el-Dhimma in Islam

We ought to demonstrate here what was recently written by Dr Mohamed Emara, El-Helal Publication, 1979. Dr Emara graduated from al-Azhar University, and Faculty of Science, then completed a Masters in Islamic Sciences. He said in an article titled 'Islam and National unity' the following:

"*The jizyah: The mind of the Islamic nation and its mental and*

---

[17] Ahl el-Dhimma in Islam, pp. 211-216

[18] Ahl el-Dhimma in Islam, p. 217

historic heritage, due to political and administrative practices which were not of Islamic origins, and due to granting the acceptance of these practices by scholars, the Islamic nation came to believe that dhimmis and Jews are second-class citizens, and at the best estimation, are not equal to Muslims in rights and obligations. Hence the jizyah was applied onto those, who, in turn, helplessly paid the jizyah. Such jizyah placed a barrier of separation in the name of religion. It is true that the Quran mentioned the jizyah, once in one location only, saying, 'fight those who do neither believe in God nor in the Judgment day, those who do not forbid what the Prophet forbids, those who don't adopt the right belief among those who received the Scripture, for then they have no option, but giving you their jizyah.'"[19]

It is also true those Muslim rulers, whose adoption of Islamic teachings is above suspicion, like Omar Ibn el-Khattab collected jizyah from Jews and Christians. Some historic sources mentioned that the Prophet reached a deal with the Christians of Negran, and the Persians of Bahrain; the deal dictated their obligation to pay jizyah to the Islamic nation.

But there are many confliciting ideas in relation to the jizyah. These deserve scrutiny, upon which we shall discover the contemporary applications are unjust and not in any way related to Islam.

It is a well-accepted belief that the jizyah is a form of tax payable by Christians, Jews and non-Muslims living in Islamic countries. The reason for imposing this tax is that

---

[19] Sooret el-Toba 29 (Chapter: The Repentance 29)

these people do not follow Islam. This is the belief of scholars belonging to el-Malky school of thought, who said "Jizyah must be imposed on non-Muslims instead of killing them for infidelity. It seems then that difference in belief is the justification of its imposition. Hence it is a must and is due as long as the difference in belief exists."

There are issues with this justification, however, for if difference in religious belief is the reason for jizyah, then it should have been imposed on all people of different beliefs. But this was not the case. It was levied on men who were capable to fight, but not on elders, women, the disabled or the sick, albeit of different belief to Islamic belief. It was also not generally applied to monks, who are also of non-Islamic faith. So religious difference was not the criterion for imposing jizyah. Rather it was a tax imposed instead of military service, according to the modern expression. This tax for soldiership was imposed on capable men, who would be paying it if they could not engage in the war, as non-Muslims could not be a member of the army. The non-Malky schools of thought agree, declaring jizyah was in place of military struggle and victory.

Jizyah, then, was not a religious tax, but an alternative for military service, depending on the needs of Islamic armies. When such a need disappears, the jizyah should also disappear. Thus is equality established between Muslims and non-Muslims. Currently, with military becoming an honourable contribution offered to all citizens regardless of faith, would there remain any justification for the jizyah to still occupy backwards-thinking minds, who believe that cancelling the jizyah is against the will of God?

Attire

It is commonly conceived that Islam commanded distinction between Muslims and non-Muslims in their attire. The Quran does not discuss the concept of attire, neither for Muslims nor for non-Muslims. The Quran's focus was on principles and intentions rather than manifestations and externals. The various decrees throughout history concerning attire - some specifying certain attire and others reversing previous specifications - therefore led to confusion regarding this matter. The confusion was further deepened through the mixing of politics and religion.

Many renowned Muslim scholars declared the need to distinguish between Muslim and non-Muslim in their attire. They recited that rulers applied that principle within societies under their rulership. For example, al-Qady Abu Yousef (731-798 AD) wrote in the book of 'Kharaj' asking Haroun el-Rasheed to show punctuality in application with Christians and Jews, commanding,

> "Not to let anyone of them to resemble the Muslims, in appearance, in 'carriage' or attire."

Abu Yousef cited that Omar Ibn el-Khattab ordered his workers to implement this principle on their dhimmisworkers, in order to enable the distinguishing between Muslims from non-Muslims. We will not scrutinise the recension of Abu Yousef regarding Omar Ibn el-Khattab, but we would like to cite some observations on el-Khattab's order:

The action committed by Omar Ibn el-Khattab and other caliphs are not established upon a religious or legislative basis.

This idea of different attire was expanded over time by the imagination of different rulers. Over time, the gap widened between these traditions and their genuine religious and legislative origins.

Most importantly, the sheikhs, over the years, expanded and modified the concept, without re-visiting its origin or its truthfulness. Had they re-contemplated it, they would have completely abandoned it.

THE COPTIC CHURCH UNDER MUSLIM RULERS
(642-868)

The Age of Muslim Rulers refers to an age where Egypt was run by the caliphate system. This means the rule by rulers appointed directly by the Caliphs. They were initially based in el-Madina el-Monawara. Then, under Ali ibn Ali-Taleb, they were based in Kufa. Afterwards, the Ayoubeans were based in Damascus. The final stage was that of the Abbassid, based in Baghdad and Samaraa. The rulers were Arabs up to the conclusion of Ummayads. During the age of the Abbyssians, the rulers were Arabs, Persian or Turks. The following are the major features of this Age:

Firstly: The Number of Muslim Rulers

It is clear that the number of rulers was enormous. Statistics indicate that there were one hundred and eleven rulers over the duration of 225 years. The rulership was too short for any ruler to introduce a constructive policy or to implement a successful plan for the welfare of the nation.

Mr Gaston Feiet researched the mosques of Cairo. He says, "Twenty one rulers ruled Egypt during the Ummyades. Two ruled twice. One ruled thrice. Five of these rulers were relatives of the Caliphs. Six had deceased during their rulership. Eleven were either killed or barred by the Caliphs. One resigned. One was excluded by his army for reducing their wages. One ruled for sixteen years. During the Abbasid era, there were sixty four rulers. The transfers among the rulers were much more than during the Ummyads. This is because of the remoteness of Baghdad. The Caliph did not allow much time to any ruler, lest the ruler win the support of the people. Fear of a recalcitrant ruler was a strong influence and motive on the policy of the Caliphs."

This instability of rulers was not in the nation's best interest. Rulers could not establish ongoing plans knowing their rulership would not be of sufficient length. During the caliphate of Haroun el-Rasheed, which lasted twenty-three years, a total of twenty-four rulers ruled Egypt. The main concern for each ruler was to accumulate wealth, typically through the imposition of new unfair taxes on the people.

The sole victims were the Copts who refused to convert to Islam and remained in their Christian faith.

Secondly: Policy of the Caliphs and Rulers Towards Egypt was Based on Financial Benefit

Abdel-Hakam quoted in his Book, 'the Conquest of Egypt' a saying of Abdalla ibn-Saleh about Egypt; "He who wants to mention the paradise or visualise any similar place on earth ought to see Egypt when its plantation and fields get green and prosper. The admiration of Egypt was voiced by each and every Arab who walked along the Nile Valley."

Omar Ibn el-Khattab once, when el-Madina el-Monawara was in starvation, ordered an urgent importation of wheat from Egypt. He said, "May Allah ruin Egypt and its constructive plans."[20] When Omar spoke about the miserable nations, he said, "Let Muslims eat them alive, if we perish, they perish, let our children eat whatever remained of their children."[21]

The above are examples of the greedy attitude of the invaders. Also, two letters were exchanged between Omar and his ruler, Amro ibn el-Ass about the rate of taxation. The amount of taxes sent by Amro to Omar was declining over the years, firstly due to the increase in the number of Christians converting to Islam, and secondly due to the

---

[20] El-Tabary, Futuh el-Buldan, Muslims and Christians p. 79

[21] Abou Yousef, Kharaj - Christians and Muslim, p. 79

dishonesty of Amro himself. Omar said in his letter to Amro, "I considered the issue. Your land is vast and great. The Pharaohs handled this land with utmost care and creativity. This is amazing. What is more amazing is that the land is incapable to produce the same kharraj." Amro responded saying, "The Caliph finds me slow in sending kharraj, hints to the deeds of Pharaohs before me, admiring the works of the Pharoahs in this regard, noting that the kharraj was greater in the previous times. The Caliph said that the river produces pearls, but I milked the river till it dried out."[22]

Omar repeated the same insult at the time of Osman ibn-Affan. Amro used to collect 12 million denarii of jizyah. The subsequent ruler, Abdalla ibn-Saad ibn Abi-Serg, increased the jizyah to 14 million. The Caliph Osman commended Abdalla's work saying, "O Abi Abdallah, the seed produced more than before." Amro commented, "You hurt its offspring."

If this was the attitude of Caliphs, what would be that of the rulers?

Financial issues were the main concern of the Caliphs. Their income from taxes was continually declining. In the meantime, the expenses were increasing. The expenses were directed towards more conquests as well as securing the Empire. Further conquest and expansions required massive, well-equipped armies. It was also necessary to establish military units to retain internal peace.

---

[22] Ibn Abdel-Hakam – Christians and Muslims, pp. 75-76

The Coptic Church Under Muslim Rulers (642-868)

The army used the most of income. The Caliphs attempted to squeeze the budget by reducing the wages of the soldiers. But they failed many times. Hence, they had to find other safe solutions, which led to imposing more taxes on invaded nations.

Ibn el-Hakam mentions an incident that happened with an Upper Egyptian Copt, named Peter, saying, "when Amro Ibn el-Ass conquered Egypt he said to the Copts, 'he who hides a treasure from me, I will kill as soon as I am able.'" Amro heard that this Peter had a treasure hidden, so he called him to ask about that treasure, and Peter denied having a treasure and was imprisoned. Amro asked other prisoners whether Peter talks or asks about anyone, and they said that they heard Peter asking about a monk at the region of el-Tore. Then Amro called Peter again, seized his seal and wrote to that monk and ordered the monk to send his possession to Peter, and stamped that letter with the stamp of Peter (as if Peter had actually written the letter). When the messenger of Amro returned with a porcelain jar (quolla) sealed with lead, Amro opened that jar, and found a letter saying "Your possession is under the big fountain." Amro sent his people to that big fountain, and removed the tiles where they found 52 bags of gold. Amro then cut off Peter's head at the door of the mosque. Ibn Rakeeba commented that the Copts, as a result of this incident, exposed their treasures, to avoid being killed in like manner to Peter.[23]

The rulership of Abdel Aziz ibn-Marwan (685-705 AD) lasted for 21 years. These years are known to have been marked

---

[23] Ibn el-Hakam: the Conquest of Egypt

by justice and fairness. Yet he introduced more taxes on monks, and these taxes continued after the conclusion of his rulership. His brother Abdallah, succeeded him, not only introducing more taxes, but additionally, he arrested and imprisoned Pope Alexander II, the 43rd Patriarch (700-724 AD), imposing a fine of 3000 denarii. Severus ibn al-Moqafaa says, "Pope Alexander went to Egypt in order to greet the ruler, as per the custom at the time. The Ruler looked at him and asked about who he was. He was told that that was the Patriarch and the Pope of all the Nazarites. He arrested him instantly, and asked his soldiers to treat the Pope in any way until he pays the sum of 3000 denarii. He was arrested for three days." The Deacon Gerga, finding out about the whole dilemma, approached the Ruler and asked, saying, "Are you after the Patriarch or the money?" The Ruler replied, "The money." The Deacon then said, "Hand the Patriarch to me, and we will go to Lower Egypt collecting the money you are after." He handed the Patriarch to the Deacon, they both toured the cities and villages collecting the money for the Ruler. Severus describes the Ruler as gluttonous and greedy for money, imposing more taxes on dhimmis.[24]

Succeeding Abdallah was Qurra ibn Shareek, who was also greedy. He asked Patriarch Alexander to pay him the same amount of money he paid to Abdallah. The Patriarch tried to convince the new Ruler that such a request is beyond his means, and that he was still indebted since the former payment. The Ruler replied, "This is nonsense. Even if you have to sell your flesh, you must to make this payment.

---

[24] Rulers and Judges, on Copts & Muslims, p 93

Otherwise, the punishment will be harsh." The Patriarch had to tour the cities and villages of Upper Egypt to collect money for the new Ruler.

We ought to mention the deeds of Osama Ibn Zeid, the Ruler of Egypt, appointed by Soliman Ibn Abdel Malek, the Umayyid Caliph. Osama was greedier than his predecessors, according to both Muslim and Christian historians. He imposed severe taxes on monks. Monks were ordered to wear rings in their fingers showing the due dates for taxes imposed on them. Whenever a monk was found without wearing that ring, he would have his hand cut off. The order was executed instantly. Monks remained hidden in their monasteries. The police soldiers searched for monks everywhere, whipping and beheading them without mercy.[25]

Third: Arabs did not have a Fixed Policy in Governing the Nation

The governors and rulers together had no overarching administrative plan for the nation. Political, social and economic decisions were reactive, based on what was needed at the moment. Some scholars attribute this to the possibility that they did not intend to remain permanently in Egypt. They solely aimed at strengthening their armies in order to conquer more nations. They were in continual need - or rather, greed - for money.

---

[25] Severus Ibn el-Moqafaa – The History of the Patriarchs p. 324-325

The plan was for Arab soldiers not to mix with the nations of the armies they defeated. Ibn el-Hakam mentions what Omar ibn el-Khattab said, "I do not want the Muslim to step in a land separated from me by water, neither in winter nor summer." The historical documents do not indicate or provide any evidence that the Arabs planned to enhance the economic situation of Egypt, improve the status of Egyptians, or to alleviate their sufferings. If any such thing had happened, it was for the benefit of the conquering Arabs, coincidentally improving Egypt's infrastructure. An example is the digging of the Canal of Trajan to facilitate the dispatch of wheat to other Arab nations. The canal was backfilled by successive sand storms in the eighth century. It was once also backfilled by the rulers on Egypt in 761-762 AD to prevent the sending of armies to Medina. The rulers enslaved the Egyptians for the cleaning of canals and the rebuilding of roads and bridges, in return for their exemption from all taxes.[26]

Although the construction of churches was prohibited in cities established by the Arabs, Abdel Aziz ibn-Marwan permitted the construction of a church in Helwan, to satisfy the resident Melkites in that area, because they worked for the Ruler. Similarly, El-Ma'mun permitted some of his Nazarite workers to build a church.[27]

When the level of the Nile River lowered in 752 AD, the Muslims and Jews prayed, without any gain. The miracle happened when the Nazarites prayed, and the Ruler

[26] El Maqurizi – Plans p. 74

[27] Ibn Batric p. 41-58, Copts and Muslims, 64

decided to reward them by reducing the imposed taxes and to guarantee them their safety and that of their possessions throughout all Egypt.[28]

The most egregious example of a ruler contradicting himself in a series of controversial decisions occurred in 785 AD. The Ruler Ali ibn-Soliman issued a creed to demolish all new churches that have been built in Egypt. He was offered the sum of 50,000 denarii in return for keeping these churches, to which he agreed. Moussa Ibn-Issa, who succeeded him in 787 AD, stated that this was merely a financial ploy by his predecessor. He asked the opinions of the sheikhs who said that these churches were an integral component of the design of the nation, and that a ruler should not be more fanatical than the rulers preceding him. They added that the majority of the churches were constructed under the Islamic rule. It should be emphasised that gangs in 735 AD revolted against El-Walid ibn-Refa'a when he permitted the construction of St Mina's church.

Fourth: Examples of Troubles Suffered by the Church

Historical sources portray a dark image of the burdens borne by the Copts and the Coptic Church. We should quote here what Dr Sayeda Ismael Kashef, Professor of Islamic History, writes in her testimony: "The Arabs changed their strategies a few years after conquering Egypt. A great deal of Copts realised that Arabization and conversion to

---

[28] The History of the Patriarchs

Islam would save them from societal and cultural burdens. Through conversion they would evade increasing taxes and retain their ranks. After the conquest, the Arabs soon started to feel superior over other nations, that their religion was superior to other religions and their language superior to other languages. This sense of superiority did not develop overnight, but over years.

Copts went through intermittent periods of troubles and burdens. The troubles were related to the establishment of churches and their attire. Scholars state that Omar Ibn el-Khattab ordered that the dhimmis should look similar to Muslims. The Caliph also commanded the destruction of all churches established since the conquest. He also disallowed the restoration of any church.

In year 235 H during the reign of El-Motawakel El-Abassi, he commanded that all Copts should wear a Tayalsah (scarf or veil) of honey colour, a girdle around their waist, use wooden seats on chariots, and must wear head covers continually. The ruler was continually ordering the destruction of their churches. The large houses of Copts were taken to be converted into mosques. If it could not be a mosque, it was converted to a tribunal. The Copts' houses were marked distinguishably from those of Muslims. He banned the hiring of Copts in governmental and administrative firms. He disallowed Coptic children from receiving any education at Muslim schools. He ordered the Copts be educated by Muslim teachers. He forbade the Copts from displaying crosses in their feasts. Additionally, he ordered that their graves be levelled to earth to distinguish them from Muslims'. His orders were distributed everywhere. Further restrictions were imposed in year 239 H, especially in relation to their chariots and attire.

Feelings of religious discrimination took root in the Arabs after the conquest. They felt their superiority over other nations, after they achieved their Islamic Empire with the sword. They sought a distinctive appearance, transport and attire, to enforce their social superiority over the other inhabitants. They were the masters. They treated the dhimmis in the most degrading way. Many Copts converted to avoid such tribulations. The Arabs also thought they need not to build any new church within their Empire. It sufficed for them to keep existing churches at the time of the conquest. The Caliph Omar ibn-Abdel-Aziz (99-101 H) tried to replace the Copts with Muslims, even to fill the smallest posts.

He soon wrote to the Copts, firing them from their jobs since they remain Copts. He who wanted to retain his job had to convert to Islam. He also sacked any Coptic governors of towns and replaced them with Muslim governors. This led many to convert to Islam in order to retain their jobs. Among troubles the Copts were exposed to in 105 H, under the Caliph Yazeed ibn-Abdel-Malek, was the destruction of crosses and statues in churches. Severus ibn el-Moqafaa described this as being a particularly Satanic attitude. In undertaking this Satanic order, even Pharaonic monuments were demolished and destroyed. Copts suffered massively during this era. When the Caliph Marwan ibn Mohamed fled to Egypt, his soldiers went 'crazy' in the land, they killed

Copts, confiscated their wealth, enslaved Coptic women, burnt churches and monasteries, and attacked nuns. The monasteries of Wadi el-Natroun were also burnt, their monks were massacred except for a few. The Copts of Egypt were exposed to similar burdens. Fanaticism toward whatever was Arabic or Muslim was the norm. Many Copts had no choice but to convert to Islam and to learn the Arabic language."[29] Now let us look at other sufferings that were visited upon the Copts of Egypt.

Concerning the religious ceremony

Caliph Abdel Aziz Ibn Marwan was described as the fairest caliph whom Egypt had seen. Yet, he ordered the destruction of all crosses - wooden, gold or silver. He ordered the insertion of signs reading "Mohamed the Great Prophet, and Essa[30] also a Prophet from Allah, who was not begotten" on the doors of the churches all over Egypt. This took place during the papacy of Isaac, the 41st Patriarch (686-689 AD). The Caliph went much further when he banned the conduction of liturgical services in churches. This took place during the papacy of Simon I, the 42nd Patriarch (689-701 AD).[31]

El-Maqrizi mentions that the Caliph Abdel Aziz Ibn Marwan became even fiercer in his attitudes. During his reign, his

---

[29] Dr Saydah El Kashef - Egypt During the Era of Governors / Rulers – p. 14 - 122

[30] Essa is the Arabic for Jesus.

[31] The History of the Patriarchs, p. 279

son, El-Asbagh went to a Monastery at Helwan where he saw an icon of St Mary carrying the infant Jesus Christ. He spat on it saying:

> "Should I live long enough, I would exterminate all Copts from this country. Who is that Christ who they worship?"

God manifested His strength that night. El-Asbagh had a nightmare and reported that dream to his father. The following night, his son suffered a sudden severe fever and died instantly. In forty days, his father died also. This took place during the papacy of Alexander II.[32]

During the Patriarchate of Kha'el I (744-768 AD), el-Kassem ibn-Abdalla, el hegab, was in charge of collecting the kharaj. He was a womaniser. He was about to enter the monastery of St. Shenouda in Upper Egypt, mounting his horse. Accompanying him was a mistress on another horse. The Abbot tried to stop him. El-Kassem refused arrogantly and went on entering the church. The other horse bolted suddenly and the mistress fell on the ground and died instantly. El-Kassem was attacked by a satanic spirit, torturing him till his death.

Concerning tribulations against the clergymen and lay Copts

There were numerous people responsibly for collecting the kharaj, as rulers had a hidden purpose they needed fulfilled. That purpose was to build massive wealth within a short

[32] The History of the Patriarchs, pp. 307-308

time span. They were fully aware that their rulership was not long by any measure. The rulers invented severe methods to torment and to torture Copts in order to obtain the maximum kharaj. Copts were robbed, tortured, and murdered. For historic credibility, we must add that this harsh treatment affected the entire Egyptian population: Copts and Muslims. But the Copts' share was greater, as they were Christians. We will now cite some examples.

IMPORTANT PERSONALITIES OF THE TIME

Pope John of Samanud
40th Patriarch (677-686 AD)

Pope John of Samanud suffered a lot under the Caliph Abdel Aziz ibn-Marwan (685-705 AD). An evil person envied the Pope. Once when the Caliph Abdel Aziz ibn-Marwan went to Alexandria to collect the kharaj, the Pope could not meet him, being ill and elderly. The evil person misinterpreted this to the Caliph as being an act of arrogance. The Caliph, accordingly, ordered the Patriarch be arrested, fined 100,000 denarii, and made to stand on fire balls. On the verge of executing these orders, the wife of the Caliph was told in a vision to ask her husband not to do any harm to the Patriarch. However, the Caliph still threatened the Patriarch by dressing him in Jewish, dirtying his face, touring him around the city in such a state. However, the Patriarch showed no fear. The Caliph gradually reduced the fine down to 10,000 denarii. The Christians donated to the Patriarch to cover the cost this fine, to save the whole church from any further persecution.[33]

Pope Alexander II
41st Patriarch (705-730 AD)

Toward the end of his Caliphate (which lasted about 20 years) he delegated full power to his eldest son el-Asbagh to run the country. El-Asbagh hated the Christians immensely, and he was bloodthirsty. He employed various means to anger the Christians. A person named Benjamin assisted him to achieve his ultimate purpose. Benjamin was a deacon who had apostatised and embraced Islam. They became intimate friends, suggesting to El-Asbagh methods to annoy and thereby reduce the number of Copts. El-Asbagh sent two messengers to the monasteries of Wadi el-Natrun to circumcise all monks! A jizyah of one denarii was imposed on each monk as well. Monasteries were ordered not to accept any new monks. Bishops were also ordered to pay a 2,000 denarii, in addition to the already imposed jizyah. The immediate effect of these policies was the conversion of numerous Copts to Islam. Among those converted were Peter, the ruler of Upper Egypt, and his brother Theodore, and many others among the laypersons. Jesus Christ did not leave El-Asbagh to continue in this manner for long.

One Bright Saturday, El-Asbagh went to a Monastery at Helwan where he saw an icon of St Mary carrying the infant Jesus Christ. He asked the bishops about that icon. He spat on it saying:

> "Should I live long enough, I would exterminate all Copts from this country. Who is that Christ who they worship?"

---

[33] The History of the Patriarchs, p. 267

God manifested His strength that night. El-Asbagh had a dream where he saw Jesus Christ sitting on His Throne, with a face shining like the sun, while he saw his father the Caliph in fetters. In the dream, El-Asbagh enquird concerning the identity of Him Who is sitting on the Throne. The following night, his son suffered a sudden severe fever and died instantly. In forty days, his father died also.

Abdallah abdel Malek (705-709 AD) succeeded Abdel Aziz Ibn Marawan. Abdel Malek was the son of the Umayyad Caliph Abdel Malek ibn Marwan. He was so cruel that Severus ibn el-Moqafaa described him saying, "he was like a wild beast, he sat and ate while his guards were killing people, and he rejoiced when blood splattered onto his plate." Pope Alexander went to congratulate him for becoming the new Ruler over Egypt. When Abdel Malek realised that the guest was the Coptic Patriarch, he handed him to his guards, ordering to humiliate the Patriarch to any limit until he pay 3,000 denarii. The Copts tried to reduce the fine. Eventually, the Patriarch was released after two months. The Patriarch toured around the cities and villages until he could finally collect the imposed fine.[34]

The Governor used to gather Christian clergymen to humiliate them, saying, "To me, you are like the Romans. The killer of any of you would be forgiven, for you are God's enemies." The governor also prohibited the burying of any Copt unless and until the family of the deceased pays the due jizyah on the deceased.

---

[34] The History of the Patriarchs, pp. 308-309

Afterwards, another governor came, named Korra ibn-Shareek (709-714 AD). The same scenario repeated itself with Pope Alexander. The governor said to the Pope who went to congratulate him on the governorship: "Whatever you paid my predecessor, you ought to pay me now."

The governor meant 3,000 denarii. The Patriarch endeavoured to explain that Christianity disallows possessions and wealth accumulation, and that what happened with the predecessor was a result of a plot, and that he was now bankrupt. He even went on saying that there was still a sum of 500 denarii due to the predecessor. After a futile conversation between the two, the governor said "all what you said was in vain, you must make this payment even if you have to sell your flesh, or else you will not escape my hands." Finally, realising that it was a hopeless case, the Patriarch asked the governor to let him go to Upper Egypt, promising that whatever he could accumulate of donations would be dispatched to the governor.[35]

The greed of Quorra the governor was unprecedented, for he seized overtook all the inheritance left by bishops, deacons and Coptic lay people. Severus said:

> *"All people, women and children, fled from one place to another, remained in a state of homelessness in order to evade the kharaj. His greed exceeded that of all his predecessors."*[36]

After Quorra, a new governor was installed, named Osama ibn-Zaid, who was before the governorship in charge of

---

[35] The History of the Patriarchs, p. 312-313

[36] The History of the Patriarchs, p. 318

the collection of kharaj. He ordered the monasteries not to accept new monks. He fitted a metal ring on the left arm of each monk, indicating the monk's name and his monastery's name. The stamp also displayed 'The Kingdom of Islam.' He then ordered that whichever monk would attempt to escape the payment was to be punished by the removal of any of his organs. Many monks became disfigured because of this punishment. The governor also shaved their beards and plucked out the eyes of others. Many died while being whipped. He even ordered the rulers to kill people and to bring their wealth to him. He directed his rulers saying,

> "I have put your people under your power, so seize whatever you can, fabrics, animals or money, from everyone and anyone. Do not make any consideration or allowance towards anyone. Any place you go to, rob it." [37]

Obeid Allah ibn-El-Habhab, another Kharaj collector, was equally unjust and greedy. He committed all kinds of unjust deeds. He stamped the image of lions on the hands of Copts. Had any Copt been found without such a stamp, his hand was to be cut off. They even tried to stamp it on the hand of Pope Alexander II, but he refused. He was so sad that he prayed to God to end his life on this earth. The Pope died soon after.[38]

Bishop Gamoul, Bishop of Oseem, was also captured and convicted of assisting in the escape of Pope Alexander. A fine of 1,000 denarii was imposed on the Bishop. But the

---

[37] The History of the Patriarchs, p. 322-323

[38] The History of the Patriarchs, p. 332-333

The Coptic Church Under Muslim Rulers (642-868)   83

Bishop was too poor to even have sufficient daily food. The governor then handed over the Bishop to be tortured. They dragged him to the Gate of Saint George Church in Old Cairo and they removed his clothes and hanged him naked. Then they whipped him savagely until the Christians collected 300 denarii, then the Bishop was released.[39]

Another kharaj collector named Abi Garrah had two brothers. The three of them went to Saint Mary's Monastery near Tinnis, and there they expelled the monks and robbed the entire place. The younger brother spat on a cross in one of the cells. An anchorite was stunned at the event, and cried towards heaven saying that if God does not avenge immediately, I will not remain in this monastery. The younger brother went to use the bathroom where his viscera spilled outside his body, as had happened with Arius the blasphemous. There was a great fear among the Muslims at that place.[40]

Then came Hafsse ibn Abdel-Walid al-Hadramy (742-745 AD). He ordered that all inhabitants in Egypt pray the Sunnite prayers. He also decreed that he who converts to Islam would be exempt from paying the jizyah. Satan misled many causing them to abandon Christianity. Due to the immense tribulations that befell the Copts, the Bishops moved to monasteries to pray to God. It is said that the number of those who had converted to Islam through this incident were 24,000. The Bishop of Ouseem prophesied

---

[39] The History of the Patriarchs, p. 332-333

[40] The History of the Patriarchs, p. 356-357

that God would take vengeance on Hafsse by burning his body in the midst of Al Fustat. This actually took place when Caliph Marwan II sent Hawthara ibn-Soheil (745 AD) to Egypt, leading a force of 5,000 soldiers in order to become the governor of Egypt. Hawthara defeated Hafsse, burnt his body and overtook all his wealth.[41]

Disturbances took place during the rulership of Abdel Malek ibn-Moussa. The ruler was hostile towards Pope Kha'el, attempting to force him to pay kharaj. When the pope could not pay, the ruler ordered the arrest of the Pope and for him to be bound in fetters. Along with the Pope, other Bishops were arrested, namely Bishop Moses of Ouseem, Bishop Theodore of Cairo, and Bishop Elijah, a spiritual disciple of Bishop Moses. They were all placed in a dark cell. Bishop Kha'el remained in fetters for almost a month, during which time he did not even see sunlight. Additionally, there were three hundred men and women imprisoned. The Pope was only released on one condition: that he heads towards Upper Egypt to collect whatever he could from fellow Copts. The ruler took all that was donated. The coming of King Cyriacus, King of Nubia, to Egypt influenced the release. The Nubian Church was under the auspices of the Coptic Church.[42]

Abdel Malek ibn-Moussa was so cruel during his term as a ruler of Egypt. Bishop Severus said in his 'The History of the Patriarchs,' that Egypt had not witnessed any safety or peace during his rulership, for he was not a descendent of

[41] The History of the Patriarchs, p. 371

[42] The History of the Patriarchs, p. 385-393

The Coptic Church Under Muslim Rulers (642-868)

Ishmael's race (the Arabs). He did not stop short of doing anything to upset the Christians. But our God restored the ruler's heart to show compassion towards Pope Kha'el. The ruler invited the Pope to the palace, as his four year old daughter was possessed by an evil spirit. The ruler asked the Pope to pray for the young girl. The Pope anointed her with oil, and the evil spirit immediately left her. The ruler, from that moment, started to show love to the Copts and began to give due respect and honour to the Coptic Bishops.

In year 750 AD, Marwan ibn-Mohamed Ali arrived to Egypt, fleeing the Abbasids. Upon his arrival, he issued the following decree:

> "Anyone who does not pray my prayers and does not follow my instructions will be crucified and put to death. I will protect anyone who converts to my religion."[43]

The army of Marwan kept run amok around Upper Egypt, pillaging it. They killed many deacons, confiscated their wealth, captured their women, their families and children. They additionally burnt monasteries and convents and captured nuns. Historic sources inform us of a story of a convent near Akhmim where thirty nuns were taken by the soldiers. After seizing the convent, they went on to rape a pretty young nun named Veronia. She thought of a trick to save herself from being raped and humiliated. She told them deceitfully that whichever body part is rubbed with oil would not be injured even by swords. She rubbed oil on her neck and asked the soldiers to strike it with a sword

---
[43] The History of the Patriarchs

to see for themselves. They did and she departed without humiliation, but as a pure virgin. The soldiers were terrified and immediately departed the convent. They left all they had seized.[44]

The History of the Patriarchs tells us the heavy burdens on people by the end of the Ummayad period, when Marwan burnt Al Fustat. People hurried to cross the Nile to Giza; many drowned in the Nile along with their cattle. Bishop Severus described the incident saying that brother abandoned brother, the blind had no one to guide them, the bed-ridden were left unaided, the elder left unaided, left behind to be engulfed by fire. People were lying on roads; starvation and drought was widespread, as Marwan had burnt all the crops.[45]

The Abbasids ruled Egypt after the Ummayads (750 AD). They initially made positive overtures to the Copts. But the rulers themselves were the actual problem. They were extremely unfair and held grudges towards the Ummayads.

They had the same motives as the Ummayads - to take the wealth and riches of the Egyptians. The Egyptian people could not complain to the Caliph who was now based at Baghdad.

Bishop Severus mentioned that during the era of Patriarch Eusabius I (830-849 AD) a decree came from Baghdad with a Nestorian messenger named Alizar, which requested the

---

[44] The History of the Patriarchs, pp. 417-418

[45] The History of the Patriarchs, p. 422

removal of all marble columns and floors from churches in order to ornament the palaces of Baghdad, for Egypt was very well known for its opulent architectural heritage. When Alizar arrived, the Chalcedonians who were living in Alexandria joined forces him. They directed him to the luxurious churches within Alexandria. The messenger ended at the monastery of Saint Mina, of Mariotis, which had been decorated by Byzantine emperors. Alizar, upon seeing the wonderful scene, uttered that this was exactly what the Caliph wanted. When Pope Eusabius heard that, he said to the Nestorian messenger, "All churches under my hands are between your hands, whatever you ask me for, I will grant." Alizar went on removing all marble and coloured porcelain, granite and sandstones, which Bishop Severus describes as of inestimable value. The Pope restored the ruined churches and monasteries afterwards. God manifested His strength, striking Alizar with sciatica.[46]

The Copts realised that they were too optimistic, that no matter the amount of love shown by Arab rulers, they would never cease collecting taxes. They started to regard the Arabs as invaders. They resolved to rid themselves of these invaders. They would not remain crippled in the face of rulers and governors. Many revolts took place in different areas of Egypt especially Lower Egypt. These revolts lasted for almost a century. The most important revolts are listed below:

1.   During the rulership of Hisham ibn Abdel-Malek, an Ummayad Caliph (724-727 AD), residents of the eastern border of Damietta boycotted the payments of taxes. The

[46] The History of the Patriarchs, p. 626-628

Caliph sent soldiers to combat them. When the soldiers found that the residents were stronger than what the Caliph thought, he went out himself to fight. The confrontation remained for three months. Many victims fell on both sides. The Copts did not give up easily, but sacrificed their lives.

2. The second rulership of Hanzala ibn-Safwan (737-742 AD), a tyrannical ruler, placed more burdens on the people. He introduced additional taxes on animals. He mistreated all people especially the Copts. He attacked the Upper Egyptians to force them to pay the kharaj. One encounter took place between his soldiers and the inhabitants where numerous Copts were killed. People complained to the Caliph who in turn isolated Hanzala, and placed Hafs ibn el-Walid in his stead.

3. During the rule of Abdallah ibn-Moussa who levied excessive taxes on the Copts, he further forced Pope Kha'el (744-768 AD) and the bishops to pay unbearable fines. The Patriarch asked for an ultimatum until he could collect the imposed fines. The Patriarch went first to Upper Egypt, where he found the Copts in an unsuitable state to make any payment. He moved from one place to another. It is said that Cyriacus, king of Nubia gathered his forces and marched to Egypt until be came near Al Fustat. Abdallah ibn-Moussa was disturbed for he had a smaller army than the Nubians. This situation was made worse with the arrival of the Abbasids. The ruler called the Patriarch and cleared him from these unfair fines and asked him to mediate between himself and the King of Nubia. Pope

Kha'el obeyed and convinced the Nubian King to withdraw from Egypt.

4. The conflict between the Ummayads and Abbasids intensified leading Marwan ibn-Mohamed to flee from the Abbasids. The Bashmurites revolted against the Arab conquest.

5. When Patriarch Kha'el was arrested and mistreated by Marwan, all Copts took the side of the Abbasids. Bishop Severus said in this regard, "The Copts said to Marwan, this is our Patriarch, held by the infidel Marwan. We do not know what the infidel is doing to him. The Bashmurites encountered the Abbasids at the Farama. They told the Abbasids about the arrested Patriarch. Howthara was with Marwan telling him that the Patriarch asked the Bashmurites to keep fighting, and God would give the rulership to the enemy of Marwan. So Marwan replied, addressing the Patriarch saying, "you are the head of our enemies." Marwan ordered his soldiers to pull the Patriarch's beard and to throw it in the sea.[47] The History of the Patriarchs, also described the defeat of the Ummayads by the Abbasids thus, "God was with the Abbasids, they relieved the Copts from excessive kharag, they treated the Copts gently." The Abbasids crucified Marwan upside down. They went to the new ruler asking him to release the holy bishop Kha'el and they glorified him greatly.[48]

---

[47] The History of the Patriarchs, p. 426-427

[48] The History of the Patriarchs, p. p. 626-628

When the Ummayads fell, the Abbasids ruled over Egypt. Their headquarters was in Baghdad. The Abbasids were more aware than Amro ibn el-Asse. They employed and made use of the services of the original residents of Egypt. The Copts were very cooperative hoping to get rid of the previous mistreatment. However, at times, the previous bitterness was relived under the Abbasids. The Abbasids soon imposed enormous taxes. Bishop Severus said in this regard, "in the third year under the Abbasids, kharaj was doubled on the Copts. They did not fulfil their promises." The Abbasids treated people in the same manner as the Ummayads did. Under the Caliphate of Abi Ga'far el-Mansour, his ruler Yazid ibn-Hatem ibn el-Mahlab (762-769 AD) harshly and aggressively treated Patriarch Mina I, and the Copts were greatly dissatisfied at what had befallen their shepherd. At Rosetta (Rashid) and Sakha, Copts revolted against that discrimination. The ruler sent his forces to combat the Copts, who were successful in defeating the ruler's soldiers. The governor became furious at the Copts and ordered the destruction of their churches. The Copts of Al Fustat offered to give him the sum of 50,000 denarii in return for the safety of their churches. He refused and insisted on destroying all churches, which he did.

During the rulership of el-Layth ibn-Fadl (799-803 AD) he sent prisoners to survey the lands and to reduce the dimensions of each block of land. The people objected to this action. El-Layth went to fight them and he was defeated. The Copts and the Arabs gathered and marched to Al Fustat where he killed many of them. He arrested about eighty of their leaders and decapitated them. They carried their heads to Al Fustat to terrify the people. This act only led to further the revolts across Lower Egypt. These revolts extended to the rulership of el-Ma'mun in 813 AD.

6. During the rulership of El-Ma'mun (813-833 AD), people exploded after their anger at discrimination had been bottled up for many years. The Copts of Lower Egypt ceased paying the kharaj and some Arabs joined them. Many fights took place between the governors and locals, and many were killed. These revolts were the severest of all revolts. El-Ma'mun was occupied with fighting the Romans. Issa ibn-Mansour (831-832 AD) was the Governor. When that Caliph met the Governor, he attributed the sufferings of the people to his deeds and to his injustice. The Caliph ordered the outer attire of the governor be removed as a sign of dissatisfaction toward his conduct. Some Muslim historians mention that when the Caliph saw the turmoil in Lower Egypt, he ordered the killing of men, the sale of women and the capture of children. The Coptic historians mentioned that Patriarch Eusebius (830-849 AD) visited the Caliph when he arrived to Egypt. The Caliph received the Patriarch with respect and asked him to address his Coptic people, advising them to remain calm to avoid bloodshed, and the Caliph would promise to look at their complaints personally. The Patriarch wrote to his people and they obeyed except the people of Bashmur. The Bashmurites refused to comply or to submit, they were more determined to resist and fight. When the Caliph heard of their stance, he sent some forces to crush them and made their village a ruin, killed their men and demolished their churches. The Caliph remained in Egypt for almost two

months, attempting to calm people down and he released the Copts of their outstanding debts. This was the last and the most significant of all Coptic revolts.

Patriarch Eusebius endeavoured to quieten the Bashmurites, without much success. Bishop Severus described the misery of the Bashmurites. He added,

> "Many died of hunger, the kharak collectors were the cruellest ever, harming and injuring people, humiliating them in order to gain the maximum kharaj out of the citizens. The Bashmurites had to sell their children for they could not pay the kharaj. They were helpless. So they revolted and ceased to pay the kharag."[49]

A state of revolt continued for over a century, especially in lower Egypt. These revolts were not technically planned or organised. These revolts were without leaders, the Copts failed to appoint a wise and strong leader; all revolts were spontaneous reactions to the burden of taxes and poverty. Partly, the revolts resulted from discrimination. El-Maqurizi said that after the Bashmurite revolt ended, the Muslims became the majority in that village as well as across Egypt. Many Copts converted to Islam following the horrifying experiences during the successive revolts. It seems that el-Maqrizi's report is greatly exaggerated.

---

[49] The History of the Patriarchs, pp. 600-601

THE PLIGHT OF THE COPTIC LANGUAGE

The Coptic language was the means of communication until the end of the last quarter of the fourth century B.C. when the Alexander the Great conquered Egypt and it was replaced by the Greek language until the Arabs came to Egypt in 640 AD. However, Coptic was still the language used among the Copts, as well as in government offices.

The Greek language prevailed over the whole world at that time, it was also used in the famous School of Alexandria, yet the Copts kept dealing in the Coptic language, and it was the official language of government departments until the Arab invasion.

During the reign of El Walid Ibn Abdelmalek Al Amawy, and the governor of Egypt Abdallah Ibn Abdelmalek in the year 705 or 706 AD the Arabic language was announced as the official language of the country instead of the Coptic language. Governor Abdallah hated the Christians intensely and deprived them of all the positions in the government. Up until that time the Copts carried high positions in the government and they were responsible for all the administrative and accounting departments under the supervision of a loyal employee named Athnas, but he was fired by Abdallah Ibn Abdelmalek, and replaced by Yarbou El Ghazawi from Syria.

The Copts then started learning the Arabic language, trying to keep their positions in the government, and books entitled 'The Ladders' were published, where words were written in both Coptic and Arabic. Also the names of cities were translated to Arabic and thus lost their original pronunciation.

In her book 'Egypt during the era of Governors', Dr. Sayyeda Kashef wrote:

> "Around 50 years after entering Egypt, the Arabs started enforcing the Arabic language across the country because they did not know the Coptic language. All the government documents started to be written in Arabic, to the extent that El Asbagh Ibn Abdelaziz Ibn Marwan ordered that the Holy Bible be translated into the Arabic language to make sure that there is nothing attacking Islam in this Book! Thus Arabic became the official language of the government departments, and Egypt became an Arabic country, politically, administratively, culturally, religiously and in all other aspects."[50]

The worst era was that of the Fatimid Governor El Hakem Be'amr Ellah (996-1021) who banned the use of the Coptic language in homes and on the street, threatening to cut the tongue of whoever speaks Coptic. Parents were also threatened to stop talking to their children in Coptic, and so this language was only used in churches and monasteries.

Fear and horror pervaded the country, and the priests used

---

[50] Dr. Sayyeda Kashef "Egypt during the era of Governors", P.119-120

to put black curtains in the churches while praying the Holy Liturgy, because the brutal governors used to attack the churches and kill whoever was attending if they hear prayers in the Coptic language.

Pope Gabriel Ibn Turek (1131-1146) was the first to set the rule of reading the Gospel and Epistles, as well as giving the sermon, in Arabic instead of Coptic at churches.

By the ninth century Arabic nearly replaced Coptic, and by the thirteenth century Christian authors started publishing their books in Arabic. Some of them were Awlad El-Assal, Girgis Ibn El Ameed known as Ibn Mekeen, Abu Shaker Ibn Elraheb the deacon at the Hanging Church, Shams Elreasa Abu El Barakat Ibn Kibr, Fr Botros El Sadmanty, Elm Elreasa Ibn Kateb Qaisar. Erudite individuals employed simplified Coptic grammar and wrote down its vocabulary to preserve the language from perishing totally.

The first Copt to publish a book written in the Arabic language was Sawiros Ibn El Moqafaa' Bishop of Ashmoneen who was a contemporary of Pope Abraam Ibn Zaraa' the Syrian the 62nd Patriarch (975-979). He also translated the lives of the Popes based on the manuscripts found at St. Macarius Monastery, in addition to the ones he found with some Christians. Someone named Boulos Ibn Ragaa' (mentioned in the life of Pope Thawfilos the 63rd Patriarch during the year 978-1003) helped him with editing the Arabic words and expression.

In spite of the spread of the Arabic language, people in

North Egypt and its surroundings kept using the Coptic language until the 17th century. In a lecture about 'The Relationship between the Egyptians in the Past and Now' given by Maspiro in 1908 he said:

> "It is clear that people in Upper Egypt kept using the Coptic language during the early years of the 16th century at the beginning of the Turks' reign in Egypt."

Al Maqrizi in the 15th century stated concerning Moosha Monastery:

> "Most of those in these monasteries speak the Upper Egyptian Coptic language, the same language of the mothers in Upper Egypt and their children."

When the Coptic language was nearly vanishing by the 18th century, the Copts started writing it using the Arabic alphabet. Although this language faced so many challenges, it still exists as the language of the church.

THE ARAB INVASION OF EGYPT

Amr Ibn Elaas came to Egypt heading an army of 4,000 warriors, while Omar Ibn El Khattab sent another 4,000 for support. Many of these soldiers were killed during the invasion which means that the number of Christians in Egypt was much more than that of the soldiers. The Arabs did not live with the Christians but rather lived in Al Fustat situated on the north of Babylon Fortress (which is the area from the River Nile up till Muqqatam Mountain). Omar Ibn El Khattab banned them from working in agriculture or owning land, so that they would only concentrate on politics and warfare, thus at the beginning the Arabs did not mingle with the Copts, and did not affect them by any means whether concerning religion or language.

During the reign of Hisham Ibn Abdallah (724-744), the situation changed when around 3,000 Arabs came and settled in the east of Delta, they were allowed to work in agriculture and so they started mingling with the Copts, and Islam started spreading in Egypt.

Historical Facts

We mentioned previously that tribulations used to come from the Muslim governors, but in fact, sometimes troubles arose from inside the church by Christian priests or laymen, some of these examples are as follows:

Pope Simon I
42nd Patriarch (689-701)

He was living in extreme piety, eating vegetables only and practising his canon strictly from before becoming Pope. Some priests envied him and four of them put some poison prepared by sorcerers in his water cup. After partaking of the Holy Communion, Pope Simon drank the water and it did not harm him. They tried several more times, but in vain. Then they put a very strong poison in some figs and insisted he eat the figs, so he was sick for around 40 days, but the Lord healed him.

When the Governor came to visit the Pope and knew about the poison, he ordered to burn the four priests and the sorcerers, yet the Pope knelt before the Governor weeping and pleaded him to forgive them saying: "If they are punished because of me, I also should be killed, and I ought not to be a Pope any more."

The Governor kept the four priests but ordered to burn the sorcerers to be an example to others.[51]

Pope Alexandros II
43rd Patriarch (705-730)

During his era there was a monk deacon named Benjamin who was a close friend to the Governor's son and used to tell him all the sensitive information about the Christians. This infuriated people, to the extent that some Christians became Muslims because of his might and pressure, including lots of priests and laymen.[52] In addition to all the afflictions that befell Pope Alexandros by the Governor of Egypt Qura Ibn Sharik (709-714), there was a person named Tawadros the administrator of Alexandria who asked the Pope to give him 3,000 denarii saying: "Even if you have to sell your flesh, you have to give me the money."[53]

---

[51] The History of the Patriarchs p. 286-287

[52] The History of the Patriarchs, p. 305-306

[53] The History of the Patriarchs p. 311-312

Pope Mina I
47th Patriarch (767-774)

Pope Mina I was afflicted badly by a deacon named Botros who desired earnestly to become a Bishop, but when the Pope refused to ordain him because of his unworthiness, he went to Syria and gave Pope Gerga of Antioch and his Bishops fake letters from Pope Mina stating that the church in Egypt is suffering great turmoil and persecution. So Pope Gerga ordered to collect a large amount of money from all the churches and to give it to Botros, who immediately went to Baghdad, which was the headquarters of the Caliph. He started giving money to the workers in the Palace of the Governor and saying that the Pope of Egypt can manufacture gold using a special chemical equation which he was privy to; thus the churches' utensils were all made of pure gold!

The Caliph Al Abbasy Al Mansour liked and was greatly attached to deacon Botros because he looked exactly like his son who had passed away, and he was ready to do anything to please Botros. In turn, Botros asked him to give him a letter to the governor of Egypt appointing him as the Pope in replacement of Pope Mina I, also giving him authority over Pope Mina I and all his Bishops.

The Caliph did so and gave him a letter to the governor of Egypt Abdallah Ibn Abdel Rahman (769-772 AD). When the governor read the letter to Pope Mina I he refused because that was contradicting the church's laws, and asked him to give him few days to assemble with the Bishops and discuss the issue.

Botros kept pestering the governor and asked him to arrest the Pope, meanwhile allowing him to enter the churches as if he himself were the Pope. So the governor arrested Pope Mina I and Bishop Tawadros, and allowed the fake Pope Botros to meet all the Bishops, while Pope Mina I issued a letter to all the Bishops supporting and strengthening them.

Botros assembled with the Bishops in Al Fustat, and as he was going into the altar to pray the Thanksgiving Prayer as usual, Bishop Mina of Sanabo and Bishop Moses of Osim snatched his hood on which was written 'Botros the Pope of Egypt' next to the text 'Caliph El Mansour' telling him: "Why are you defiling the churches of Egypt?"

He was so angry and asked the soldiers to imprison all the Bishops. There, they met Pope Mina I who kept comforting them by saying:

"My beloved, He Who is defending us is greater and more powerful than those who attack us, the Lord will save us from the hands of our enemies." Then the governor released the Pope and the Bishops asking them to give him the golden utensils of the church as advised by Botros.

This governor was a kind one who liked the Christians, so when Botros noticed his compassion towards the Pope and the Bishops, he threatened him to tell the Caliph that he was not carrying his orders. The governor did not like Botros' threatening attitude and imprisoned him for three years,

The Coptic Church Under Muslim Rulers (642-868) 101

after which another governor ruled Egypt who sent him back to the Caliph.

Botros did not achieve anything whatsoever, he denied his Christianity and became a Muslim.[54]

Pope Yousab
52nd Patriarch (830-849)

According to the decision of the Holy Synod, Pope Yousab he was obliged to excommunicate Bishop Isaac of Tinnis and Bishop Tadros of Cairo after they were accused by their congregation, who threatened to deny their Christianity if these two bishops were not excommunicated. These two Bishops seized a chance when there was a big gathering at St. Mary's Church at Kasr El Shame' on Palm Sunday, where a righteous man was ordained as a deacon and he had been nominated for the Papacy before Pope Yousab. They went to the chief general of the army, who had just calmed down an uprising of the Bashmors, and informed him that it was Pope Yousab who had fomented the uprising and that he was gathering with the people at the Church hatching a plot to kill the general.

The General was drunk at that time so he asked his brother to head to the church accompanied by a huge number of soldiers in order to kill the Pope. Isaac the Bishop of Tinnis led them to the Pope. As soon as the General's brother dragged his sword to kill the Pope, the sword accidentally hit a marble pillar in the church and was broken. He was so

---
[54] The History of the Patriarchs p.476-493

mad and got another knife which he had and stabbed the Pope, but again the Lord protected him and the knife just cut the leather rope around his waist and did not touch his body.

Seeing this miracle, he just decided to take the Pope to his brother the General, but as the congregation were shouting and weeping he hit the Pope with a knocker on his head, which hurt his eyes.

Standing before the General, Pope Yousab explained the issue of the Bashmors' outrage, as well as the excommunication of the two Bishops; thus the General was turned against the two bishops and asked his soldiers to kill them. The Pope pleaded him saying:

> "My religion orders me to reward with good those who do evil to me, I ask you please to forgive them and let them go."

The General was greatly astonished at the Pope's kind heart and let them go.[55]

Also during the era of Pope Yousab, a person named Tawadros wanted to be ordained Bishop of Osim despite the congregation's refusal. When the Pope refused, Tawadros headed to the Governor and asked him to convince the Pope. When the Pope would not budge, the Governor was greatly annoyed and ordered that all the churches be demolished, starting with the Hanging Church in Old Cairo. The wise Christian elders advised the Pope to ordain Tawadros and

---

[55] The History of the Patriarchs p. 604-615

save the rest of the churches, so he agreed and the Governor asked him to pay an amount of 3,000 denarii as a fine, which he gathered from the righteous Christians.

But God the Almighty took vengeance on this brutal Governor and he was killed by the Romans when the Caliph sent him to invade their city.

Another incident which took place with Pope Yousab concerned a bishop named Bana. He wanted to have a higher rank over the other Bishops, and as the Pope refused, he went and befriended a wicked judge named Muhammad Ibn Abdullah, who in turn gathered the other Bishops and asked the Pope to come.

He asking the Pope, "Who appointed you to rule over all the Christians in this country?" The Pope answered: "God", so the judge addressed the Bishops saying: "Do not listen to or obey this Pope. From now on, your Pope is Bana." The Bishops agreed and that was because of a previous agreement between them and the judge who had already taken a sum of money. But Pope Yousab rebuked them in Coptic and someone translated his words to the judge who was greatly annoyed for disobeying him.

The Pope told him that he could not object to the decision of God and the Caliphs, and showed him letters from the Caliphs giving him full authority over the Christians as their Pope. The judge's face turned red and he was greatly ashamed.[56]

---

[56] The History of the Patriarchs p. 637-641

IMPORTANT PERSONALITIES OF THE TIME

Pope Benjamin I
38th Patriarch (623-662)

Born in the Bershout village in Boheira, he was from a very wealthy family, but since his childhood he leaned toward monasticism, so at an early age he became a monk at Canopus Monastery (recently known as Abu Qir-Alexandria). It was revealed to him in a vision that he would tend to the flock of Lord Christ, and since then God was preparing him for this task. He was ordained as a priest by Pope Andronicus the 37th Patriarch and was his assistant, and he recommended him to be his successor after his departure.

The era of Pope Benjamin is characterised by three distinctive periods:

First Period: Starts at his ordination in the year 623 AD until his disappearance 631 AD

He was ordained during the last 5 years of the Persian rule in Egypt which was a relatively calm period. He made a pastoral visit to Babylon Fortress in Old Cairo, and sent a pastoral letter to the Bishops to be stricter with the newly ordained priests, and he also suspended those of distorted spirituality.

After the withdrawal of the Persians, the Romans came back

to rule the country; the Pope spent 3 years in total calmness because Emperor Hercules was busy sorting some problems left by the Persians.

Second Period: From 631 AD- 644 AD

Pope Benjamin disappeared during this period until Amr Ibnelaas sent him a letter that he would be safe if he came back. This period was characterised by many problems and divisions due to the Emperor's political policy, trying to impose a new doctrine by force, in addition to appointing Al Mukawkas as the Chalcedonian Patriarch.

It is said that the Lord had revealed to Pope Benjamin what was about to happen and ordered him and his Bishops to disappear in order to be able to guide and shepherd their congregation secretly. Actually, he wrote a letter to the Bishops stating this fact and advising them to strengthen their congregation that they may maintain their strong faith until the last breath.

Pope Benjamin stayed in hiding in Wadi El Natroun Monasteries, and then headed to Upper Egypt Monasteries. He was in hiding for 13 years. During this period the Arabs invaded Egypt and occupied it.

Third Period: From 644 AD until his departure in 662 AD

Egypt started being ruled by the Arabs, and Pope Benjamin

continued shepherding his flock, especially after gaining favour in the eyes of Amr Ibnelass. He therefore gave the Pope authority over all the churches as the legal Patriarch of Egypt; giving him back all the Coptic churches taken by the Romans particularly in Alexandria.

The Pope's achievements during this period include;

1- Strengthening the Orthodox faith among the Copts of Egypt and restoring those who had gone astray towards the Chalcedonian faith.

2- Calling the Bishops who – under pressure - followed Al Mukawkas and lots of them came back to the Orthodox Church repenting.

3- He replaced the Chalcedonian bishops with Coptic Orthodox bishops after the Romans were unable to send a new Patriarch to Egypt from 651 to 728.

4- Returning St. Mark's head after a sailor stole it from his church in Alexandria thinking it was a treasure as it was wrapped in satin cloth. However, his ship would not move from the Alexandrian harbour, so the Pope took the head back to St. Mark's Church praising and glorifying the Lord. This church was burnt up during the Arab invasion of Alexandria in 646 AD and was rebuilt by his successor Pope Agathon the 39th Patriarch.

5- He consecrated St. Macarius Church at his monastery in the Scetis Wilderness. It is said that during the consecration, Pope Benjamin saw St. Macarius among his monks, and he decided in his heart to ordain him as a Bishop whenever a bishopric needed one, but a seraphim appeared and revealed the true identity of St. Macarius. During the consecration of the church with the Mayroun,

Pope Benjamin saw the Hand of the Lord Jesus anointing the altar with him.

Pope Khaeil
46th Patriarch (744 - 768)

The Papal Seat was empty for around one year and a half before his ordination, and then heavenly signs pointed to this monk who was at St. Macarius Monastery. This Pope tolerated severe persecutions and tribulations and he was a contemporary of the last era of the Umayyad rule and the beginning of the Abbasids. The Chalcedonians tried to occupy St. Mina's Church at Mariout, and they became even stronger after having a Patriarch named Qesma (728-756 AD), supported by Thawfilex the Roman Patriarch in Syria who was a close friend to the Umayyad Caliph Marawan Ibn Muhammad. He tricked the Caliph and made him write a letter to the Governor of Egypt Abdel Malik Ibn Marawan to occupy the previously mentioned St. Mina Church.

The Governor investigated the issue personally at the beginning, then delegated a Judge whom they bribed and thus he started procrastination. Some suggested that Pope Khaeil would give some money to the Judge, yet bishop Moses of Osim rejected and declared that they would never bribe anyone and that God would never abandon them. On the same week the bribed Judge was suspended, another Judge took over who was a just one issuing a decree assuring that the Copts the owners of this church.

During that time the first conference of Christian unity was held between the Copts, the Romans and the Chalcedonians in March or April 749 AD. The Chalcedonians were the ones who called for this conference after their failure in St. Mina's Church issue.

Pope Khaeil sent two delegates from his side: Father Mina who succeeded Pope Khaeil and he was very knowledgeable concerning the church books; and Deacon Yehnes the writer of the lives of the Popes. They both assembled with Qesma the Chalcedonian Patriarch and Constantine the Chalcedonian bishop of Egypt, who both confessed the One Nature of Lord Jesus Christ after Incarnation and not two natures. When they were asked to write down their confession and send it to the Pope, they asked about what their position and that of their bishops would be after the unity with the Coptic Orthodox Church. Qesma wanted to be treated as a Pope exactly likely Pope Khaeil, so they told him they would have to check with Pope Khaeil first but Bishop Moses assured him that after the unity it was not proper to have two Popes, and he suggested for Qesma to be the Bishop of Cairo and a brother to the other Bishops. Qesma accepted, but after evil advice from a deacon who wanted to be ordained as a bishop the idea was rejected. And so here was the failure of the first meeting towards unity. The only good result of this meeting was restoring Constantine the Chalcedonian bishop of Cairo to the Coptic Orthodox Church.

Pope Khaeil was imprisoned for a month from 8th September to 9th October 749 AD, together with Bishop Moses of Osim and Bishop Tadros of Cairo. In the prison, the Lord gave him favour in the eyes of all the prisoners, whether Christian or Muslim, they used to come and confess their sins, and he used to comfort them saying that if you offer true repentance, the Lord will deliver you before the end of the year. The Pope was released and went to Upper Egypt to gather the sum of money to be offered to the Governor; in this tour, many miracles were performed because of his continuous prayers.

On the day of his release from prison, the congregation asked him to pray a Holy Liturgy which he did at St. Sergius and St. Bacchus Church (Abi Serga) in Old Cairo. During partaking of the Holy Communion a man approached but the Pope refused to give him the Communion. After the service, the man came asking for the reason, but the Pope informed him that it wasn't the Pope who prevented him, it was Lord Jesus Himself. The man confessed that he used to have breakfast first and come to the church and partake of the Holy Communion. Accordingly, the Pope ordered the clergymen to warn the congregation and explain the correct rituals of the Holy Communion.

Another miracle took place in St. Mary's Church in Alexandria. A non-Christian youth entered the church and saw the Crucifix icon with the soldier piercing Lord Jesus' side, asking about that picture he was told that it expresses the salvation of the world. Mockingly, he took a rod and pierced the left side of the Lord. Immediately the young man froze and his hand was stuck to the rod. He kept screaming all day out of pain while the congregation were praying "Lord have mercy". He then confessed that this was the icon of Christ the Saviour; he headed to a monastery and was baptized there.

Pope Yousab
52nd Patriarch (830-849)

After the departure of Pope Simon II, the congregation of Alexandria tried to ordain a wealthy man named Isaac Ibn Andona who was a married layman. Unfortunately, the Bishops of Cairo and Osim encouraged that decision, but the rest of the bishops called for a meeting where they rebuked the two bishops saying: "Where is the fear of God in your hearts? Why are you contradicting the law and accepting the ordination of a married layman as the Pope of the See of St. Mark?"

The idea was rejected then they recommended a monk-priest named Yousab from St. Macarius Monastery. On their way, they decided that if the Lord had chosen Yousab, they would find the door of his cell open, and it so happened and they became sure it was the Lord's choice. The tribulations and details of the era of his Papacy were mentioned earlier in this book.

Pope Yousab ordained two Bishops for Tinnis and Cairo replacing the two excommunicated Bishops, as well as ordaining many other Bishops for Africa, the Five Western Cities, Ethiopia, Egypt, and Nubia.

During his era the Abbassid Caliph Al Mo'tasem ordered the removal of all the decorations inside the churches and

The Coptic Church Under Muslim Rulers (642-868)

the demolition of the alabaster pillars, and immediately a person named Lazarus who was a follower of Nestorius carried out this decree at St. Mina Church in Mariout.

It was a custom of the kings of Ethiopia and Nubia to send Christian youth from their countries to the Pope, who used to teach them in preparation to become preachers and missionaries when they go back to their countries. He inaugurated a special school for them in the residence of the Patriarchate. But one of the excommunicated bishops informed the judge of Egypt that these youth were Muslims.

The judge called the youth and rebuked the Pope in front of them saying: "It is not appropriate to kidnap the Muslim youth to convert them to Christianity and baptize them"; but the Pope answered: "They are Christian youth of Christian parents sent to me by the kings of Ethiopia and Nubia." Under severe pressure, the youth proclaimed that they were Muslims in front of the judge and the Pope, and they ended up becoming slaves owned by the Muslims in high position in the government!

Pope Yousab bore many tribulations and departed in peace during the Holy Communion on a Sunday.

Bishop Moses of Osim

Bishop Moses of Osim was one of the great scholars of the church during the 8th century. He became a monk at an early age at Scetis monasteries, taking an elder monk as his guide for 18 years, obeying his instructions and following his guidance in great submission, asceticism and humility. Being a pious monk he was chosen to become the Bishop of Osim (Al Boheira Governorate). His lifestyle as a bishop was a continuation of his monastic life in the monastery, spending lots of his time in prayers and worship. It is said that he never met anyone except on Saturday and Sunday. He also had a strong holy zeal for protecting the Orthodox faith.

He was granted the gift of performing miracles and healing the sick, as well as the gift of prophecy. When the church was experiencing great tribulations, most of the bishops used to go back to their monasteries and isolate themselves in prayers and pleadings, but Bishop Moses stayed in his diocese headquarters strengthening his congregation and warning them from the snatching wolves.

Some Christian elders came to him asking to lift his heart to the Lord with prayers as the number of those who converted to Islam had reached 24,000, yet he answered:

> *"I want you to believe, my dear children, that this governor who is persecuting you will perish in a month from now"*, and it was so.

Bishop Moses was a contemporary of Pope Khaeil, the 46th Patriarch. He objected to the advice of paying a bribe to the judge and demolishing the alabaster pillars in St. Mina's Church.

During the riot of the Bashmors, one of his disciples asked him about the end of this turmoil, so he answered: "Be sure my son that God never abandons His Church but always saves It. This kingdom of Umayyads will fall and another one will come after". And it was so when the Abbasids took over from the Umayyads.

Bishop Moses accompanied Pope Khaeil when Marawan Ibn Muhammad the last Umayyad governor persecuted the Pope, as he wished to become a martyr shedding his blood for the Name of the Lord Jesus Christ. As soon as they came before Marawan the soldiers hanged Bishop Moses upside down hitting his sides and neck with thick copper nails. The soldiers were asking for a bribe in exchange for his release, but as he did not understand their Arabic language he never said a word to them.

Marawan ordered for Pope Khaeil to be beheaded, so Bishop Moses ran after him, and kept clinging to the Pope; the soldiers failed to stop him and again started hitting him with the copper nails. He was imprisoned with the Pope tying their legs with chains along with many others prisoners, but Bishop Moses prophesied that they would come out of the jail safely, and this was fulfilled as Marawan was defeated by the Abbasids.

He fell sick for a while and knew the time of his departure, so he blessed the priests and the congregation of Osim and departed in peace.

THE HERMIT SAINTS, WILDERNESS AND MONASTERIES

It is very hard to count the number of hermit saints who strove hard to hide their virtues in their continuous struggles for self-denial; but we will just mention some of them:

St. John the Hegumen of Scetis (different from St. John the Short) to whom Christ and St Mary used to appear whenever he was praying the Holy Liturgy; also his disciple Hegumen Epimakhos whom people likened to Moses the Prophet because of the his many gifts among which was healing the sick, he lived for 100 years. St. Abraam and his friend St. Gawergi and St. Aghathon who was a monk in St. Macarius Monastery, then lived in solitude in the wilderness, and many others.

SCHOLARS AND BIOGRAPHERS

John of Niqusia

We know a little about his life through what was written in 'The History of the Patriarchs' by Bishop Severus Ibn El Moqafaa'. He lived during the second half of the 7th century. Straight after the Arab invasion in Egypt he was ordained as the Bishop of Niqusia and he was responsible for the monasteries of Scetis. Once he punished a monk who committed adultery hitting him roughly until the monk died. As a result the Holy Synod excommunicated him.

He is famous for the book which he wrote about general history, in which he recorded the world's history since the creation up until the 7th century. He is considered a contemporary of the Arab invasion of Egypt and he wrote about this experience in details, which made his book a great resource. The original copy of this important treasure written in its original language was lost but there is a full manuscript of the book in the old Ethiopian language (Al Ge'ez).

Mina Bishop of Niqusia

He wrote the life of Pope Isaac the 41th Patriarch.

Deacon Gerga

He lived during the second half of the 7th century and the beginning of the 8th century. He wrote the lives of the Patriarchs from the Council of Chalcedon in 451 AD until 717 AD

Bishop Zacharias of Sakha

He was a monk at St. John the Short Monastery and had a spiritual relationship with St. Abraam and St. Gawerga. Pope Simon I, ordained him around 693 AD. He wrote many biographies and his most famous was the coming of the Lord Jesus to Egypt.

THE TULUNIDS AND THE IKHSHIDID (868-969)

Egypt was under Abbasid rule until divisions started between the two sons of Haroun El Rashid: Al Amin and Al Ma'moun, thus the Abbasid Cailph sought help from the Turks. One of these Mamluk Turks was named Tulun; the father of Ahmed Ibn Tulun was given to Al Ma'moun as a gift. The Turks ruled Egypt from 856 AD.

Ahmed Ibn Tulun was sent to Egypt by Amir Bakbak in 868 when he was 22 years old, and by that time Egypt was an Islamic country ready to be ruled by Turks. He combined Syria to Egypt and ruled both, and established a Tulunid country which lasted for 38 years. This was the first time for Egypt to be independent after the Arab rule.

Ahmad Ibn Tulun

Ahmad Ibn Tulun ruled Egypt for 16 years; he died in 884 just before reaching 50. Historians recorded his piety, kindness and charitable deeds, yet he used to commit violence with his sword. It is said that he killed around 18,000 people whether by the sword in battle or after imprisonment. He memorised the Quran and chanted it all the time as he had a beautiful voice. As soon as he started ruling Egypt he started attracting people to himself by his sensible attitude, for example he dismissed all the foreign tax collectors and appointed Egyptian citizens instead. There were yet some rebellions in Alexandria and Upper Egypt but he maintained control of these situations.

In spite of what was recorded concerning his justice and kindness, there arises a big question mark: Where did Ahmad Ibn Tulun get all this money to carry on all the buildings and establishments which were achieved during his short period of reign (16 years)?

In the year 870 he established a new capital city called El Qatae which means 'The Sections', north of Al Fustat expanding till Al Muqqatam Hills. It was called 'The Sections' because each nationality such as the Sudanese, the Greeks etc. lived in a special area of this capital. He also built a huge luxurious castle for himself in the middle, as well as the famous mosque carrying his name, which took two years to be finished (867-877). Then he ploughed the area surrounding it, which formed a cemetery for the

Christians and Jews, and built an enormous headquarters for the government. His followers also built houses all around this area.

Muslims living during that time forbade people from praying in that mosque claiming that they did not know where Ibn Tulun got the money from, so he gathered the people and gave a sermon defending himself. It was said later that he had found a treasure and used it in building this mosque.

He also adjusted the Nile measurement at El Roda area, as well as establishing an aqueduct and a well in El Basateen area. In addition to all of these buildings, when Ibn Tulun passed away he left behind the amount of 10,000 denarii. So the big mystery was where did he get all the money?

In answer to this query, the historian Stanley Lane-Poole stated that most probably Ahmad Ibn Tulun used to collect expensive tributes and fines from the Coptic Pope.[57]

Ahmad Ibn Tulun and Pope Shenouda I

Pope Shenouda I the 55th Patriarch was a contemporary of Ahmad Ibn Tulun (859-880). He was from Batanon county, Menoufia Governorate. He became a monk at St. Macarius Monastery during the era of Pope Yousab I the 52nd Patriarch and he became the Abbot of the Monastery. When Pope Quzman the 54th Patriarch departed, monk Shenouda was chosen as his successor.

---

[57] Stanley Lane-Poole, "History of Egypt in the Middle Ages" p. 66

Severes Ibn El Moqafaa the author of the lives of Patriarchs says about Pope Shenouda I:

> "His words were exactly as humble as his attitude. His tears were always flowing before everyone. When people tried to comfort him he used to say: "When I see the Bride of Christ, i.e. the Church with its beauty and high spirituality compared to my sinful self and iniquities I can't stop weeping.""

He cared about restoring the heretics; the Copts living in Mariout used to believe that the physical pains and sufferings of Lord Jesus were just a myth and mirage, not a true fact, so he changed their wrong belief, as well as going to El Balyana and changing another wrong belief that the Divinity could suffer pain.

This Pope suffered many tribulations at the hands of his congregation:

A Coptic deacon asked the Pope to ordain him as a Bishop through bribery, but when he refused and threatened to demote the deacon, the latter got a Syrian monk who was his friend and asked him to act as if he were the Pope, then he brought some witnesses who did not know the actual Pope and claimed that the Pope took from him some money and did not want to give it back to him, and that he had a document proving this fact.

The Pope knew about the trick and informed a good Muslim man who was a friend. The Pope asked the man to bring the witnesses, while he sat among other Bishops, and of course the witnesses couldn't point to which one was the Pope out of all the Bishops sitting. This incident was kept a secret from the deacon. A few days later the deacon came to the judge and asked him to summon the Pope, showing the Judge the fake document. He went to bring the witnesses, yet they cursed, insulted and dismissed him, so he came back to the judge claiming that he couldn't find any of them.

The Judge postponed the case until the next day and released the Pope, yet the deacon was so ashamed of himself and did not show up to the court case. Everyone knew about what had happened and he was so disgraced and embarrassed. He disappeared for a while then he came back, confessed to the Pope who accepted him and advised him with verses from the Holy Bible.

Unfortunately, many Coptic Christians used to do the same; accusing their brethren falsely to get closer to the Muslim Governors, and this often provided a good pretext for the Governors to persecute the Christians and loot their money and possessions.

A monk from Al Bashmoor took off his monastic garments, got married and addressed a complaint to the Governor against the Pope, so the Governor wrote an order to arrest Pope Shenouda I and some of the bishops. The soldiers arrested the Pope – who was suffering at that time from gout - and jailed him with the robbers and criminals for 40 days. As for the Bishops, they took off their priestly garments and clothed them in laymen clothes and mocked them in front of everyone. Finally, the Governor discovered the vanity of the complaint and set the Pope free.

Amazingly, after all the hardships which the Pope suffered because of this monk who abandoned his monasticism and got married, the Pope later forgave this monk, gave him some money, a donkey to take him back and three robes, and a place to live near Sana Al Hagar, yet again he kept annoying the priests and complaining about them to the Governor. Finally, the Lord avenged as he had not offered repentance, so some tradesmen complained about him to the Governor of Alexandria who ordered his hands be tied with iron chains, that he be struck with thick rods and whipped until he approached the point of death. Then they released him, so he took his wife and children and went back to his hometown Al Bashmoor.

Pope Shenouda I faced many temptations coming from a monk in Abu Yehnes Monastery in Scetis wilderness who had a bad reputation. He wanted the Pope to ordain him as a deacon, yet he was sure the Pope would refuse because of his well-known bad manners. He made some Coptic elders write a letter of recommendation and headed to the Pope, who at that time was suffering from gout and couldn't meet anyone. When the Pope's disciple informed the monk about the situation asking him to wait for a while, he refused to wait and started shouting and yelling, then he left going back to his city Mariout.

Around the year 871 AD Ahmad Ibn Tulun was visiting Alexandria, so when passing by Mariout the monk met him and claimed that Pope Shenouda I was baptising Muslims in the wilderness and converting them to Christianity to become monks. Ibn Tulun ordered his scribe to investigate the issue under the monk's guidance. The latter took two soldiers from Ibn Tulun's guards, headed to the monastery and arrested a monk with whom he had enmity from before. The arrested monk did not know the reason for his arrest, but when they came before Ibn Tulun the other monk kept saying that this monk was a Muslim and the Pope baptised him and ordained him as a monk. The arrested monk kept telling them that he was born Christian and asked them to go and check with his parents and neighbourhood, but as the scribe of Ibn Tulun was corrupt and loved bribery he got two false witnesses who also witnessed that this monk confessed to being a Muslim and was baptised by the Pope and became a monk.

The soldiers took off his monastic garments, clothed him in Islamic attire, yet the arrested monk never denied the Lord and tolerated torture and jailing. The aim of this trick was to condemn the Pope and ask for a large sum of money from him.

The scribe sent some Turkish soldiers with the evil monk to bring the Pope who was very sick, they arrested him together with Bishop Simon of Benha and his spiritual brother Maqqara the deacon after tying them with chains. Before leaving, the soldiers stole everything in the Pope's cell, including the holy utensils, spiritual books, clothes etc. There were also some closed boxes including books, but the soldiers thought they might be treasures, so they broke the boxes to find only books. The scribe thought that the evil monk stole the money so he turned against him and took him to the Governor. In front of the Governor the evil monk claimed falsely that the Pope's two disciples stole the money. When Bishop Simon and deacon Maqqara came to be investigated about the money, they informed him that the Pope always gave the money to the poor and to the needy churches, yet they kept hitting Maqqara until he bled badly, but the Pope signed him with the Cross and he became whole immediately.

Pope Shenouda and his two disciples were in jail for thirty days, and after a large amount of money was collected and paid, they were released. While all the Coptic elders asked the Pope to give them permission to avenge him, the Pope prevented them and interceded for the evil monk. As for the arrested monk, after investigating his case and finding out the false accusations against him, they released him from jail gaining the crown of confessing his true faith and holding fast to his Christianity and he went back to his monastery.

The evil monk went back to Scetis and started making trouble with other monks, becoming a great stumbling block to everyone. Noble Muslim tradesmen who used to come to the monasteries to purchase their handiwork knew about this and witnessed some incidents of him dealing rudely and cruelly with other monks. They complained about him to the Governor of Alexandria who arrested him together with his layman brother for a year. He was then struck with leprosy (that was the last thing mentioned by Pope Severus Ibn Al Moqaffa concerning the History of the Patriarchs as he did not write anything about the last 8 years of Pope

Shenouda I papacy).

In his book 'Golden Gardens and Valuable Jewels' Al Massoudi wrote that in the year 873-874 AD Ibn Tulun knew that there was an old Coptic man aged 130 years, still living in Upper Egypt; this man travelled a lot around the world and was very knowledgeable - he lived with the Mamluks and knew a lot about Egypt and the River Nile. When they brought the man to Ibn Tulun he asked him about the secret of his good health and memory, although he looked so old, the man answered: "I was moderate in eating and drinking, I never drank wine. I was also moderate in my lifestyle with clothing, cared about physical cleanness of my body and never followed my lustful desires." Ibn Tulun tried to offer him delicious food, yet he refused, then he asked him about the sources of the River Nile, so the man answered: "I think the sources of the River Nile come from the high mountains where there is a big lake, and night and day are of equal hours all around the year." Scientists called this the 'Straight Line'; this meant the Equator. Ibn Tulun admired the answers and great knowledge of the Coptic man and allowed him to go back to his country.

It is really strange that the European researchers discovered the sources of the River Nile around nine centuries later!

It was mentioned that Ibn Tulun used to go for meditation and a retreat in 'The Short Monastery' (which was a Monastery East of Turah and was later demolished), and so he befriended the monks who asked him to relieve them from the high taxes, so he gave them many other privileges and stopped his men from irritating them.

On 24th Baramudah 597 AM corresponding 19th April 880 AD Pope Shenouda I departed in peace after being a Pope for 21 years, 2 months and 11 days. He was the last Pope to live and be buried in Alexandria as the headquarters of the Patriarchate.

Pope Khaeil III (Michael III)
56th Patriarch (880-907)

The last Pope whose biography was written by Bishop Severus of Al Ashmonin was that Pope Shenouda I the 55th Patriarch (excepting the last 8 years of his life). Bishop Michael of Tinnis wrote the biographies of subsequent Popes. He wrote the biography of Pope Khaeil the Third after around 150 years of his departure. Although he spent 27 years as a Pope, very little was known about his biography. Bishop Michael wrote at the beginning of recounting his biography: "Pope Khaeil had three beautiful qualities resembling gold melted in fire because of the tribulations which he endured during his Papacy".

Together with some bishops the Pope headed to a city called Denother to consecrate a church for St. Patlumius (affiliated to the Diocese of Sakha in Kafr El Sheikh Governorate whose bishop was known for his cruelty). This bishop was supposed to come to church to start the Holy Liturgy with the Pope and the other bishops, yet he did not show up because he was too busy preparing food for the congregation. When they sent someone to call him, still he did not come for the same reason, finally, as he was too late, everyone told the Pope just to start the offering, so the Pope did. Suddenly, the Bishop entered the church shouting and yelling at the Pope: "How dare you offer the Lamb without my permission and presence?!" Then he took the Lamb off the Paten, broke it and threw it on the floor. As the consecration prayers had not yet been prayed on this Lamb, they got another one and prayed the Holy Liturgy. Next day the Pope called for a meeting and this Bishop was excommunicated and another one was appointed.

This excommunicated Bishop wanted to avenge himself, so he contacted Ibn Tulun and claimed that Pope Khaeil had a lot of money. At that time Ibn Tulun was preparing for an armed invasion of Syria around 882 AD and he needed lots of money, so he brought the Pope and asked him about this matter saying: "You Christians, you do not need money for anything, you just need food and clothes. I know that you have a large amount of money in addition to the gold and silver utensils, silk material and other precious items." The Pope answered him humbly: "There is no injustice in your honourable kingdom, you know that I am a poor weak person who owns nothing; you have been informed falsely about those possessions of mine. Your highness knows that according to our religion, we are ordered not to have any treasures on earth and not to concern ourselves about tomorrow. Here I am, do whatever you like; you only have authority over my body but my spirit is in the Hands of its Creator."

Ahmad Ibn Tulun was so angry and ordered for the Pope to

be put in prison. The Pope spent a year in prison until nearly the end of 883 AD. Two Coptic employees of Ibn Tulun, scribes named Bassous and Abram, the sons of Moses, tried to convince Ibn Tulun to release the Pope and allow them to keep him in their house, yet he refused. Another Coptic scribe named Youannis pleaded to Ibn Tulun's mother to release the Pope but in vain. He then tried with Minister Ahmad Ibn Aly ElMazraei, Ibn Tulun's scribe, who went and mediated with Ibn Tulun. Finally, Ibn Tulun called this Coptic scribe and his son, and ordered his soldiers to give them the Pope, on the condition they pay 20,000 denarii - 10,000 to be paid after a month and the other 10,000 four months later. The scribe and his son signed the agreement.

The Pope headed to St. Mary's Church at Qasr El Shame (Kasreyet El Rihan) where he spent 20 days trying to collect some money, but he could not. Then he held a meeting with the Coptic elders, they identified 10 dioceses without Bishops, and so they decided to ordain 10 bishops for these dioceses in return for some money. The scribe and his son obtained 2,000 denarii for the Pope, some rich Muslim scribes collected 7,000 denarii and an employee gave them 1,000 denarii. They gave Ibn Tulun the first instalment of 10,000 denarii. As for the second instalment the scribe and his son, together with Bishop Bakhoum of Tema and another disciple promised to secure its collection.

The Pope held a meeting with the Holy Synod and discussed the money that was already borrowed from the above mentioned people, as well as the rest of the money owing to Ibn Tulun. They decided to raise the money from whoever wants to be ordained as a Priest or a Bishop. This practice of simony is obviously against the rules of the church and the commandments of the Apostles.

The Pope then kept going around the monasteries in the desert of Scetis forcing the monks to pay him money, and then went to Alexandria to sell the church assets and buildings, yet the priests there added a condition that the Pope must give them 1,000 denarii annually; they signed a document stating this condition should also be followed by his successors. Finally he managed to collect 10,000 denarii which was the amount borrowed for the first instalment. Trying to solve this financial crisis, the Pope sold one of the churches to the Jews (which still exists to this day), next to Kasr El Shame, next to the Hanging Church. He also sold them a piece of land in Al Habash area, which the Jews are still using as a cemetery east of El Basateen area. The Pope was in very worried and restless because of the rest of the money he had to pay.

Through God's guidance he went to the city of Tinnis (where El Manzala Lake, next to Port Said, now is today) trying to collect some money from the Christians living there. One day later after arriving to Tinnis, some of its congregation came to receive his blessings. Among them was a monk who was covering his face, very skinny and wearing poor clothes. He asked the Pope's disciple, "Why is the Pope so depressed and not happy? Just tell him that after 40 days the Lord will tear the document and nothing will be asked from him to pay." The disciple informed the Pope who asked them to bring this monk, yet they looked everywhere for him, even in the neighbouring cities but could not find him.

Forty days later on 10th May 884 AD, Ahmad Ibn Tulun passed away, and his son Khamarweih succeeded him, so Minister Ahmad Ibn Aly ElMazraei gave the document to Youhanna El Meligy his scribe, and ordered the Pope to come from Tinnis. The Pope came back to St. Mary's Church and the Coptic elders presented the document to him, which he tore with both hands. Finally, he went back to his cell glorifying the Lord, grieving for breaching the rules of the Church and for what might happen with his successors.

When Ahmad Ibn Tulun fell sick and was about to die, he gathered his government members and asked them to tell everyone to go out to the mountain and pray for God to heal him. So, Muslims took the Quran, Christians the Bibles and Jews the Torah and they all went up on the mountain pleading and crying with a very loud voice, to the extent that when he heard them he wept.[58]

Pope Khaeil lived during the era of Khamarweih the son of Ibn Tulun (884-895 AD). Khamarweih was a different personality from his father. When he knew about the monasteries of Scetis he went there, visited St. Macarius Church and saw his coffin. When he asked who it belonged to they told him it is the body of the owner of this church, so he ordered them to unwrap the shroud and he touched St. Macarius' beard. Immediately the saint opened his eyes

---

[58] The Life of Ahmad Ibn Tulun written by Al Balwy – Tarton, Christians in Islam 175 from Al Kanady, Governors and Judges

so Khamarweih fell on the ground and fainted for an hour, after which they took him back to his tent. Then they took some holy oil from the lantern in front of St. Macarius and put it on his forehead.

Khamarweih had another experience in this church. While he was walking in the church carrying a bunch of basil herbs, he saw an icon of St Theodore, so he threw the basil on the icon saying, "Take it, O knight of the courageous ones." Miraculously the saint's hand came out of the icon and took the herbs, and people witnessed this incident. Khamarweih was greatly scared and ordered that this icon be marked as a commemoration of what had happened, so they drew a cross on the saint's other hand. It seems these two miracles made Khamarweih respect the bishops and monks.[59]

Khamarweih used to visit the Monastery of the Short in the eastern mountain (east of Turah). He always admired the icon of St. Mary carrying Baby Jesus with angels surrounding them, and the icon of the twelve disciples. He built a room on top of the roof of the monastery for retreat, with four openings in the four directions.[60] Most probably this is the Monastery of the Short built by Emperor Arcadius, son of Theodosius, on top of the tomb of his teacher St. Arsanious. It is called 'The Short' after St. John the Short.

---

[59] The History of the Patriarchs Part 2 p. 77

[60] El Shabeshti: The Monasteries p. 284; Abu Saleh El Armany – Churches and Monasteries in Egypt p. 49

Pope Khaeil departed in 20 Baramhat 623 AM, corresponding to 16th March 907 AD after spending 27 years on the papal throne. From what Abu El Makarem wrote in his book 'Churches and Monasteries in Egypt', he is most probably buried in Shebas the Martyrs (Desouq – Boheira Governorate).

Pope Gabriel I
57th Patriarch (909-920)

In his book "Life of Ibn Tulun", El Balawi (who might have been his contemporary) wrote that Ibn Tulun dealt with different people differently. A Turk himself, he preferred the Turks to the Muslims, and the Melkites to the Copts. He also mentioned that as Ibn Tulun used to go to the Monastery of the Short for a retreat, his son Khamarweih did the same, and the friendship between him and the Christians increased. It is written in "The History of the Patriarchs" that Khamarweih was a close friend to Bishop Pakhoum of Tema to the extent that Khamarweih entrusted him to defend the western borders of Egypt from his side. The Bishop was a trustworthy person so he appointed 300 soldiers who were excellent in shooting for this task. He also prepared some ferries for easy transportation from one bank of the river to the other if needed, also scheduling roster shifts for these guards that they might be ready to defend in case of any attack.

As a result of Ibn Tulun's preference for the Chalcedonians,

The Tulunids And The Ikhshidid (868-969)

they successfully appointed a Pope for themselves in Alexandria, after having failed to do so for around two centuries. No doubt the church was in tranquility during these two centuries, but as soon as this Pope was appointed, troubles started again, especially after the departure of Pope Khaeil the 56th Patriarch, as there was no Pope appointed for two years and two months due to the instability of the country.

Bishop Pakhoum of Tema who was a close friend to Khamarweih was able to convince the latter that having a Chalcedonian Pope was not in Egypt's best interests, as he might be a spy from the Byzantine Emperor preparing to invade the country. Khamarweih was pleased at the loyalty and patriotism of Bishop Pakhoum, and gave him permission to go to Alexandria and do the best for the welfare of the country and the Christians. So the Bishop took a letter from Khamarweih to the governor of Alexandria and was successful in removing the Chalcedonian Pope and six of his bishops from their seats. Then he decided to go to the Scetis Wilderness with a group of bishops in search of an appropriate Pope.

During his visit to Damascus in 895 AD, Khamarweih was assassinated by a group of women who conspired against him. He had fallen in love with them, gathering a great number of them in every palace. It was said that some of them became jealous and planned his assassination. This was the beginning of a series of conspiracies, murders and troubles.

In the meantime, the Bishop had decided to ordain a monk named Gabriel from the Monastery of St. Macarius, about whom an elder prophesied saying that he would abandon his solitary life, and he was ordained as Pope Gabriel on 21st Bashans 652 AM, corresponding to 16th May 909 AD. Although it seemed that the reason he spent most of his time in the Scetis Wilderness was his love for the life of solitude, but it may have been due to the unsettled situation of the country at that time. The country was in chaos with constant riots and disturbances; Khmaraweih's son was a spoilt 14-year-old boy when he ruled the country and the Caliph in Baghdad wanted to destroy the Tulunid family because of their expanded authority and wealth.

The government in Baghdad also doubled the taxes to be paid by the Egyptians; El Maqrizi mentioned that minister Aly Ibn Issa came to Egypt and ordered the Coptic monks, bishops and poor citizens to pay taxes. In response, a Coptic delegation went to Baghdad presenting a petition in this regard, which was accepted, and so minister Ibn Issa was instructed to waive Coptic taxes.

It is mentioned in the 'The History of the Patriarchs' that this Pope was fought by sexual desires in his old age, so he headed to one of the elders of St. Macarius Monastery and confessed his struggle asking for advice, and the elder said to him, "You can only conquer through humility and being lowly in spirit." So, every night when he was sure that all the monks were in their cells he used to clean all the bathrooms and toilets in the monastery, until the Lord had mercy on him and lifted up the fight.

Pope Gabriel I departed on 21st Amsheer 636 AM corresponding to 15th February 920 AD after being Pope for 10 years and 9 months. He was buried in St. Macarius Monastery in Scetis Wilderness.

THE REIGN OF THE TULUNIDS AND THE IKHSHIDID (868-969)

After the death of Khamarweih in 896, the Tulunids started getting weaker and losing control over the country. Khamarweih's son, Abul Asaker Habash (895-897), was ousted by military forces, followed by his brother Abu Moussa Haroun (897-905) at the age of 14, being of course unfit for this responsibility. Then the Abbasid Caliph Al Mote sent his commander Mohammed Ibn Suleiman El Kate to restore Egypt to his Caliphate. He conquered the Egyptian Fleet, and his uncles Sheban and Oday killed Haroun. The soldiers were not happy with this move, and when Sheban was appointed as a governor for Egypt, they contacted Mohammed Ibn Suleiman, who came in 905 to Al Fustat then to El Qatae', the capital of the Tulunids. They burnt all the buildings of this area; the only thing that was left was Ibn Tulun Mosque. Copts suffered a lot during this time because of Ibn Suleiman's soldiers who used to attack and rob the Copts. With the fall of the Tulunids in 905, Egypt went back to the control of the Abbasids, yet because of the weakness of the Abbasid Caliphs the internal disturbances did not stop until the rise of the Ikhshidid rule after 30 years (935-969).

The Christian historians never pointed to the forbearance of the Ikhshidid as they did to that of the Tulunids. Rather, they accuse Mohammed Ibn Tafh El Ikhshidid of forcing Christians to pay more taxes when he could not pay his soldiers' wages. These demands forced the Christians to sell some churches, which appears to be a common event historically. It is mentioned in 'The History of the Patriarchs' that during the papacy of Pope Mina II the 61st Patriarch (956-974) there was great inflation for 7 years because of the low level of the River Nile for 3 years and the Nubian invasion of Egypt. It was such a hard time to the extent that many people left Egypt, others died of hunger, many dioceses were bankrupt because of a lack of congregation. Hence, there were no bishops appointed, and they had to amalgamate these dioceses to neighbouring bishoprics.

In her book 'Egypt during the reign of Ikhshidid', Dr. Sayeda Ismail Kashef writes:

> "We did not hear about any obligation for the Christians to wear different clothes from the Muslims or to use different means of transportation during the reign of Ikhshidid; the relationship between Muslims and Christians was mostly fine. Riots only erupted between the two groups if Muslims wanted to stop the interference of Christians in financial issues in the country, or in the case of Byzantine victory over Muslims in Levant, or when the Muslims objected to giving permission for Christians to build churches. It is said that Muslim riots erupted and they kept destroying and burning churches when news came about the victory of the Byzantines in the Levant in 960. In the following year when

the Byzantine Emperor Nikephoros Fokas invaded Akrtish Island (Crete), he destroyed many mosques there and arrested many of its citizens, and, in reaction, the Muslims destroyed one of the churches in Old Cairo.

It is true that many riots took place during the reign of Kafour El Ikhshidid, but it is fair to say that his government always rejected the disturbances and churches' destruction at the hands of the Muslims. They always tried to defuse the situation, and in 952 the Caliph issued a decree for reconciliation and waived the tribute to be paid by the bishops, monks and the needy Christian laymen."

This is also confirmed by Lane-Poole who recorded that the Egyptians were loyal to Kafour El Ikhshidid, even when the Nubians invaded Egypt, because he was just and fair in treating his citizens, regardless of religious or cultural differences.[61]

Pope Cosmas III
58th Patriarch (920-938)

After the departure of Pope Gabriel I the See was vacant for only 14 days, then all the clergymen and Christian elders agreed on ordaining a monk named Cosmas on 4th Baramhat 636 AM corresponding 28th February 920 AD.

The most important incident during his era was in regard to Ethiopia. He ordained Metropolitan Botros for Ethiopia, and when the King of Ethiopia was about to depart, he entrusted

---

[61] Stanley Lane-Poole, "History of Egypt in the Middle Ages" p87-88

his two sons to Metropolitan Botros to look after them, that after becoming adults he might ordain whoever he felt was the most appropriate one to become the king, no matter who was older or younger. Bishop Botros ordained the younger brother. Two monks from St. Anthony Monastery named Mina and Boqtor went and asked for some money from the Bishop, and as they were not of a good reputation he refused. So Mina wore Bishopric garments as if he was the Bishop while Boqtor played the role of his disciple. They wrote a forged message and signed it with Pope Cosmas' signature, saying that he never ordained Bishop Botros and that he was a fake Bishop, and that the legal Bishop was Mina, asking for Bishop Botros' suspension and for Mina to be enthroned as Bishop. The forged message added that the elder brother was supposed to be the King not the younger one.

Mina and Boqtor took the forged message to the elder son of the reposed king, so the latter prepared an army to fight his brother the king of Ethiopia. He gained victory and removed his brother the King together with Bishop Botros and replaced him with Mina. After a short while there was a dispute between the two monks, so Boqtor stole all the possessions of the Mina's bishophric and fled, and after he had spent all that he had stolen he converted to Islam.

As soon as Pope Cosmas knew of these sad events, he excommunicated Mina, and when the King of Ethiopia was informed of the decision he killed Mina the fake Bishop. When Pope Cosmas wanted to return Bishop Botros to his bishopric he found out that he had already departed and so he refused to ordain another Bishop for Ethiopia until his departure. The five Popes succeeding Pope Cosmas followed the same decision and they never ordained any Bishops for Ethiopia. Pope Cosma departed on 5th Baramhat 648 AM corresponding to 27th February 932 AD, after spending 12 years as Pope.

Pope Macarius I (Maqar El Shabrawi)
59th Patriarch (932-952)

One month after Pope Cosmas' departure, a monk named Maqar from St. Macarius Monastery was ordained on 1st Baramudah 648 AM corresponding to 27th March 932 AD. He was from a village called Shubra Qabala close to Qwesna Governorate.

A beautiful story is recounted about this Pope: during one of his trips accompanied by the Bishops and Christian elders he passed by his place of birth to see his elderly mother who was sitting in her home spinning yarn. When he entered, however, she did not rise to greet him, but rather was weeping. Everyone was embarrassed because of the poor welcome from his mother; he thought she did not recognise him. Finally she said: "Of course I know you my son, but the thing which you do not know is what you are doing with yourself... You are proud because of your high position, but I rather grieve; I would prefer to see you in your coffin which would be better than all the vainglory surrounding you now. Do not rejoice in your position, but rather weep and lament, for you are responsible for this congregation and their sins from now on..."

How powerful and deep were these words, which reflect the true spiritual awareness of simple people such as this old mother. Pope Macarius departed in peace after sitting on the see of St. Mark for around twenty years and was buried in St. Macarius Monastery.

Pope Theophilus
60th Patriarch (952-956)

The era of Pope Theophilus was a dark time for the Coptic Church. He was a monk at St. Macarius Monastery, and was ordained on 1st Mesra 668 AM corresponding to 25th July 952. He was ordained at an old age approximately four months after the departure of Pope Macarius. As mentioned before in the life of Pope Khaeil III, when he was under financial pressure from Ahmad Ibn Tulun he sold the endowments of the churches in Alexandria, and the priests agreed on the condition that he would give their churches 1,000 denarii each year, with the same arrangement to be honoured by all his successors. Pope Theophilus used to pay this amount of money until he started refraining from paying. The priests disputed with him saying: "You have to respect and honour these garments and Eskeem; we were the ones who chose you to be our Pope. Either give us the amount of money or give us these garments. He became very angry, took off his priestly clothes and Eskeem and threw it saying: Take them, they are yours and I do not need them."

It is mentioned in the 'The History of the Patriarchs' that as soon as he took off the priestly garments and Eskeem a bad spirit haunted him, and he was under its bondage as if tied with iron chains for the rest of his life. Different stories are told about his death, but they all agree that he became insane and blasphemed. His Papacy lasted for around 4 years and a half. He departed on 10th Kiahk 763 AM corresponding to 965 AD.

Pope Mina II
61st Patriarch (956-974)

Pope Mina was ordained on the day after the departure of Pope Theophilus on the 11th Kiahk 763 AM. He was a monk from St. Macarius Monastery. Before becoming a monk, he was forced by his parents to get married, but he lived in virginity with his wife for the first three days following the wedding ceremony, talking to her about the vanity of this world. When she was convinced, they agreed that she would stay at home and keep their secret, while he would head to Scetis Wilderness. He was chosen as the Pope, but when the elders of the church and the Bishops knew about his previous marriage they were so confused because they had broken the church laws. Thus he called his wife and when she came they revealed their secret and everyone glorified the Lord. This Pope was a contemporary of the end of the Ikhshidid and the beginning of the Fatimid rule.

People suffered financially during the final years of the Ikhshidid rule; Egypt experienced seven years of inflation because of the decreasing level of the River Nile for three consecutive years in 967. As a result, there was a great famine and many plagues, which led to the death of around 600,000 persons in Al Fustat and the surrounding cities. People therefore started immigrating to neighbouring countries for a better life.

After the death of Kafour El Ikhshidid in 967, his son became ruler at the age of 11. The country was in chaos because of the weakness of its ruler. This presented a good opportunity for the Fatimids – who were now well established in Morocco - to invade Egypt. The Fatimid Caliph Al Mo'ez Ledin Ellah sent an army headed by Gowhar El Saqqali to invade Egypt in 969. This army consisted of more than 100,000 armed fighters, with more than 1,000 camels and horses.

It is worth mentioning that Gowhar El Saqqali was the one who established the city of Cairo as the capital of Egypt under the Fatimids, and he built Al Azhar Mosque, which exists to this day.

No one resisted the Fatimids except the Bashmurs, who joined the Ikhshidids, but Gowhar Al Saqqali conquered this uprising with great efficiency. This served as a lesson for whoever might consider rebellion at a later stage.

Gowhar sent a messenger to Girgis the King of Nubia reminding him about the tribute he was supposed to pay. Gowhar suggested that if he were to convert to Islam, he would waive the tribute, but the King sent the requested amount of money.

Similarly to Gowhar, Caliph El Mo'ez had good qualities, he used to treat the Egyptians fairly, not differentiating between Christians and Muslims. He kept the Christian minister Abul Yemen Qozman Ibn Mina in his position during the reign of Kafour which lasted for 22 years; moreover he befriended him and gave him more authoritiy than he had during the reign of Kafour.

There were many waves of rebellion against the Fatimids, such as the cooperation between the Syrian army and the Iraqi Prince to attack Egypt - they actually reached its borders and surrounded it for two months. Gowhar, however, defeated them, sending them back in shame. The Syrians attempted to attack again but it also failed. This was because of the arrival of the Fatimid Caliph Al Mo'ez Ledin Ellah to Egypt in 972 in a great ceremony among ministers, army generals and soldiers. They were carrying the coffins of his predecessors whom he had resolved to be bury in Egypt to affirm his Egyptian family roots.[62]

It is mentioned in the book 'The History of the Patriarchs' that during these incidents Pope Mina II resided in the countryside, but when the inflation became so intense, he moved to a region called Mahalet Daniel, where a rich pious woman named Dina looked after him and his companions. He would not go to Alexandria or Wadi Habib to make the Mayroun, thus he built an altar in Mahalet Daniel by the name of St. Mark.

On 16th Hatour 691 AM corresponding to 13th November

---

[62] Stanley Lane-Poole, "History of Egypt in the Middle Ages" p. 108

974, Pope Mina II departed after sitting on the See of St. Mark for around 18 years. By then, the conditions in Egypt had improved and prosperity prevailed in the country.

IMPORTANT PERSONALITIES OF THE TIME

Said Ibn Kateb El Farghani

He was a Coptic engineer during the era of the Tulunids, and was probably from Farghan in El Sharqeya Governorate, or El Faragon in Kafr El Sheikh Governorate, which had been destroyed and replaced by Sidi Salem. El Farghani was responsible for the rebuilding of the measurement of the River Nile in El Roda Island in 864 AD, following the Abbasid Caliph El Motawakel's orders. When Ahmad Ibn Tulun became the ruler of Egypt, he delegated the building of some installations to El Farghani, starting with the Ibn Tulun Aqueduct and the well at Lake Habbash to enable the water to reach El Qatae' city between the years 872 and 873.

El Maqrizi wrote: "It was a very talented Christian engineer who built this well for Ahmad Ibn Tulun. There was a part that needed some lime and 4 bricks, which El Farghani made, and when he finished everything he invited Ibn Tulun to come and inspect it. Ibn Tulun really admired his work, but because of the moistness of the lime, the foot of the horse on which Ibn Tulun was riding slipped in the lime.

He thought that this was a trick from the Christian engineer to harm him, thus he ordered for his clothes to be torn off and that he be whipped 500 times, then he imprisoned him. The poor engineer thought that he would be rewarded by a large sum of money for his construction, but instead he was punished."[63]

Ibn Tulun then decided to build the biggest mosque in Egypt with a foundation of 300 marble pillars. El Maqrizi wrote:

'When Ahmad Ibn Tulun wanted to build the mosque on 300 marble pillars he could not find sufficient marble. Some advisors suggested going to the old churches in the countryside to salvage enough pillars from the debris but he refused. When the Christian engineer who built the Aqueduct knew about this matter, he sent a message to Ibn Tulun informing him that he could build the mosque with only two pillars for the Qibla. Ibn Tulun brought him from prison, his hair was so long it fell over his face, so he said, "I can make a model and show you how it would look like." They brought him the material and when Ibn Tulun saw the model he really liked it, and decided to give him the job. He released him and gave him 100,000 denarii, promising to give more if needed. The Christian engineer started the building in Shukr Mountain, and when he finished Ibn Tulun inaugurated the first Friday prayer in the mosque, after which the Christian engineer mounted the platform and shouted: "O Ahmad Ibn Tulun, the prince of safety, your servant wants his prize and asks to live safely and not to be treated like the first time." Ibn Tulun answered, "Come

---

[63] El Maqrizi Part 4, p. 338

down, you are safe." He gave him 10,000 denarii and kept providing for him until his departure.'[64]

The Ibn Tulun Mosque is witness to the genius of this Christian engineer; he started building it in 876/877 and it took two years to be completed. You can see the pointed ends in the architecture of this mosque two centuries before they were known in England.[65] As for this engineer's end, some sources recorded that Ibn Tulun asked him to convert to Islam, but when he refused, holding strongly to his Christianity, he beheaded him and was counted as a martyr. His body was kept in St. Qolta Church, which has now been destroyed, but used to be situated in the area of Al Hamra Al Wosta (between St Abu Sefein Church and St Mina Church in Fom El Khalig close to Old Cairo).[66]

Abul Makarem

Abul Makarem Saadallah Ibn Girgis Ibn Masoud was the husband of the honourable lady Set Eldar, niece of Seif El Dawla. He was one of the most renowned Coptic historians. In 940 AM (1208 AD) he wrote a book about the churches and monasteries of Egypt.

Unfortunately, we know very little about this great historian. Much of the information we do have was found by a Catholic

---

[64] El Maqrizi Part 4 p. 26-27

[65] Stanley Lane-Poole p. 64-66

[66] Abu Saleh El Armani 33b-34a (quoted from El Maqrizi, El Sebouti and El Eshaqi)

monk named Vansleb who came to Egypt in the 17th century and bought the manuscripts for three piasters for the Civil Library in Paris. This book is mistakenly attributed to Abu Saleh El Armani because the person who bought or transcribed it wrote his name on the book.

Hegumen Philothaous Ibrahim El Tantawi, the head priest of the Church of St. Mark in Cairo, found the rest of this book. H.G. Bishop Youanis of Gharbeya has a photocopy of the full book in his library, taken from the copy owned by Girgis Philothaous Awad the scholar. In 1895 the English Professor Evetts published the book, while historian Alfred Butler wrote the footnotes.

Severus Ibn El Moqafaa'

Born in the 10th century, He was one of the greatest personalities in the history of the Coptic Orthodox Church. Born around 915 AD, his father was named El Moqafaa' (which means with a bowed head or stiff hand), and was probably brought up in Old Cairo. He had great knowledge about both in both theology and the secular sciences as seen in his many theological and doctrinal publications. Severus may have been the first to publish Christian books in the Arabic language. He recorded the lives of the previous Popes by collecting information from Greek and Coptic manuscripts in St. Macarius Monastery in the Scetis wilderness and Nahia Monastery (near Giza, since destroyed). He finished editing this book when he was 80 years old.

His books show him to be well acquainted with Greek and Islamic philosophy, being full of intricate philosophical observations. He was also knowledgeable in medicine and astronomy.

During the reign of the Ekshidids he rose in the government ranks until he became a very skilful scribe. It was a condition at that time for scribes to master the Arabic language, which he had mastered together with the Greek and Coptic languages. This position was a very honourable one, and Severus was known as 'Abi El Bashr Ibn El Moqafaa' the Scribe. This was just a metaphor; it did not mean that he had a son named El Bashr, but was a customary way of denoting that he was an honourable man.

After reaching such a high respected position, he forsook everything and became a monk in one of the monasteries, we are unsure which. He made use of the period of his monasticism to grow. He primarily depended on the Holy Bible and the biographies of the saints; he excelled in learning both.

Historians mention that his knowledge of the Holy Bible was amazing and his knowledge about the fathers of the church surpassed all his contemporaries. His book 'The Precious Jewel in Explaining Belief in Religion' (Al Dor Al Thameen Fi Idah Al Eteqad Fil Din), was published in 925. Another book, published in 971, showcases his detailed knowledge of the Holy Bible, arguably unmatched by any other Arabic author. His theological writings also witness to his familiarity with the writings of the Greek and Coptic

Church fathers.

He was ordained as a Bishop for Ashmooneen (a great Bishopric full of churches and monasteries, mentioned in the list of the dioceses since the 4th Christian century under the ancient name Great Harmopolis). It is now a village affiliated to the Assiut Governorate north-west of Mallawi. It is not known who ordained him, but probably it was Pope Maqar the 59th Patriarch (932-953).

He was famous for debating the learned Muslims in his day and age. He ran a debate in the year 955 with one of them, and recorded their discussion which was about the Holy Trinity in a book 'The Book of Councils' and unfortunately this book was lost. We only know about this book as he mentioned it in his book 'Explanation of the Creed', when he wanted to defend the Christians from the accusation that the Holy Bible has been distorted.

Undoubtledly, Severus Ibn El Moqafaa is considered the most erudite in Christian theology and doctrine in the 10th century. He was a friend to Pope Abram Ibn Zara'a the Syrian the 62nd Patriarch. Al Mo'ez Ledin Ellah Al Fatemy also used to invite him for debates with the Muslims and Jews in his palace. Severus surpassed them all by his intelligence and skilful reasoning; thus he had a very good relationship with them, mingling his discussion with some light-hearted humour and jokes in their meetings.

It is said that once on a Friday he was sitting with the Supreme Judge and many others when a dog passed by.

The Supreme Judge asked him: "What do you think, is this dog Muslim or Christian?" Severus answered, "Ask him and he may tell you", so the Judge said: "Dogs do not talk, you tell us." Severus then said: "This is a test, we have to test this dog. Today is a Friday on which Christians fast and do not eat meat, but rather drink some wine at dinner when they break their fast; while the Muslims do not fast or drink wine, but rather eat meat. So let us offer both wine and meat to the dog, if it eats the meat then it is Muslim and if it drinks the wine then it is Christian." They all wondered at his intelligence and good answer.[67]

He also had many debates with the Jews, such as the one with Moses the Jew in the presence of Al Mo'ez Ledin Ellah in 975, which was related by deacon Mikhail Ibn Bedeir El Damanhory.[68] Moses the Jew was a friend to minister Yacoub Ibn Kalas who was a Jew who converted to Islam. On the assigned day, they both came to the palace in the presence of the Caliph. After a long silence the Caliph Al Mo'ez asked them to commence their discussion; then he addressed the Pope, "Speak, Pope, and let your vicar [Bishop Severus] also speak." So the Pope said to his vicar: "Speak, my son, and God will support you." Bishop Severus said to the Caliph "I cannot talk to a Jew in the presence of the prince of the believers". So Moses was upset and said: "Are you implying my ignorance in front of the Caliph and his minister?" So Bishop Severus said: "If it is the truth that is revealed there should not be any anger." Al Mo'ez said: "No one should be upset in a discussion, each side should say whatever they

[67] The History of the Patriarchs, vol. 2, part 2, p.92-93

[68] The History of the Patriarchs, vol. 2, part 2, p. 93

like in order to justify and prove their point."

Bishop Severus said: "It is not me who says you are ignorant, but it is the witness of a great Prophet". The Jew asked, "Which prophet?" Bishop Severus answered: "Isaiah the great Prophet who wrote at the beginning of his book 'The ox knows its owner and the donkey its master's crib; But Israel does not know, my people do not consider.' (Isaiah 1: 3)." Al Mo'ez asked Moses: "Is this true?" Moses answered: "Yes that is what is written". So the bishop said: "Did not God say that the animals understand more than the Jews, so it is not appropriate to talk to the Caliph in the presence of someone than whom the animals are more knowledgeable, someone described by God as ignorant." Al Mo'ez admired Bishop Severus' answer and ordered everyone to be dismissed. There was great enmity between the two parties; the Jewish minister was furious and kept trying to scrutinise the Pope for any wrongdoing because he exposed and disgraced the Jews before King Al Mo'ez.[69]

Abul Barakat, known as Ibn Kibr the priest of the Hanging Church (1324 AD) mentioned that the publications of Severes Ibn El Moqafaa' were around 26 books in theology, doctrine and history.[70] His books were renowned in the Arabic countries, to the extent that the Iraqi Nestorians kept debating his doctrinal writings tens of years later.[71]

[69] History of the Patriarchs, vol. 2, part 2, p.93, 94

[70] Fr. Samir Khalil – Ibn El Moqafaa'- Book 'Lantern of the Mind'- Cairo – 1978

[71] Mentioned by German historian George Graf in his book 'History of the Christian Arabic Literature' published in German language Part 2 in Rome 1947

THE FATIMID RULE
(972-1171)

The Fatimids ruled Egypt for around 200 years (972-1171 AD). Their policy fluctuated wiildly from complete clemency to severe persecution; each ruler dealt with the Christians according to his mood and personality. Thus the Christians lived in peace sometimes, while suffering bad treatment at other times.

Gowhar El Saqali who came from Morocco, invaded Egypt and built the city of Cairo. He was a Greek slave offered as a gift to Caliph Al Mo'ez. For this reason he was also known as Gowhar the Roman. Yacoub Ibn Kalas was another assistant of Al Mo'ez; he was a Jew from Baghdad who converted to Islam for personal benefits. He came to Egypt during the era of Kafour the Ikhshidid. The historian Ibn El Qalans mentioned that Yacoub was very tricky and cunning. It is written that Kafour one day said: "If he was a Muslim I would have made him one of my ministers". So he entered the mosque and converted to Islam, then fled to Morocco and helped the Fatimids in their invasion of Egypt. Al Mo'ez appointed him the head of his consultants and made him the Minister of Finance.

Here are four personalities who ruled Egypt as an example of how each treated the Christians: Al Mo'ez, Al Aziz, Al Hakem Be' Amr Ellah and Al Mostanser.

Al Mo'ez Ledin Ellah (969-976 AD)

He was one of the most merciful and broad-minded rulers, as well as being both experienced and cultured. In addition to the Arabic language and poetry, he spoke Greek, Sudanese and the Barbarian language of North Africa, as well as Slavonic language to talk to his slaves whom he brought from Eastern Europe. He was an eloquent orator to the extent that people used to cry while hearing his speeches. He was also a just and unbiased person. Al Mo'ez was also fond of theology and spirituality, and so he used to invite the Christians, Muslims and Jews to debate frankly before him. Yet, in spite of all those beautiful qualities, politics requires a certain tough attitude. Al Mo'ez was facing much enmity because the Egyptians were Sunnis, while Shia like himself were not welcome. He tried to befriend the Sunnis by showing a bit of disinclination towards the Christians. He cancelled the tradition set by the Ikhshidids to attend Christian celebrations, forbade the Christians from collecting donations from noblemen at El Nairuz Feast, as well the customs of sprinkling turbid water and shooting rockets. He also banned them from erecting tents and sailing in the River Nile during the Epiphany Feast celebrations. He threatened to hang anyone who would disobey and so the Christians stopped celebrating these feasts.[72]

Dr. Gamal El Din Seror wrote in his book "The Fatimid Rule in Egypt" an opinion which contradicts the above: some of the Fatimid Caliphs who are Shia unlike the Sunni Egyptian population needed some extra support to strengthen their grip on power. When they found it impossible to depend on the Sunnis in Egypt – who had been the supporters of the Abbasids - they befriended the Christians and showed them a lot of clemency, and appointed them to high positions in the government. Yet sometimes the Fatimids had to change their policy.[73]

Al Aziz Be'Amr Ellah: (976-996 AD)

All historians agree that this Caliph was kind to the Christians whether the Melkanites or Yacoubites, despite the fact that he would often demand a monetary gift in exchange for jos permission to build or reconstruct a church. During his era the government used pay close attention to this and guard the workers if needed. He also tried to get rid of the social

---

[72] Jack Tager: "Coptic and Muslims" p. 120 from Ibn Eyas Badae Al Zohoor Fi Waqe' Al Omoor (Beautiful Flowers of True Ages)

[73] Dr. Gamal El Din Seror wrote in his book "The Fatimid Rule in Egypt" p. 86

differences between Muslims and Christians. So, without exaggeration, we can definitely say that his era was an important turn in the history of Islamic Egypt, because Al Aziz – for the first time - called for total equity between Muslims and Christians.

Al Aziz married a Melkite Christian lady, among their children was a daughter named Set El Malek who was so compassionate with the Christians. He loved his Christian wife and daughter heartily and always consulted them on different issues. Further, he issued an order, which was admittedly in breach of the law, appointing two of his wife's brothers as Melkite Popes: the first, named Orestes, as Pope of Jerusalem; the second Arsanious as Metropolitan of Cairo, who was promoted to the position of Pope of the Melkites in Alexandria during the rule of Al Hakem Be'Amr Ellah.

The personality of Al Aziz was not weak; he fought many defensive wars to protect the eastern borders of his Empire, and maintained very strict administration measures inside the country. He fixed the wages of his employees and prevented them from accepting presents or bribes. His huge army included soldiers from Ethiopia and Turkey; he was engaged in many wars with the Byzantines. Generally speaking, the Fatimid government was at its zenith during his reign.

When Al Aziz depended on the Christians and those who converted to Christianity (or Muslims by pretence only such as Yacoub Ibn Kalas), the Muslims started taking

The Fatimid Rule (972-1171)

action against him, for Yacoub Ibn Kalas was Al Aziz's right hand for 15 years, to the extent that when Ibn Kalas died, Al Aziz grieved deeply. In tears, he visited his home and uncovered him to see his face. He ordered that he be buried under a dome which he personally built in his house. He attended his funeral and ordered government departments and shops to be closed for days, mourning his departure.[74]

After the departure of Yacoub Ibn Kalas in 991, Al Aziz also trusted the Christian Issa Ibn Nastoros who later became a minister, and appointed the Christian doctor Aba El Mansour, who had been Al Mo'ez's personal physician, as his assistant, granting him a very high position in the government.

This incident proves the Muslims' anger at Al Aziz's trust in the Christians: Once Al Aziz was walking in the city, then a Muslim pushed his way into the procession, gave him a letter then disappeared. The letter read as follows: "The Jews are proud of Mansha; the Christians are proud of Issa Ibn Nastoros, while the Muslims are ashamed of you."[75]

As a result, and to calm down the Muslims, Al Aziz arrested these two men and dismissed them; he also got rid of some of his Christian employees.[76] Shortly after, he pardoned

[74] Ibn El Kalanas, "Copts and Muslims: History of Damascus and Said Ibn Yehia El Antaki" p. 123

[75] Mansha Ibn Ibrahim El Farrar whom Al Aziz appointed as governor of Syria, Dr. Gamal Seroor "The Fatimid in Egypt" p.87

[76] Adam Metz, Vol. 1, p. 114 from "The Complete History" for Ibn Al Atheer.

Issa Ibn Nastoros and made him the minister and returned some of the Christians to their jobs, either under pressure from his wife and his daughter Set El Malek, or because he could not maintain sound government without their honest service. He returned Issa Ibn Nastoros on the condition that he would appoint Muslim employees in the government departments.[77]

During the reign of Al Aziz we witness the peak of sympathiy with the Christians, as he refused to punish converts from Islam to Christianity. A story is recounted about a Muslim nobleman who became a Christian. When he was arrested, many renowned personalities interfered including Al Aziz's wife, thus he was released without any harm. This man lived for the rest of his life in a monastery in Upper Egypt.

Generally speaking, Al Aziz showed an honest intention of spreading the spirit of forbearance and tolerance between Muslims and Christians; he frequently invited Bishop Severus Ibn Al Moqafaa for debates with renowned Muslim personalities such as the famous judge Ibn No'man.[78]

Yehia El Antaki narrates a very strange story:

> "Al Aziz decided to invade Rome in 996 and he ordered his minister Issa Ibn Nostor to prepare the Navy for this purpose. They were to set off after Friday Prayers, but the

---

[77] Dr. Gamal Seroor "The Fatimid in Egypt" p.87; Copts and Muslims p. 124

[78] Stanley Lane-Poole,"History of Egypt in the Middle Ages" p.119; Copts and Muslims p. 125

fleet was burnt in a blaze of fire and 16 ships were totally destroyed. People blamed the Roman merchants who used to come to Egypt and sell their products, and so there were riots everywhere including in Morocco. They killed around 160 of these merchants and the Melkite church of the Archangel in Qasr El Sham' was looted as well as the Nestorian Church. Minister Ibn Nostor went to the scene of the looting and asked them to stop harassing the Roman merchants, asking people to bring back what was stolen. Some agreed but some did not, so Ibn Noster paid each of the Romans what was equivalent to the stolen property and arrested and imprisoned 63 of the robbers. Al Aziz ordered that one third of them be set free and one third be killed. The method used was a lot, so he wrote on some papers 'hit', some 'kill' and some 'free'. He put the papers under a cloth and each prisoner chose a paper randomly. Thus whatever was written on the paper was carried out. During these riots the Bishop of the Nestorians was fatally wounded."[79]

Al Hakim Be'Amr Ellah

He was the harshest and most cruel ruler in his persecutions and humiliation of the Christians.

After the death of Al Aziz, Al Hakim his son ruled the country at the age of 11; Borgwan El Saqqali was his guardian (as he was under age). A person named Abu Muhammad El Hasan Ibn Ammar was appointed in a position a little

---

[79] Copts and Muslims p. 125, 126. Al Maqrizi retold the story in a summarized version (Adam Metz, from the Omia Civilization, p.114)

lower than a minister as well as Chief Army officer; he was the leader of El Katameen, which was the main group of the Fatimid. They asked for Issa Ibn Nostoros' resignation and for the appointment of Ibn Ammar. Ibn Nostoros then became responsible for the Caliph's personal office, but he did not enjoy this position for long. Some people envied him and alleged that he was misusing the country's money. They convinced Ibn Ammar to kill him.[80]

As there was great enmity between Ibn Ammar and Borgwan, the conditions in the country never settled down. Ibn Ammar was killed when Turkish troops defeated his troops in battle, formed of the North African tribes. Borgwan then gained control and appointed Fahd Ibn Ibrahim, who was a Christian, as his personal scribe and close assistant, granting him the title 'The President'. Soon the Caliph gave orders to kill Borgwan in the year 1000 AD, feeling that the latter wanted to have more authority by preventing Al Hakim from having a direct connection with the members of his cabinet. Again, people rioted after the killing of Borgwan, and al Hakim dealt with the situation in a very inexperienced way.

He called for Fahd Ibn Ibrahim the Christian, and dressed him in a robe of honour saying, "Do not be disturbed at what has happened". Ibn El Qalansi recorded the minutes of that meeting in detail: 'At dinner, Al Hakim called Al Hussein Ibn Gawhar and minister Abi El Alaa' Ibn Fahd Ibn Ibrahim. He also asked all the other scribes of the cabinet

[80] Dr. Gamal Seroor "The Fatimid in Egypt" p.87; (from the history of Yehia Ibn Said El Antaki)

to come. Then he addressed them saying: "This is Fahd. He was previously a scribe for Borgwan but now he is my minister - listen and obey him. He is above all of you. Carry out your duties carefully, protecting the country's monetary resources'". Fahd bowed and kissed the floor and so did everyone saying, "We are obedient to our ruler". Then Al Hakim addressed Fahd saying: "I am so pleased with you. All these scribes are my servants. Be aware of their rights and treat them nicely. Reward whoever is extremely honest and respect them."'

Shortly Fahd was a target for various plots, because those who envied him feared his growing authority, thinking he would be biased in favour of the Christians. They started stirring Al Hakim against him; Abu Taher and Ibn Addas the scribes accused him of stealing money. They greatly envied the Christians in Egypt and Syria, but when Al Hakim did not listen to them they incited others to present similar accusations. Although Al Hakim knew the truth about these accusations, he still ordered Fahd's execution, explaining to his followers that he took his decision under extreme pressure.

In order to make up for this, he called the sons of Fahd, and giving orders that they should be harmed nor their houses looted. In this way, Al Hakim wanted to challenge Ibn Addas and Abu Taher who were behind this plot and by then had reached higher positions.

The personality of Al Hakim Be'Amr Ellah

As he started ruling the country when he was younger than 16 years of age, he used to make confusing and contradictory decisions, such as:

He loved walking around in the streets at night, and in order to make these walks easier he ordered for lanterns to be hung on shops and yards at night. Accordingly, lifestyle became completely different; people started buying and selling at night, and sleeping in the morning. When he was informed that some people started making use of the lit streets for hooliganism and illegal activities, he issued a strict curfew for citizens from evening until dawn. He also forbade men from sitting in cafés, and decreed no stores may open at night.[81]

When he discovered that these rules did not reverse the alteration in people's lifestyle which was by now long-standing, Al Hakim issued new rules in 1002 AD. forbidding women to appear in public without veils and to walk after coffins in funerals. Then, in 1006 AD. he ordered women not to go to the shops or public baths, nor to look out from windows and balconies or to go on the roofs of houses. This reached such an extreme extent that he ordered shoemakers not to make any ladies' shoes, so as to ensure women would be stuck at home!

Some historians tried to defend Al Hakim's strange attitude

---

[81] Stanley Lane-Poole, "History of Egypt in the Middle-Ages" p. 125-126

The Fatimid Rule (972-1171)   163

by claiming that he wanted a more conservative religious atmosphere to prevail over the country, and to thus purify the souls of his citizens.[82]

But we actually disagree with this analysis, because it is unlikely his attitude was springing from religious intentions, given no Muslim ruler in history has issues such decrees.

Some of his instructions were:

- He prevented any fun activities on beaches, closing all the routes leading to the beaches;
- He forbade exporting raisins or selling them for fear that people would make wine. He ordered the destruction of all vineyards;
- He prevented people from eating a popular Egyptian green soup (Molokheya).
- He prevented fisherman from catching any fish without scales.
- Slaughtering cows only at Bairam Feast
- People should not store a greater amount of food than what they actually needed.

He threatened very strict punishment upon whoever disobeyed his orders, which sometimes reached death, and he was keen to personally follow up the fulfilment of his orders so that people might fear him and obey. Even his closest friends, staff and governors were under this pressure, but they asked him to give them a written document stating

---

[82] Dr. Gamal Serour "The Fatimid Country in Egypt" p.93

they were safe and he could not harm them. He did so and they lived in security.

Although Al Hakim was so strict, he lived a life of austerity, preventing people from using the term 'our master' or 'your highness' when addressing him. Moreover, no one was to kiss his hands, and he refused to hang any decorations or lights in the streets for his procession to the mosque.[83]

Following the footsteps of Al Mo'ez and Al Aziz, Al Hakim practised astrology; he consulted all the fortune tellers and gave them a lot of money. As these fortune tellers were thus able to manipulate the minds of many people, in 1007 he prevented any fortune teller from plying his trade. However, he had a personal telescopic site in Al Moqqatam Mountain to follow the routes and movements of the stars.

In order to give people the impression that he was aware of every single issue in their lives, he was known for his intense curiosity in other people's business. He sent spies everywhere in the markets and streets updating him secretly about different issues. In this way, people believed that he was a fortune-teller.

Some Persians came to Egypt, they were of the Sheia' Fatimid sect. Among them was a person named Hamza Ibn Ali El Zorni who was secretly calling people to venerate Al Hakim as a god. The extremists among the Sheia Ishmaelite sect would gather around Al Hakim, becoming close to him and gaining his favour. But the Sunni Muslims in Egypt

---

[83] Dr. Gamal Serour "The Fatimid Country in Egypt" p.94-95

The Fatimid Rule (972-1171)

rebelled, after one of the extremist groups openly declared that we should venerate Al Hakim in a sermon in Ibn El Aas mosque. Soon, the person declaring this was killed.

Among those calling for Al Hakim's veneration was a person named Muhammad Ibn Ismail El Dorzi. He was close to Al Hakim, and announced his belief openly in Al Azhar mosque. Again, the Sunni Egyptians and some of the moderate Sheias rebelled. They kept following him until they knew that he was hiding in Al Hakim's palace. They asked Al Hakim to hand Muhammad El Dorzi over to them, but El Dorzi kept delaying and finally secured his escape to Syria after giving Al Hakim a large sum of money. In Syria he also spread the call for the veneration of Al Hakim, and he formed a group, which were known later as the Druze.

As for Al Hakim, he was angry with those living in Al Fustat who objected to the idea of venerating him. He was particularly infuriated after the killing of one of his followers, and he took vengeance by burning Al Fustat city.

Many stories are told about the end of Al Hakim's life, as he was last seen in Al Moqqatam Mountain and then disappeared. He probably wanted to live in isolation as a great prophet or religious leader. Perhaps he wished to himself become the Mahdi whom the Ismailites (from the Al Sheia sect) are waiting for to come and rule in justice and peace.

This belief in venerating Al Hakim Be' Amr Ellah stems from the beliefs of the extremist Sheias who consider Ali

Ibn Abi Taleb and his Caliphs to be greater normal human beings. Some of these denominations even believe that Ali did not die and that he would return once more to the earth and rule in justice. Some of these groups in Iran idolise Ali's grandchildren and consider them rulers who never err (Al Khoumeiny, Ayyat Allah, Roh Allah).

Al Hakim Be' Amr Ellah and the Christian Coptics

Although Al Hakim was solely responsible for the brutal incidents that the Christian Copts suffered endured during his rule, there were a group of plotters who wanted the Christians to lose the privileges they had obtained during the era of Al Aziz. They made use of Al Hakim's young age and love of bloodshed to achieve their goal.

It started with the killing of Isa Ibn Nastoros who was Al Aziz's Prime Minister, then the killing of Fahd Ibn Ibrahim who had served Al Aziz for six years. He had been close to him and was granted security, but finally Al Hakim killed him to please some close friends. Many other Christians were also targeted.

It is mentioned in 'The History of the Patriarchs' that the reason for the killing of Fahd by Al Hakim was that Fahd refused to convert to Islam at Al Hakim's request. He was beheaded and his body placed in fire for three days. His body was not burnt and his right hand looked normal, as if nothing had touched it. Fahd was such a kind generous person who never let anyone down who asked him for anything. This was manifested through this miracle, since it was his right hand with which he performed all his charitable deeds.[84]

He also arrested ten of the renowned Coptic Orthodox elders and their scribes. One of them was named Abul Nagah El Kabir whom Al Hakim ordered to convert to Islam. He asked for one day to think about it, but in reality he did not need any time to think about the matter. Rather, he wanted to contact his brethren and encourage them to shed their blood for the Lord Christ. When he met them he said: "My brethren; do not esteem the vain glory of this world and lose the everlasting glory of Christ our Master. For He has filled us all with His goodness, and because He is Merciful He is calling us now to join Him in the Heavenly Kingdom. So be strong and steadfast in faith".

The next morning he went to Al Hakim and refused to convert to Islam. Al Hakim threatened and tortured him, taking his clothes off and lashing his body 500 times, and then ordered he be put through the two-wheel machine. His blood was flowing everywhere and his skin was lacerated and cut into many pieces. Al Hakim then ordered another 500 lashes, and when they reached 300 he asked for some water. Al Hakim said: "Give him some water and ask him again to join our religion". When Fahd knew it, he said: "Take his water back to him for my Lord Jesus Christ has quenched my thirst."

Some witnesses said that they saw water dripping from his

---

[84] Life of Pope Zacharias the 64th Patriarch, The History of the Patriarchs, 2nd Vol. Part 2, p. 123

beard, after which he gave up his soul.

The soldiers informed Al Hakim that he had died, but he ordered that the remaining lashes be completed, and thus he was martyred.

As for the rest of the ten whom he had arrested, they also refused to renounce Christianity, so he ordered them to be whipped. Four of them announced their conversion to Islam when they could not tolerate the torture, but returned to Christianity after the era of persecution. One of them died the same night, while the other five were martyred and gained eternal life.[85]

Al Hakim kept torturing the Christians, even his staff in the government; he dismissed most of them and only kept those whose service he considered absolutely essential. In 1004 AD, persecution was a public ordeal; in order to facilitate their marginalisation, he ordered the Christians to wear distinct clothes. He also afflicted the Sunni Muslims, and wrote insulting sentences on the mosques targeting Abi Bakr, Omar, Osman and Ayesha. In 1008 AD, he put additional restrictions on clothing. He banned the rich Copts from having Muslim slaves, he also issued a decree to destroy and loot all the churches. When he knew that the Christians visit the Church of the Resurrection in Jerusalem on feast days, especially on Palm Sunday and Easter, he ordered for this church to be destroyed.

---

[85] The Life of Pope Zakarias the 64th Patriarch, The History of the Patriarchs Vol. 2 Part 2, pp.122-123

The Fatimid Rule (972-1171)

This decision was a shock to the entire world, one of the believers in Europe said: "Every Christian wept". It is believed that this action was one of the reasons for the Crusades. The person who wrote Al Hakim's decree to destroy the Church of Resurrection was a Nestorian Christian named Ibn Sherin;[86] he died of grief 15 days later.

In the year 1009 AD, he cancelled all the Christian feasts and forbade any celebration in the country. All the real estate of churches and monasteries were taken over by the Monetary Institute of Muslims.[87] It was forbidden to ring church bells and the crosses were removed from the top of churches. His brutality reached the extent of asking Christians to remove the tattoo crosses from their skin.

In 1011 he ordered Christians to hang wooden crosses on their necks, one arm in length and 5 Libra in weight. In 1013, he again ordered to destroy and loot all the churches in Egypt without exception; the total number of churches pillaged reached 30,000.[88] Al Hakim then gave the Christians two options: either to convert to Islam or to leave the country.[89]

What really made the situation worse were the gangs who carried out Al Hakim's orders; they were fuelled by intense hatred and envy toward the Christians. They not only destroyed the churches, they demolished them completely;

---

[86] Copts and Muslims p. 129, 130

[87] Dr. Qasem Abdu Qasem, "Christians in Egypt-Middle Ages", p. 56

[88] Copts and Muslims p. 130, 131

[89] Copts and Muslims – El Antaky p.131

they even dug the Christians' tombs and used the bones of the dead as fuel for furnaces of the public baths.

Al Hakim also ordered the sailors not to take any Christian on board their boats; finally he ordered them strictly either to become Muslims or to face death.

As a result, a great number converted to Islam, while some others secretly fled to countries affiliated to the Byzantine Empire, and a third group hid their belief and used to gather secretly where they had hidden the holy utensils saved from destroying and looting.

Historian Yehia Ibn Said El Antaky who died in 1066, who started writing his history a short while after the disappearance of Al Hakim, described a touching incident that took place in Cairo in 1012 AD:

> *"A group of diverse professions from authors, workmen and doctors etc. gathered with the bishops and priests bareheaded and barefooted and headed to the palace of Al Hakim crying and pleading for his pardon. He sent them one of his men so they wrote their petition on a piece of paper and gave it to him. The messenger came back to them and answered them softly."*

Since the Arab invasion of Egypt, the Copts never experienced such persecution as in the era of Al Hakim. The Muslim historian Al Maqrizi recorded the following about the brutality of Al Hakim in dealing with the Christians in Egypt:

"Pope Zacharias sat on his throne for 28 years, 9 of them during the reign of Al Hakim with all its turmoils. Al Hakim arrested the Pope for 3 months, then he ordered him to be thrown to the lions with Susana the Ethiopian but they did not harm them. During his papacy the Copts suffered great tribulations and persecutions, because many of them were rich and reached high positions in the government, e.g. ministers. This gave them a degree of authority over the Muslims and annoyed them. Al Hakim could not tolerate such a situation; he always lost control whenever he got angry."

After mentioning some persecutions that the Christians faced, Al Maqrizi wrote:

"Al Hakim Be'Amr Ellah kept destroying and looting the churches and building mosques above their ruins; he even mounted the top of St. Shenouda Church and used the microphone to call the Muslims to prayers, and surrounded The Hanging Church in Old Cairo. He also wrote letters to officials to give Muslims permission to destroy the churches and monasteries, and they did so from 1013 AD to 1015 AD destroying around 30,000 churches and monasteries in Egypt, Syria and the surrounding countries, in addition to looting the golden and silver utensils and taking all their real estate. The Christians gathered in front of the palace of Al Hakim asking for his clemency, so they were pardoned from being exiled. During all these horrible incidents, many of Christians converted to Islam."[90]

Al Hakim kept persecuting the Christians for 9 years, the

[90] Al Maqrizi 'The Plans', Part 4, p. 398-400

last 3 years were the worst because he forbade prayers in churches except the monasteries in the mountains, so people used to bribe the governors to let them secretly gather and pray the Holy Liturgy in their houses. Al Hakim was so frustrated that his orders were not carried out accurately, so he tightened his grip on the Christians especially the priests. When they fled to the churches in the wilderness he followed them there and killed them.

As we have mentioned before, many Christians converted to Islam, but on the other hand there were a large number who refused and openly declared it; among them was a deacon named Bokira El Rashidi who was a chief scribe in the government. He resigned, carried his cross and went to Al Hakim's palace crying out "Christ is the Son of God". Al Hakim ordered him to renounce Christ and become a Muslim, but he refused. The more Al Hakim talked to him, the more he screamed, "Christ is the Son of God!" Al Hakim ordered for him to be imprisoned in iron chains, where he kept praying all the time. One day, a person visited him in prison, and he asked him to inform his family that before the sun sets he would be with them in his house. It indeed happened that Al Hakim released him that day, giving orders that Bokira should be treated fairly and reasonably by all.

After being released, Bokira went around comforting the Christians, assuring them that after three days things would ease, and it was so, for on the fourth day Al Hakim issued a decree allowing business dealings with Christians once more. He also allowed them to leave the country if they wished to go to Rome, Ethiopia or any other country. Bokira consecrated his time to serve the needy and strengthen the weak; he was so merciful and pious. He abstained from food daily until sunset, spending most of the night praying. A story is mentioned about his merciful deeds: Once he bought some bread and distributed it to the poor sparing one loaf for himself. As he started eating, someone knocked on his door. His disciple opened the door to find a poor man who said: "Tell Bokira that he has forgotten me today and I have nothing to eat!" He gave his loaf of bread to the poor man and slept without eating until the sunset of the following day.

A very rich man became poor as his circumstances changed, to the extent that he hardly had any clothes to wear. When Bokira knew about him, he sent much wheat. The man was not at home so Bokira's disciple left the wheat with his wife. When the man came back and knew about the wheat, he was so upset and kept weeping because his poverty was disclosed and people were helping him. His wife calmed him down and asked him to pray and the next day he would return the wheat. During his sleep he saw the Lord Jesus standing before him saying: "Why is your heart distressed?", the man answered: "Of course my heart is distressed. How could it be after all my wealth, riches and merciful deeds that I am asking alms now from others? It is better for me to die out of hunger rather than to live in such a situation."

The Lord Jesus said: "Do not be upset. This wheat is mine; I sent it to you through my messenger." The man answered:

"My Master it is not Your messenger who came, it was Bokira El Rashidi", the Lord said: "As if you did not know up to now that Bokira is My messenger!." When he woke up he informed his wife and they both rejoiced.[91]

Many announced their willingness to return to Christianity despite Al Hakim's aggression. It is written in the 'History of the Patriarchs' that some of the Christians who had converted to Islam came asking him to allow them to go back to their religion, so he agreed and many others did the same and returned to Christianity.[92]

Among them was a monk named Bimen who returned to Christianity and the Lord gave him grace in the eyes of Al Hakim so he asked the latter to give him permission to rebuild St. Mercurius Monastery known as Deir Shahran[93] (it is now St. Barsoum El Erian Monastery in Helwan). Al Hakim agreed and Bimen did so and he lived in the monastery with other monks.

Al Hakim and the monk Bimen became very close friends and Al Hakim used to go frequently to the monastery spending a few days there eating of their humble food, and whoever needed any favour from Al Hakim would go

---

[91] The Life of Pope Zacharias 64th Patriarch, The History of the Patriarchs, Vol. 2, Part 2, p. 128-131

[92] The Life of Pope Zacharias 64th Patriarch, The History of the Patriarchs, Vol. 2, Part 2, p. 135

[93] This was the name of the village where the monastery was built, and then it was destroyed.

The Fatimid Rule (972-1171)

and ask Bimen to talk to him.[94] It was Bimen who mediated between Pope Zacharias and Al Hakim when the Pope was in the monastery.

Al Hakim also completely banned using the Coptic language. (It had already been banned in government departments in 705 or 706 during the era of El Walid Ibn Abdel Malek El Amawy and the governor of Egypt Abdullah Ibn Abdel Malek. The latter hated the Christians with a passion, and ordered the exclusive use of the Arabic language in government departments, considering it the official language of the country). Al Hakim additionally banned using the Coptic language in the home and on the street, threatening to cut the tongues of whoever would dare to speak it. This order had to be followed very strictly by mothers while talking to the children, otherwise her tongue would be chopped off. The rulers succeeding Al Hakim followed the same policy.

Finally, after shedding the blood of around 18,000 people, and after claiming himself to be divine, he pardoned the Christians and allowed them to worship openly. Moreover, he encouraged them to re-build their churches and monasteries, and to increase the number of their monks.[95] He issued a decree saying:

> *"In the Name of the Merciful God... this is a note from*

[94] The Life of Pope Zacharias 64th Patriarch, The History of the Patriarchs, Vol. 2, Part 2, p. 135

[95] The Life of Pope Zacharias 64th Patriarch, The History of the Patriarchs, Vol. 2, Part 2, p. 131

Abdullah and his governor El Mansour Abi Aly, the Imam Al Hakim Be'Amr Ellah the Prince of Believers, son of Al Aziz Be'Allh, to the Christians in Egypt: when he knew about the fear and horror they were living in, he gave them a note assuring them of their safety, that they were surrounded by the safety of God and His prophet, and the safety of the Prince of Believers Aly Ibn Abi Taleb. Your souls, lives, children, wealth, all your possessions are safe."[96]

Al Mostanser Be'Allah

He ruled Egypt for around 60 years, from the age of 7 years old. For 7 years during his era there was a horrible drought because of the low level of the River Nile and this was called 'The Great Tribulation' (1066-1072). Famines and plagues prevailed over the country, and as a result of inflation a civil war arose in Egypt. The worst years were 1069 and 1070. It was said that around 10,000 people died daily. People ate their pets and they kidnapped each other to sell human bodies to the butchers. Clashes took place between the the Turks and the Sudanese who were supported by Caliph Al Mostanser's mother as she was a negro slave bought by his father Al Zaher from a Jewish merchant (1020-1026), but the Turkish soldiers won victory and the mercenary soldiers looted the Caliph's palace taking all his possessions. The Caliph used to sleep on a mat on the floor as he had no furniture left. Chaos reigned and around 35 ministers were change during just 12 years in the government. This

---

[96] Dr. Gamal Serour "The Fatimid in Egypt" pp.88, 89 from the History of Yehia Ibn Sad El Antaky

The Fatimid Rule (972-1171)

instability added to the country's miserable circumstances.[97]

Al Mostanser had an imprudent minister named Muhammad Al Bazori who severely hated Christians, particularly the Copts, because of the Caliph's preference for them. He kept seizing any chance to put them in trouble during the Papacy of Pope Christodoulos the 66th Patriarch. A new judge named Abdel Wahab Aba El Hussein was appointed in Alexandria, and he expected the Pope to give him a donation as a gift from the Copts. When this did not happen and he was informed about Al Bazori's hatred for the Copts, he went and told Al Bazori that the Pope was unjust to some people. He alleged that the Pope had stolen their money and built an extravagant palace and some churches in a place called Damro,[98] which had become a second Constantinople. He also claimed that the Pope despised the Islamic religion.

Immediately the minister gave orders to destroy the 17 churches in this area. Pope Christodoulos lived in a house

---

[97] Dr. Aly Ibrahim Hasan "Egypt in the Middle Ages" p. 120

[98] It is called Damro the Churches an affiliate of El Mahala El Kobra – Muhammad Ramzy – The Geographic Dictionary – Part 2, vol. 2, p.11; Some Popes used Damro as their headquarters after the seat was transformed from Alexandria. Pope Shenouda 1 the 55th Patriarch was the last one to stay in Alexandria headquarters, and then they moved to Damro. Pope Macarius 1 the 59th Patriarch, Pope Philothaous 62nd Patriarch, Zacharias 64th Patriarch, Shenouda II the 65th Patriarch, Christozolos 66th Patriarch was the last one to stay at Damro then the Hanging Church in Old Cairo became the headquarters of the Patriarchate.

which he had built, on the front it was written: "In the Name of the Father, of the Son and of the Holy Spirit", so the first thing which the delegate of minister Al Bazori did was scratch this writing off the wall. In response, the Pope – boldly and courageously - said to him: "You have taken it off the wall but you cannot take it off my heart."[99]

He kept annoying the Copts and attempting to aggravate Muslims against them, but nobody heeded this, as the people were busy with the bad circumstances of the country, the inflation and the plague. Finally he arrested the Pope and the other bishops with a false accusation and sent them to Cairo. Caliph Al Mostanser could not find any accusations against them, so he sent them back to their home towns with honour. The minister was infuriated at the Caliph's attitude, so he ordered for all churches in the country to be closed. This led to an uprising by the Christians which almost degnerated into outright conflict. The Caliph arrested this minister and exiled him to a place called Tinnis. The Caliph killed him later because he used to spread false rumours against the Caliph. He would have died a horrible death anyway as he was suffering from a serious disease.

Among the injustices of Al Bazori towards the Copts were his attempts fleece them of their money. He claimed that Pope Christodoulos was inciting the Christian King of Nubia not to carry out his duties towards the Fatimid Caliph. Thus, Al Bazori arrested the Pope without investigation and fined him 100 denarii. After the Pope was brought to Cairo, he was sent to Abdullah the governor of Upper Egypt. He

---

[99] The History of the Patriarchs, vol. 2, p. 167

The Fatimid Rule (972-1171)

found the Pope to be innocent so he went to Al Bazori and had permission to release him.[100]

The Head of St. Mark the Evangelist was kept in the house of Abi Yehia Ibn Zakareya. When he was very sick, the Christian elders assembled in his house for fear of the Muslims taking all his possessions after his departure, including St Mark's holy head. Finally they decided that the head should be kept in the house of Abi Al Fateh, the father of the historian who wrote 'The History of the Patriarchs'. As the Caliph had already persecuted Abi Al Fateh, Al Fateh was afraid lest the latter should persecute him again. For this reason, he refused to have the box with the holy head in his house. Thus the box was taken to the house of Seror Ibn Natrouh in front of Abi Al Fateh's house. Then father Simon the pastor of St. Mark Church wanted to take the box to his house, to look after it together with his brother.

When Al Bazori heard this news, he arrested Abi Al Fateh and all the Christians who were involved in transferring the holy head. He made Kawkab El Dawla, the governor of Alexandria, to issue a decree returning the head to Alexandria, along with a payment of 10,000 denarii which he claimed were with the head when it was taken. All those who were arrested succeeded in releasing themselves except Abi Al Fateh who was sent bound to Al Fustat and was asked to pay the amount of money (the governor said that the Romans were ready to pay the money and take the head for themselves). Abi Al Fateh was in prison for 37 days. He kept telling himself that all he was going through was because he

[100] Copts and Muslims p. 138

refused to keep the head of St. Mark at his house at the very beginning. The prison guard was a Muslim named Barakat who came on the 37th day of his imprisonment and said: "I had a dream today that a youth with a black beard and a mark on his forehead came and knocked on the prison gate. He said 'Abi Al Fateh, I am Mark the Evangelist. You have won yourself with your patience', and he also said many other things which I did not understand. Then he said 'take this and you will be saved', and then he threw a rock with three heads saying in three days you will be saved. Abi Al Fateh took the rock, kissed it and held it tight." Three days later he was able to gather 600 denarii and was released. He headed to Alexandria where the head was kept, and took its blessing.[101]

Some Muslims helped the Christians at certain times, such as in the above-mentioned incident with Abd el Dawla. Another example is Hesn El Dawla, the Governor of Alexandria, who used to love the Christians. When Al Bazori ordered all the churches in Alexandria closed, with all their possessions and utensils seized along with a fine of 10,000 denarii levied on the Christians, Governor Hesn El Dawla called a person named Mawhoub Ibn Mansour (the writer of the biography of Popes) and his uncle Sadaqa Ibn Serour. They were already serving him and he said to them, "Al Bazori has issued an order to close all the churches and seize all its possessions along with an additional 10,000 denarii fine. Go now and remove everything from the

---

[101] The History of the Patriarchs, Vol.2, p.174-176,'Copts and Muslims' p. 138-139

The Fatimid Rule (972-1171)

churches". The next day all the churches were closed and they paid 2000 denarii. When they came to him complaining about their inability to pray the services, he secretly gave them the keys of St. George Church which was originally the house of Ananias the second Pope, saying: "Go, open the church, carry out your prayers and pray for me." When they went to try to open the church, it took them six hours, from 3pm to 9pm. As they were struggling, they cried and pleaded to the Lord saying: "We know that we have sinned and trespassed against you, this door is locked because of our iniquities, please Lord forgive us and have mercy upon us". Immediately the door was opened, we prayed the Holy Liturgy and partook of the Holy Communion.[102]

Chaos prevailed the country after the death of Al Bazori. The Lewana tribe members seized their opportunity. Al Mostanser was weak after the defeat of his army by the Turkish leader Nasser Al Dawla. The Lewana therefore arrested Pope Christodoulos, tortured him, looted his house and robbed money that had been dedicated to the churches of St. Mark and St Macarius.

One of the Christians named Abul Tayeb Al Zarawi who was the secretary of Nasser Al Dawla asked him to negotiate with the head of the Lewana tribe to release the Pope. He succeeded in this endeavour, after paying a ransom of 3000 denarii for the Pope's release. This did not stop this tribe from spreading chaos, stealing and looting. They invaded the Scetis wilderness and its monasteries killing most

[102] The History of the Patriarchs, Vol.2, p.178-179, Copts and Muslims p. 139-140

of the monks there. They also committed horrible crimes throughout the whole country, killing the men, raping the women and slaughtering infants, destroying churches and scratching the saints' faces on icons.[103]

The spread of famine from 1066-1072 worsened the situation, and Nasser Al Dawla kept challenging the Caliph. The Caliph at the time was named Badr El Gamaly (who was an Armenian slave of the Syrian Prince Gamal Al Dawla Ibn Ammar, that had then converted to Islam). El Gamaly was known for his strength and intelligence. Militarily, he depended on some Armenian forces and local groups. He agreed to come to Egypt on the condition that he could replace the Turkish soldiers with Syrian ones in order to guarantee peace and safety in the country. The Caliph accepted his condition and gave him the title of "The honourable master, prince of the armies, sword of Islam, supporter of Imam, head of the Muslim judges, preacher of the Imams of the believers".

Badr El Gamaly started his job by killing the Turkish princes in a banquet which he had prepared for honouring them. When he got rid of his opposition, he worked hard to improve the financial situation of the country, lower inflation. This created peace and stability within the country.

Generally speaking, the relationship between Muslims and Christians is likely to be healthy in a country with a wise government. The Christians liked this Armenian man who

---

[103] The History of the Patriarchs, Vol.2, pp.183-184, Copts and Muslims p.140

The Fatimid Rule (972-1171)

ruled the country, because they considered him one of them although he had converted to Islam. From his perspective, he also liked them and was fair in any dispute that would arise. They even asked for his intervention in one of their religious arguments. In 1082 AD, five bishops and a Coptic elder came to Badr Al Gamaly complaining about Pope Kyrillos II (1062-1078 AD). The complainants were led by Bishop Youhanna Ben Al Zalem of Sakha. Badr Al Gamaly decided that it was not his job to deal with these issues, so he ordered the Pope to call for a general assembly for all the bishops in the country. And so 47 bishops assembled together with Al Gamaly. He started by calling them to unity, dealing with one another in love, and to respect their religious leader. He also warned them not to collect money for the sake of accumulating it, but rather to spend it on the charitable needs of their dioceses. He ended the assembly and let them go giving each one of them a document protecting them from any injustice.[104]

Being kind to the Christians did not mean that he was biased towards them. Once some Muslim merchants complained to him that Bishop Boqtor of Nubia had destroyed a mosque, so he immediately ordered Pope Christodoulos' arrest, accusing him of being responsible for this act. He also issued a decree ordering the Christians and Jews to wear a black belt and pay a special tax at the rate of a denarius and one third for each person.

Minister Badr Al Gamaly died in 1092 AD, so the Caliph appointed Al Afdal Ibn Badr and granted him the title

[104] Copts and Muslims pp. 141-142

'Shahinshah'. A few months later Caliph Al Mostanser died. The war of the first Crusade took place during the era of Al Afdal, which we will explain in detail later.

The End of the Fatimid:

By the death of Al Mostanser's caliphate, the Fatimids began to become weaker, while the authority of ministers whom the weak rulers relied on became stronger, e.g. Shawer, Asadeddin Shakouh and Salah Eldin. The Fatimid Caliph Al Aded was the last to rule the country (1160-1171 AD). During his era a major disaster happened to the Christians, namely the burning of the old city of Al Fustat in 1168 at the order of Shawer the minister of Al Aded. He was trying to prevent Amoori, the ruler of Latin Jerusalem, from invading it. Al Fustat's residents were mostly Christians. Shawer decided to pour 20,000 barrels of flammable substances on the city, igniting it using 10,000 flames to burn it. The fire blazed for 50 consecutive days. This was one of the side effects of the Crusades on the Christians.

Social Life of the Copts

The Fatimids left behind a prosperous civilisation in many aspects; for example, they founded the city of Cairo. Dr. Aly Ibrahim Hasan mentions: "We are sure that the specialised artistic forms seen during the Fatimid era were due to the skill of the Coptic craftsmen. This is clear in the beautiful portraits and artworks in the museums, including pictures, clothes, antiques etc. The Copts also excelled in medicine, and so the private doctors for the Caliphs were Christians. Among them was Sahel Ibn Kisal who was very close to Caliph Al Aziz and Abul Fateh Sahel Ibn Maqshar the private doctor of Al Aziz and Al Hakim.

Most of the craftsmen were Christians, such as jewellers, tanners, carpenters, tailors, engineers, builders etc. We can still see their brilliant work in the old churches at Haret El Room, Haret Zeweila, and also the churches in Old Cairo such as the Hanging Church and St. Mercurius Abu Sefein Church."[105]

As for the Coptic Feasts, Dr. Aly Ibrahim Hasan wrote:

> *"The Fatimid Caliphs shared with the Christians in celebrating their Coptic Feasts in great splendour and pageantry, especially the Epiphany Feast where the Muslims used to keep vigil all night. They also lit candles, played on the drums and celebrated. The Fatimids also celebrated El Nairuz Feast, where they distributed money, clothes, watermelon, pomegranate, bananas, dates and a special meal made of chicken, beef and lamb. They also appointed a prince whom they called 'The Prince of Al Nairuz' to go out in a great procession on this feast to distribute presents to statesmen from different ranks. The Fatimid also celebrated Maundy Thursday where they also gave gifts to highly ranked statesmen and renowned personalities. In celebration*

---

[105] Dr. Aly Ibrahim Hasan "Egypt in the Middle Ages" p. 480

of Maundy Thursday, they minted 500 denarii in gold to be given as gifts. Christmas was also celebrated by the Fatimids."[106]

Al Maqrizi mentioned that, in celebrating Christmas, the Fatimids used to distribute sweets and different meals to the scribes and officials in the government, and sold decorated candles and statues. Rich and poor alike bought these things for their children and families at Christmas time. They called them lanterns and they produced an unbelievable quantity, which were hung in all the houses, streets and shops.[107]

IMPORTANT PERSONALITIES OF THE FATIMID ERA

Twelve Popes were contemporary to the Fatimid reign which lasted for 200 years in Egypt, the first was Pope Abram Ibn Zaraa' the 62nd Patriarch (975-978 AD) who was a contemporary of Al Mo'ez Ledin Ellah, and the last was Pope Mark the 3rd who was a contemporary of Al Aded, the last Fatimid Caliph, and Salah El Din El Ayyoubi.

Pope Abram Ibn Zaraa' (The Syrian) (975-978)

He was a Syrian merchant living in Egypt named Ibrahim

---
[106] Dr. Aly Ibrahim Hasan "Egypt in the Middle Ages" p. 486-487
[107] Al Maqrizi Copts and Muslims p. 149

Ibn Zaraa'. He was a pious man known for his charity towards the needy, orphans, widows and destitute. He was an old man with his beard coming down reaching his chest. He had a good friendship with Caliph Al Mo'ez and the high statesmen in the government, as well as the senior Copts in Egypt. During a feast he entered to pray in St. Sergius and St. Bacchus Church in Old Cairo. Everyone noticed his piety and devotion and they decided to choose him as the Pope. He was pleading that he was not worthy of this honour, but they chained him with iron bars and took him to Alexandria and ordained him as the 62nd Pope.

It is mentioned that after his ordination he donated all his money and possessions. He also banned paying money to acquire a position in the church – a practise that was allowed by previous Popes. The Lord granted him favour in the eyes of Al Mo'ez who used to ask for his counsel in certain matters and took his blessings.[108] He also asked him to live in Cairo.

It was commonplace at that time for elders to have concubines and children, so the Pope announced that anyone practising this should be excommunicated; everyone obeyed except a rich elder who had many concubines. The Pope made many prostrations begging him yet the elder refused to obey. The Pope decided to visit the elder in attempt to convince the him, yet as soon as he knew that the Pope was paying him a visit, he refused to open the door and left the Pope standing outside for 2 hours. Finally the Pope excommunicated <u>him and shook</u> the dust of his shoes on the doorsteps of

---

[108] The History of the Patriarchs, Vol. 2, Part 2, p.92

the elder's house. It was made of granite stone which was split into two pieces. Many people witnessed this incident, praised the Lord and honoured the Pope. A few days later this elder passed away, losing all his possessions.

The greatest miracle performed through Pope Abram for which everyone glorified the Lord was moving Al Moqqatam Mountain. A Jewish minister who had converted to Islam incited Al Mo'ez against the Christians saying: "In their Bible it is written, "If you have faith as a mustard seed, you will say to this mountain, 'Move from here to there,' and it will move", so their Bible is either true or false." Al Mo'ez asked the Pope if this was written in the Bible and the Pope affirmed it was. The Caliph asked him then to move Al Moqqatam Mountain, otherwise he would destroy all the Christians. The Pope was perplexed and asked him for three days days.

In St. Mary's Hanging Church, the Pope assembled with all the priests, Coptic elders, the congregation and informed them of the matter while in tears. He called for a 3 day fast with only bread, salt and water, and along with corporate prayers in the church. As for himself, he totally abstained from food for the 3 days, and as a result he nearly fainted on the third day as he was standing in the church. At this time, he saw St. Mary asking him, "What's wrong?" When he narrated the story to her, she calmed him down saying, "Do not be afraid, I will consider all the tears which you shed in my church." She then asked him to go ahead to the market where he would find a one-eyed man carrying a jar of water - he would be the one to carry out this miracle.

The Pope did what St. Mary asked, and when he met the man that had been described, he informed him about St. Mary's message, asking him to tell him more about himself, the man said: "Forgive me father, I am not worthy of this honour, I am a tanner, I plucked out my eye following the Lord Jesus' commandment as I coveted something that was not mine. Here I am working for a tanner; I eat a little bread and spend the rest of the day helping the needy and destitute. Each morning I bring water in this jar to the poor people in the area. I work all day and spend the nights in prayer. Please do not tell anyone about me for I cannot stand people's praise". The man asked the Pope to go with him to the Mountain, wherever the Caliph would appoint. The Pope, together with the priests and congregation, carrying candles, censors and crosses would stand on one side of the mountain, and the man would stand behind the Pope, not recognised by anyone. Al Mo'ez, his soldiers and his followers would stand on the other side. They would then cry out to the Lord saying 'Lord have mercy' for a while. Then after being ordered by the Pope to be silent, everybody would bow with the Pope three times, while the Pope would sign the mountain with his cross every time they bow. Thus they would witness the miraculous glory of the Lord.

The Pope informed the Caliph that they were ready to go to the Mountain. The Caliph went, accompanied by his soldiers and the Jewish minister, and the Pope did exactly what the one-eyed man had told him. Every time the Pope signed the mountain with the cross, it would move up, and every time they bowed, the mountain would come down to the ground.

Al Mo'ez and the Muslim people accompanying him were greatly terrified and finally cried out: "God is Great; there is no God except You." Then he said to the Pope, "Now I know that your religion is true."[109]

Caliph Al Mo'ez asked the Pope whether he needed any favours from him, yet the Pope answered, "I do not wish for anything except that the Lord may strengthen you and give you victory over your enemies". When the Caliph repeated his question three times, the Pope finally said, "I ask your highness to permit us to rebuild St. Mercurius Abu Sefein Church and St. Mary's Hanging Church as they were destroyed". Al Mo'ez wrote a decree ordering the rebuilding of the two churches, with all the expenses to be paid by the Muslim Ministry of the Treasury. The Pope returned happily, but refused for the churches to be built with this money, saying that the Ministry of Treasure should spend this money on their own business.

When the local merchants heard about the rebuilding of the churches, they started a riot threatening that they would give up there lives to block it from taking place. The Pope went back to the Caliph and informed him of this. The became furious, came with his soldiers and ordered for the work to commence. There were no objections from anyone except for a Sheikh who was leading the prayers at a neighbouring mosque, who threw himself in the hole that had been dug, shouting, "I want to die today for the name of God and never let anyone build this church". The Caliph ordered for building to commence regardless, throwing the rocks and

[109] The History of the Patriarchs, Vol. 2, Part 2, p.94-96

The Fatimid Rule (972-1171)   191

lime over him. When they did so, he tried to move and get up, but Al Mo'ez ordered that he be left to get buried in this hole. The Pope pleaded with Al Mo'ez to get him out, and finally he was lifted from the hole, and the building of the church continued without any objections. Similarly, the rebuilding of St Mary's church was completed successfully. Many churches in Lower Egypt were renovated.

Mystery surrounds the circumstances of the departure of this saintly Pope. It is said that a rich Coptic elder named Abi El Serrour El Kabir had many concubines, and when the Pope rebuked him and ordered him to set them free, he refused. Consequently, the Pope prevented him from entering the church and receiving Holy Communion. As a result it is said that he poisoned the Pope. He departed after spending 3 years and 11 months on the See of St. Mark. People deeply mourned him after his departure.

We would like to mention that the miracle of moving Al Moqqatam Mountain is written in detail in the book 'The History of the Patriarchs', which was written contemporary to this miracle. It is also mentioned by Abul Makarem in his book 'Churches and Monasteries' in the 10th century, and also by Marco Polo who was an Italian merchant from the Republic of Venice in the 13th century. The first mention of this miracle was it recorded by Dr. Aly Ibrahim Hasan in his book 'Egypt in the Middle Ages' where he wrote: "the first one to write about this miracle was the writer of Al Kharida Al Nafissa". Anyway, there is another proof of the occurrence of this miracle, which was the change of attitude of Al Mo'ez towards the Christians. Later, his son Al Aziz

Bellah married a Christian woman.

Alfred Butler was a British historian who wrote a book in two volumes about the churches of Old Cairo. He wrote that Al Mo'ez ordered for the mosque which was facing St. Shenouda Church in Old Cairo to be demolished. Al Mo'ez was baptized in the baptismal font next to the altar of St. John the Baptist then he gave his throne to his son Al Aziz Be'Amr Allah, spending his last days in worship in one of the monasteries.[110] Ibn Al Makin mentioned the same story in the 14th century; it was also mentioned by Marcos Pasha Smeika. Although the Muslim historians deny this miracle, given the fact that the conversion of Al Khalif Al Mo'ez was not mentioned by a famous historian, we believe that all the surrounding circumstances assure the veracity of the story. In his book 'Al Tarikh Al Magmou Ala Al Tahqiq wa Al Tasdiq' (The Gathered History of Investigation and Confirmation), Yehia Ibn Said Al Antaki who died in 1066 AD, did not refer to the miracle of Al Moqqatam Mountain. Importantly, however, he wrote that news of the death of Al Mo'ez was kept secret for 8 months, and that one day before his departure he pledged allegiance to his son Al Aziz as the ruler of the country. In his book 'Copts and Muslims' Dr. Jack Tager wrote:

> "Yet there is one point about which we worry: Al Mo'ez – the first Caliph to arrive to Egypt - spread rumours about his death, which the Coptic historical record never doubted, saying that this Caliph abandoned ruling the country after becoming a Christian. On the other hand, the liberality of

---

[110] Alfred Butler "The Ancient Coptic Churches" vol.1, p. 126, 127

his son and successor Al Aziz with the Christians was very astonishing. Caliph Al Mo'ez disappeared after visiting the monasteries and spending time there. He also rebuilt and renovated many churches and monasteries, neglecting the battle with the Crusaders. Finally Al Khatar risked his life to protect his Christian Minister Bohram. Can it seriously be suggested that their good treatment of the Christians was solely due to the Christians' loyalty to the regime?"

Pope Philothaous (979-1003)

He was the 63rd Pope, serving for 24 years, chosen from the monks of St. Macarius Monastery, and was a contemporary of Caliph Al Aziz Bellah and Al Hakim Bi'Amr Ellah. Nothing in this Pope's era is worth mentioning; although he witnessed around 8 years of the reign of the tyrant Al Hakim Bi'Am Ellah, nothing was recorded about this.

The History of the Patriarchs mentions that his life ended miserably as he was not living in asceticism appropriate for a monk and a Pope. Once he entered into St. Mark's Church in Alexandria to serve the Holy Liturgy with a number of bishops, but as soon as he started, he halted and could not say a word, so bishop Marcos of Al Bahnasa completed the service. They carried him to the house of one of the Christians where he kept silent for 9 hours. After others insisted to know what had happened, he told them that as soon as he started the Holy Liturgy, before signing the Lamb with the cross, the wall to the east of the altar was split, a hand came out and signed the Lamb with the cross, and he became silent. As he was saying this, one of his limbs shrivelled up and after a little while he departed.

It was said that after his departure his family found a large amount of money that he had collected during his papacy. They were 4 brothers, and they divided the money amongst themselves. But later they lost the money and the author of this Pope's biography wrote that he saw one of these brothers going around the streets begging. The most important events in his biography was the faith of Al Wadeh Ibn Abu Al Ragaa' and the martyrdom of St. George Al Mozahem.

Al Wadeh Ibn Abu Al Ragaa[111]

He was a fanatical Muslim youth living in Egypt. One day he saw a crowd surrounding a Muslim youth who had converted to Christianity. The soldiers had prepared some coal to burn him after killing him, so Al Wadeh came closer to this man and said to him, "Why would you expose yourself to destruction for the sake of a religion which makes you deny your Muslim beliefs and hurt your God. You will thus be burnt both with the everlasting fire and the fire here on earth, as you are making the One God Three personalities, whereas he is only One. Now listen to me and forget about this Christianity, go back to your religion and I will consider you my brother and let everyone honour you." So the youth who had converted to Christianity answered; "We, Christians, worship One God; The Father, The Son and The Holy Spirit. The Son is not estranged from God the

---

[111] The History of the Patriarchs, Vol. 2, Part 2, p.101-112

Father, He is His Word; neither is the Holy Spirit estranged from God the Father, He is His Spirit. The Mystery of our religion is too sublime for you to comprehend. I can see that after a little while you will come closer to the Light of Christ, and you will also struggle for the sake of the One for Whom I am struggling now and sacrificing my body and soul. You will also be tortured exactly like me." Hearing these words, Abu Al Ragaa' became more furious, he took his shoes off and kept hitting the youth on his mouth, head and face, slapping him harshly while saying: "I will never be like you, you wretched person". The youth answered: "One day you will remember that my words came true."

The Christian youth was beheaded, then they piled coals and bark on him and lit the pile, the fire kept blazing for three days while the guards were guarding his body. This should have been enough to turn the body into ashes, yet they found his body shining like gold; not a single part was burnt.

Ibn Al Ragaa' went back home and spent his night in total depression and anger because of what he had heard from the youth who was martyred for Christ's sake. His family tried to cheer him up, yet in vain. Then he heard that some friends were going to Mecca for the Hajj; he asked his father to join them and his father agreed and asked one of his best friends to look after his son during the trip.

On their way to Mecca he had a dream of an elderly man resplendent in white saying to him: "Follow me and you will save yourself." When he woke up, he narrated the dream to his father's friend who calmed him down saying "The monk was the devil who is trying to tempt you. Just ignore the whole matter and do not think about it."

After performing their pilgrimage, six or seven days through their trip on their way back, they stopped for a break. His father's friend mounted the camel and left him behind. He ran after them trying to track them but he could not; he was left alone in the desert frightened of the dark night and the wild beasts. Suddenly he saw a handsome knight in spendid garments mounting a horse, asking him: "Who are you and how did you lose your way in the desert?" When he told him the story, the knight asked him to mount the horse behind him. Doing so, they flew in the air, quickly reaching St. Mercurious' Church in Old Cairo. The door was opened by itself without anyone opening it, and then the knight disappeared.

He was stunned as if he were in a dream, as he saw the lanterns and candles lit in the church. In the morning, the church guard entered and saw him, and started shouting, thinking he was a robber. Yet Abu Al Ragaa' asked him to tell him what this place was, the man told him that it was St. Mercurius' Church in Egypt. When he could not believe he was in Egypt, the church guard said: "I can tell that you are an insane person and you seem completely disorientated". Then Abu Al Ragaa' informed him about his full story, yet the man still was in doubt, suspicious that he was a robber and St. Abu Sefein had tied him up in the church. Showing him an icon of the saint, he screamed: "This is the knight who appeared to me in the desert and brought me here!" He then informed him that he was Al Wadeh Ibn Abu Al Ragaa' and he was ready to become a Christian. Yet the church would be burnt because of him if he revealed his identity openly. He asked the church guard to do him a favour and hide him until he finds a solution. He also asked to be introduced to a priest as his heart was yearning to become a Christian and he wanted to know more about Lord Jesus.

Abu Al Ragaa' asked the priest to baptize him. The priest feared it was just a devilish trick; he asked him to first spend some time in the Scetis wilderness. But Abu Al Ragaa' pleaded vehemently with many metanias, arguing that he might pass away before reaching the wilderness. And so he was baptized and named Boulos. Because of much fastings, prayers, and spiritual devotions his complexion changed, and so he put on different clothes so that no one could recognize him and he left.

As for his father and his family, when they were told that he got lost in the desert, they grieved and mourned him deeply. Yet a friend who used to live next to St. Mercurius' Church saw him entering and leaving the church, first he doubted it was him because of his change in appearance, so he informed his brothers, who kept watching him from afar. Finally, they became sure he was their brother and they approached him saying: "What have you done to us?" They took him home to their father and he told him: "I am now called Boulos". His father blamed him saying: "You have disgraced me among the people of honour". They kept arguing with him trying to convince him to go back to Islam, but when they failed they locked him in a dark room for three days without food or drink.

They had resolved to kill him, but then changed their minds, took him to Giza and said, "Just stay away from us." He headed to the Scetis wilderness, becoming a monk after spending some time as a disciple to a pious, elderly monk.

One day, a monk said to him, "The Lord will not accept you as a Christian unless you go to Cairo and declare your Christianity." He went back to his father's house, deciding to sacrifice his life for the sake of the Lord Jesus. Seeing him in monks' garments, his father was furious and ordered him to be locked in a dark room, banning him from any food or drink. His mother kept crying and lamenting; she secretly tied some food and drink on a rope and put it down for him, but he never ate any of it.

He kept praying for six days, after which he became very weak, and on the seventh day, the monk who appeared to him on the way to Mecca appeared again carrying some bread for him. At first, he did not want to eat lest it was a mirage. But he recognised the monk when he informed him that he was St. Macarius, the father of the Scetis wilderness, coming to comfort and strengthen him. He ate from that bread and regained his strength.

As a last resort, Abu Al Ragaa's father ordered his brother to have sexual intercourse in front of him with a concubine with whom he used to live with before becoming a Christian. And so he conceived a son. Again, failing to return him to Islam, his father drowned his son before his eyes, yet Abu

Al Ragaa' said to his father: "Truly I love my son, but I love God more than him."

Finally, he presented a complaint about him to Al Hakim Bi'Amr Ellah who was the Caliph at that time. The Caliph ordered him to come with his father before the judges and the witnesses, yet as there were no verdicts against him, he was released.

Abu Al Ragaa' named himself Al Wadeh and became a friend to Bishop Severus Ibn Al Moqafaa of Al Ashmonin who taught him a lot about piety, the church books and the lives of the church fathers. Abu Al Ragaa' wrote a book, now lost, in which he mentioned the story of a martyr named Al Hashimi. We are retelling the story here as written in 'The History of the Patriarchs':

> *'There was a famous person in Baghdad named Moqadem. Known as Al Hashimi, he was the son of a king, but he never cared about the kingdom. Every day, accompanied by his soldiers, he would enter Christian churches during the Holy Liturgy, take the Lamb from the altar, break it and mix it with dust, and then pour the wine in the chalice on the floor. There were nearly no Liturgies held in Baghdad at his time, as most of the priests refrained from praying because of him. One day, he entered a church, and the Lord opened his eyes - instead of the Lamb he saw a beautiful baby in the paten. During the Fraction Prayers, he saw the priest slaughtering this baby and squeezing His Blood in the Chalice, cutting his flesh into small pieces in the paten. Al Hashimi was shocked and froze in his place. When the priest came out to give the*

> Body and the deacon to give the Blood, Al Hashimi asked his soldiers if they could see the child in pieces and His Blood in the chalice. They told him that all they could see was just bread and wine. He was stunned. In the meantime, all the congregation was wondering: why he is he not desecrating the church as usual? After the Holy Liturgy ended and everyone left the church, Al Hashimi told the priest what he had seen. Knowing that he was the only one to see this, he asked the priest to tell him about the Mystery of this Flesh and Blood. The priest explained how Lord Jesus established the Mystery of the Eucharist, then said to him, "The Lord has revealed to you this mystery for the salvation of your soul.'

The priest kept reading more religious books, explaining the Christian dogma to Al Hashimi. This greatly attracted Al Hashimi to the faith. He ordered his soldiers to leave, then the priest baptised him and he spent the night in the church. The next morning, his friends came to pick him up with a mule, yet he dismissed them derisvely. So they went and informed his father, who came and took him out of the church by force. He tried convincing him gently to return to Islam, but finally he ordered that he be tortured harshly. Al Hashimi bore this with patience, refusing to deny the Lord Jesus Christ. He was beheaded and won the crown of martyrdom. People in Baghdad honoured his body by burying him and building a church named 'Al Hashimi Church'.

Al Wadeh (Boulos) spent two years in the Scetis wilderness. When the monks saw his piety, they ordained him a priest against his will. When his father knew about it, he bribed some people to kill him. Some monks, however, when they had heard about this plan, advised him to escape to the countryside to a place called Sandafa.[112] He lived there for two years in St. Theodore church where he served night and day. About two days prior to his departure, some cruel people began spreading the fact that he had originally been Muslim throughout all Sandafa and Al Mahalla Al Kobra. At this time, he had a severe fever, and God sent a deacon to him named Tidar Ibn Mina from Menouf. So Boulos said to him, "Do not depart from me before taking the blessing of burying my body. I have just two more days to live. Please bury my body before the Muslims come and burn it". He said this in the spirit of prophecy, for indeed after two days, he passed away. The devil announced this news in Sandafa and Al Mahalla, so the people came and surrounded the church where he was lying dead. The Lord guided deacon Mina to bury him in a place in the church, and when the people came in they looked everywhere but could not find his body.

Al Wadeh once said: "Although I faced horrible tortures and went through many afflictions, yet nothing worried me more than three things: when my brother slept with my concubine before my eyes, taking my son from her forcedly while I was watching, and even more than that, when the Pope was watching his disciples attempt to extract money from me after for ordaining me a priest without rebuking them." These people had asked Boulos for money, but as

---

[112] It was a part of Al Mahalla Al Kobra - Geographic Dictionary written by Muhammad Ramzy Vol.1, p. 185

he had none, they were really annoyed and hurt him. Some Coptic elders who were watching paid the money on his behalf.

St. George Al Mozahem[113]

His martyrdom was on 19th Baounah 695 AM corresponding to 26th June 979 AD during the era of the Fatimid ruler Al Aziz Bellah, and the papacy of Pope Theophilus (63rd Patriarch). As we have mentioned before, the era of Al Aziz was characterised by dealing nicely with the Christians, however every now and again a dispute would boil over, such as the following incident with this martyr in Talkha.

He was named Mozahem, the son of a Muslim man named Gom'a Al Atwy who had married a Christian girl named Mariam, both against her will and her parent's will. They were living in Talkha, Daqahleya Governorate.

He was a Muslim until the age of 12, but his mother used to go to church regularly. He always asked her for a piece of the 'blessing morsels' to eat, which tasted like honey in his mouth. This was the beginning of his yearning towards Christianity. He started going to church with his mother, then he went secretly to Bishop Zacharias of Damietta where he was baptized, partook of the Holy Communion and was named George Al Mozahem.

He got married to Sweila, the daughter of father Abanoub,

---

[113] From the manuscript published by the Church in Damietta in 1969

the priest of Bosat Al Nasara Church in Talkha. The devil stirred up some people against him, so they went and informed Metwally Al Harb in Demeira that he was a Muslim and had converted to Christianity. George admitted this when Metwally asked him about the truth of this story. He was tortured, bleeding profusely from his mouth. He was then imprisoned, but later released miraculously; the angel of the Lord appeared to Metwally and asked him to release George, then the angel unlocked his handcuffs. His wife was also severely tortured. Amazingly, wherever this saint went, the devil would enter into someone's heart to announce his arrival and the fact he was a Muslim who converted to Christianity.

One day they tied a rope to his neck and dragged him throughout the streets of the city, one of the people watching came and hit his head with his sword but the sword was split, the saint only falling on the ground. At this time he was working at an oil-press, and the owner of the press was informed that one of his workers had been killed, so he went and dragged him out of their hands and took him to his home. He decided to wait until Friday prayers to take him to the mosque, and if he refused to pray with them, he would burn him alive. A Christian worker in the oil-press knew about this plan, and informed George who secretly escaped to Qalyoubeya with his wife where he lived for 3 years.

Again, the enemy of goodness announced his arrival through someone, so they moved to a place called Ekhna where he spent 3 years. He fell sick with a very dangerous disease, so together with his wife they headed to Al Mahalla Al Kobra, then to Digoway (now known as Demiana), spending another 3 years. There he and his wife vowed to live as brother and a sister. From there they went back to Bosat A Nasara, and he lived with his father-in-law. He struggle had in his prayers, making 500 prostrations every night.

As he was tired of moving from place to place because of the threat of persecution, he considered joining St. Macarius Monastery in the Scetis wilderness. That night he had a vision of heaven, where he was sitting on the right hand of the Lord Jesus Christ. He heard a voice saying "George be courageous in your witness. Blessed are you because you deserve to be counted among the martyrs. The toil is difficult but the everlasting joy is forever." Hearing these words he was strengthened and informed his wife. She answered and said to him: "My brother, what you have seen in this vision means that the Lord does not want you to become a monk, but to witness for His Holy Name, to gain the crown of martyrdom and the everlasting joy. Thus, I would be named 'the wife of the martyr'." She kept encouraging him to struggle patiently until his martyrdom.

George then headed to a monk priest and informed him about all these thoughts concerning monasticism and martyrdom. He advised him: "Blessed are you, my son George. If you have patience for one punishment it is more beneficial for you than spending a whole year in the monastery." Being strenghthened by his advice concerning the vision, he began preparing to witness to the Lord Jesus.

His second opportunity to witness came in Demeira in front of one of the governors. While he was living in Bosat Al Nasara, an evil person had revealed the truth about his Christianity. The people brought him to Demeira where they hit him harshly, tied a rope to his neck and took him to the Persecutor who ordered him thrown into a dark room. Then they brought him again before the Persecutor, torturing him physically and financially. Some of them were spitting on his face, others were beating him on his head mercilessly, one man hit his neck and shoulders with an iron rod, breaking his bones. Bound and tortured, he never ceased from calling upon the Name of Lord Jesus with joy.

Metwally Al Harb called for him in Demeira and he witnessed to the Lord Jesus saying: "My Lord is the Living God, no matter how much you torture me, I will never renounce my Master and Saviour Jesus Christ". They tied him with iron chains and tortured him brutally, one of them hit him on the head and split his head, then they jailed him. At midnight, Archangel Michael appeared to him, shielding George with his wings and strengthening him, and wiping his whole body. Instantly he was healed then Archangel Michael ascended to heaven.

St. Mary the Mother of God appeared to him in the shape of a dove, spreading her wings above his head and kissing the site of the head trauma. When he tried to catch her right wing she flew away, the place being full of light. His wounds were all healed and he felt strength going through his entire body. His saintly wife visited him in prison encouraging him, so he related to her what St. Mary and Archangel

Michael did with him.

Archangel Michael appeared to him another time and filled the prison with strong light. Another time the Lord Jesus, accompanied by Archangel Michael and Archangel Gabriel, appeared to him with a strong sharp light to the extent that he could no longer open his eyes.

They tortured him a lot in the prison, his wife always visiting and encouraging him. Archangel Michael - whom he was pleading to help him - appeared to him another time saying: "I have been pleading with the Lord on your behalf for a week, and He is sending this robe to you to give you strength. Come forward and I will cover you." The saint went closer and as soon as the Archangel covered him with the robe it became one with his flesh; he signed it with the cross and he was healed immediately.

Some Christians visited him in prison to take his blessing and asked for memorabilia to keep in their houses. He gave them the bloodstained bandages which were wrapped around his hands and legs. Knowing this incident, his wife came to him straight away to strengthen him lest he fall into pride, saying: "Who are you to deserved to give your bandages for people as a blessing? Maybe you are like St. Paul whose garments used to heal people?" George wept bitterly when he heard her words and promised not to do it anymore.

People who were full of envy kept pushing Metwally to deliver George to them to kill him; some of them even threatened to become Christians if he refused their request.

Finally, after much suffering, he was informed in a vision that his martyrdom would be completed on 19th Baounah. The Lord Jesus appeared to him again in the form of a prince carrying an open book saying: "Peace to you my beloved George, the sweet name in every mouth, be strong and comforted. All the pains and sufferings which you tolerated for My Name are written in this book. Blessed are you, but lift up your eyes and look upwards." George lifted his eyes to heaven and saw a handsome youth wearing white like a great angel, followed by an entourage who were also wearing white clothes. They all bowed to the Carrier of the book. George asked the Lord: "Who is this great king followed by such a multitude?" The Lord Jesus answered: "This is my beloved George from Palestine, after whom you were named, those following him are the martyrs and saints, they all came to interecede on your behalf that you may complete your martyrdom." Then the Lord Jesus disappeared.

The next morning Metwally came to George in the prison saying: "What's the point of staying here now? Ask your wife to get a guarantor to pay me 20 denarii and you can go home, and I will not deliver you to the citizens of Demeira." George answered: "I have no money to give you nor do I have a guarantor. Let them do whatever they like, whether they burn me or drown me."

On the next day, which was 17th Baounah, news spread about a letter sent from Cairo to release George. The people gathered promising to fight to the death to prevent his release, and rather burn him alive. They kept pressuring Metwally until he promised to give them George the next day. People headed to the prison where they saw a congregation praying with George, so they thought they were some Christians. Some went to inform Metwally so he told them to kill any Christians they might find with George. To their astonishment, when they went back, there was no one with George. Apparently, these were some martyrs and saints who came to strengthen him at this difficult time.

They wanted to take him immediately without waiting until the next day for fear that he would escape, but he calmed them saying: "I cannot escape from the service of my Saviour, I am totally ready". When they did not believe him, they gave him to a monk named Mina to guarantee he would not escape. The monk did so and prevented them from torturing him, and he was the one who wrote George's biography.

In his last meeting with his wife, he asked her to stay away from him lest they should torture her, but she answered: "My brother and master, please remember me when you meet My Master Christ." The saint signed himself with the cross saying: "May the Lord Christ reward you, my sister, for your constant toil with me. Now I ask you to remember me in your prayers so that the Lord may strengthen me unto the end." She kissed his feet saying: "Be strong, fix your eyes on the Lord, do not be afraid of death lest you lose everything."

People tried to convince him to deny his faith until his last moments, yet he refused. Finally, they took off his clothes, scourged him, and escorted him bleeding to the place of martyrdom. They were hitting him without mercy or compassion, some with rods, others with iron bars, fulfilling the Lord's words, "the time is coming that whoever kills you will think that he offers God service."

A mob of about 1500 gathered around him with iron bars, rods, arrows and swords, torturing him while he was repeating the Name of the Lord Jesus Christ. When they noticed that he had not died yet, one of them suggested that the Name that he was repeating was keeping him from death. So they put a sharp rock in his mouth, and he was repeating the Blessed Name in his heart.

They kept shooting arrows at his body, striking him several times on his head, till at 3.00pm on 19th Baounah he yielded up his soul between the hands of the Lord.

Pope Zacharias
64th Patriarch (1004-1032)

After the departure of Pope Theophilus, there was no Pope for two months and 8 days. The bishops in Alexandria elected an old celibate priest named Zacharias, who was serving at the Church of the Archangel in Alexandria. He was beloved by all the bishops and oversaw many churches. The reason for choosing him over one of the monks was the following: There was a rich merchant in Alexandria named

Ibrahim Ibn Bishr. He was a close friend to all the governors in Egypt, and so was looking forward to become the Pope, because of his connections with the nobles. He was able to obtain a decree appointing him as Pope; even some of the citizens of Alexandria nominated him.

The bishops convinced the citizens of Alexandria to choose Zacharias as their Pope saying: "He is better than a Pope sent to us by an order from the Sultan, to whom we would become slaves."[114] They ordained him as Pope Zacharias (64th Patriarch), during the reign of Al Hakim Be'Amr Allah and Caliph Al Zaher.

On the eve of his ordination, Ibrahim Ibn Bishr came with the decree apppointing him Pope, but someone informed him that they had already ordained priest Zacharias as the Pope. He was greatly disturbed to the extent that he fell sick. The bishops, trying to avoid the Caliph's anger, suggested that Pope Zacharias might ordain Ibrahim as a bishop. They soothed him saying that the ordination was God's will, and as soon as any bishopric should require a bishop they would ordain him. And so they ordained him as a Hegumen, and then the Bishop of Upper Menouf.

During the first 7 years of Pope Zacharias' papacy there was peace and tranquility in the church. Then the wrath of the Lord fell upon the pastors who were practising simony in the ordination of priests and bishops.[115]

---

[114] The History of the Patriarchs, Vol. 2, Part 2, p.116-117

[115] The History of the Patriarchs, Vol. 2, Part 2, p.117-118

The Fatimid Rule (972-1171)

'The History of the Patriarchs' mentions one example of the chaos in the church at the time. One of the housekeepers of the church used to drink the pure wine, while mixing the unfiltered wine with water and giving it to the priest to use as the offering. He did this even if the wine had expired, because the bishops used to ordain priests who were not suitable for priesthood by any means.

During these days, there was no spiritual education or ecclesiastical discipline; rich people were ordained just because they paid a lot of money, while those suitable for ordination were not ordained if they were poor. This was why God's wrath came upon the church, just as when God's wrath came upon Jerusalem and it was destroyed, its children taken as captives.[116]

The History of the Patriarchs mentioned that this Pope was as meek as a lamb, nothing mentioned above was carried out by his own decision. Even his food was given to him by others; if they forgot, he would never ask for it. He was passive in his papacy, never talking or discussing anything with anyone, being ruled by his family and his disciples - They were the ones who took money from people to ordain them. If the Pope wanted to give charity to anyone, he had to ask them first. If any one approached him to be ordained as a priest, the Pope would refer him to them.[117]

This Pope suffered many tribulations, such as the trouble

---

[116] The History of the Patriarchs, Vol. 2, Part 2, p.119-120

[117] The History of the Patriarchs, Vol. 2, Part 2, p. 120

from the incident concerning a monk named Youannis from St. Macarius Monastery. He came to the Pope asking to be ordained as a bishop for Kharab city. As usual, the Pope referred him to his disciples, so Khaeil the Bishop of Sakha and the Pope's nephew insulted him because he wanted to be ordained without paying any money. The monk was furious and headed to Cairo to present a complaint about the Pope to Caliph Al Hakim Be'Amr Ellah. When the Christian elders in Egypt knew about this, they stopped the monk and sent him to meet the Pope in the Scetis Wilderness with his letter of complaint. The Pope referred both the monk and his letter to Khaeil the Bishop of Sakha, who asked some Bedouins to kill him. They threw him in a deep well and started throwing stones on him, yet he managed to hide in a groove in the well. Hearing about this incident, the Pope was so upset and excommunicated Khaeil. He sent his disciple to take the monk out of the well, promising to ordain him as soon as there were any vacant bishoprics. Later, two bishoprics were vacant yet he did not ordain the monk, and the his disciples kept annoying the monk until he went again to the Caliph to complain about the Pope.

In Cairo, monk Youannis wrote a scandalous complaint against the Pope, he headed to the mountain knowing that the Caliph was there. He kept yelling: "You are the Caliph of God on earth, so please support me." He gave him the complaint which read, "You are the king of the earth, yet the Christians have another king who does not accept you because he is so rich by collecting money from those ordained as bishops; he is disobeying God..."

As soon as the Caliph read the complaint, he ordered for all the churches to be shut and summoned the Pope, who was by then an old man.[118]

Al Hakim ordered the Pope to be thrown the lions, yet He Who saved Daniel from the lions' den saved Pope Zacharias. He also threw an Ethiopian monk named Shebshee with the Pope, but the lions used to come and sit under his feet, licking his legs. Having heard about this miracle, Al Hakim thought that the lions were not hungry, so he commanded that the lions should be starved, took off the Pope's clothes, and killed a lamb, staining the Pope's body with his blood. They did this but the lions never touched the Pope or the Ethiopian monk.

Then they imprisoned Pope Zacharias for three months, burnt him and threw him to the lions in an attempt to convince him to convert to Islam, luring him with promises of positions and wealth. Then a man named Madi Ibn Maqrab interceded for those in prison, so the Pope was released with many others. The Christians rejoiced and suggested that the Pope should go to the Scetis Wilderness, for fear that the Khalif might change his mind. The Pope lived in Scetis for nine years.

It was mentioned before that, during the reign of Al Hakim, a Coptic monk named Biemen converted to Islam but then returned back to Christianity. He was a close friend of the Caliph who allowed him to build Shahran Monastery to live in with some monks. Al Hakim used to visit this monastery

---

[118] The History of the Patriarchs, Vol. 2, Part 2, p. 120

frequently and eat with the monks. Thus monk Biemen asked him to permit Pope Zacharias to rebuild the churches that had been destroyed and he approved. Biemen brought the Pope and hid him in the monastery.

When Al Hakim came as usual to visit Shahran Monastery, Pope Zacharias and some bishops came and greeted him. Al Hakim asked the monks who he was; when he knew that he was their Pope and these were the bishops, he kept gazing at the Pope who was of a short stature wearing very humble clothes, while the bishops were tall and wearing clerical garments. Then he asked: "Is this your leader?" They answered and said, "Yes your highness may the Lord prolong your reign". Then he asked, "Which areas are under his leadership?". They answered: "Egypt, Ethiopia, Nubia, Pentapolis, Africa and other countries." Al Hakim was amazed and added: "How would everyone obey him without soldiers or any money given to them?" They answered: "With one cross, everyone obeys him." He asked: "What is that cross?" They answered: "It is the cross on which our Lord Jesus Christ was crucified."

Finally he said: "Truly there is no religion in the world whose members are steadfast like the Christians. We shed blood, spend money and send armies, yet we are not obeyed. Yet this poor, dishevelled elder is obeyed by all the residents of these countries with only one word from his mouth!"[119]

In this meeting Al Hakim told the Pope and the bishops accompanying him: "Stay here until I fulfil all your requests."

[119] The History of the Patriarchs, Vol. 2, Part 2, p. 125-126

Then he issued a decree to rebuild all the churches that had been destroyed, and to return all the pillars, wooden bars and bricks that had been looted. He also ordered to return the real estate and gardens, which had been taken away from the church. He waived the requirement for Christians to wear a special uniform and necklaces with crosses, and allowed the ringing of church bells.

Pope Zacharias spent the rest of his papacy in peace until he departed on 4th January 1032, after being a Pope for 28 years: 7 years before the persecution of Al Hakim, 9 years during the persecution, and he spent the last 12 years in rebuilding and the churches. He was a pious man and 'The History of the Patriarchs' mentioned some of his miracles.

A Miracle:

One of his miracles was that Bishop Markora was struck with leprosy. He went to the Pope who informed him that he was very compassionate about his situation and his pain, but warned the bishop against serving the Holy Liturgy until he was completely healed. The bishop wept and asked the Pope to pray for him, then he headed to St. Mary's Church. There, he spent three nights fasting and praying in front of St. Mary's icon, after which he was totally healed. Then he went and told the Pope that he had healed through his prayers. The latter said: "It is because of your prayers and your honesty."[120]

Another Miracle:

---

[120] The History of the Patriarchs, Vol. 2, Part 2, p. 148-150

A married deacon committed adultery and was struck with leprosy. He was weeping fervently, so his pious wife said to him: "You have sinned my dear. Go and cling to Pope Zacharias' feet and with his prayers you will be healed." The man did so and confessed everything to the Pope who said: "My son, in the name of God, are you willing to follow my advice?" He answered: "I will do whatever you ask, my father, with God's help and grace, as well as your prayers." The Pope brought him to a dark room and asked him to pray and plead to the Lord continually, offering repentance resolving not to return to this sin. He used to feed him every three days with some bread and water, visiting and praying with him.

After 40 days, the deacon was healed from leprosy, so he had a shower and the Pope anointed him with holy oil saying: "My son, now you are healed so always remember your promise not to fall into this sin any more. Do not think that I asked you to fast while I was not; but during those 40 days I ate exactly what you ate at the same time."[121] Then he prayed for him and the man went back happily to his blessed wife.

Once a lady came and offered him some money as donation; he took the money and only said: "My daughter, may the Lord accept your donation." The lady was waiting for some more kind words from him but he said no more, then she left a bit unhappy. His disciple noticed this so he went and informed the Pope who asked to bring the lady again. Then he brought pair of scales and put her donation on one pan,

---

[121] The History of the Patriarchs, Vol. 2, Part 2, p. 148-150

and on the other pan of the scale he put a paper on which he wrote, "May the Lord accept your donation". The pan with the paper was heavier, so he said to the lady: "My daughter, take whichever you like." She wept and took the paper, keeping it as a blessing.[122]

Pope Shenouda II
65th Patriarch (1032-1046)

He was the 65th Pope who was a contemporary of Al Zaher and Al Mostanser. After the departure of Pope Zacharias, some tried to be ordained for this position by coming closer to the Caliph and pushing him to issue a decree in their favour. When the pious man Boqeira Al Rashidy (mentioned earlier) heard of this, he went to the minister Ali Ibn Ahmad together with some elders. The minister was a wise man, and compassionate with the Christians. The minister said to them:

> "It is the custom that whoever is ordained as a Pope should pay 3,000 denarii to the Ministry of Finance. We will waive this for you, on the condition that you should allow the Pope to be chosen in Baghdad through the following procedure: they filter the nominees down to three, then they write the names of those three nominees on three pieces of paper and the Name of the Lord on the fourth. They put the papers on the altar and pray the Holy Liturgy, then a little child picks up one paper. If this paper happens to be the one with the Name of the Lord, that means that the three nominees are not

---

[122] Iris El Masry, "Story of the Coptic Church", Part 3, p. 73

suitable for the position, so they put another three names and so on until the Lord chooses the appropriate person. So, you also should do the same."[123]

Everyone was amazed because of the wisdom and understanding of this Muslim minister; they thanked him and left.

The bishops had a meeting with some of the elders of the Scetis Wilderness, but they did not follow the minister's advice and kept thinking who to choose from amongst the monks to become their Pope. Someone mentioned a monk named Shenouda who was ordained at the age of 14 in St. Macarius Monastery, who was very knowledgeable of the holy books, but by then he was an old man. One of the bishops reported that he had been advised in a dream that "The first person to enter the church tomorrow and kiss the holy relics is your next Pope; ordain him." This person was Shenouda, who said that he had a dream that night of St. Paul and St. Peter giving him some keys. He mentioned this dream to another monk who informed him that he would be the Pope. It was said that Shenouda greatly yearned for this position; because he had previously tried to be ordained as a bishop but was rejected because he had no money.

It is very clear that this was an inappropriate method of choosing the Pope. How would we know whether the bishop's dream is from God or Satanic? The behaviour of this Pope later proved that it was definitely not God's choice.

---

[123] "The History of the Patriarchs", Vol. 2, Part 2, p. 151-152

The Fatimid Rule (972-1171)

Before ordaining him, the bishops placed a condition that he would ordain bishop Youannis for Al Farma to placate him. This was the person who envied Pope Zacharias and because of whom the Pope was thrown to the hungry lions and imprisoned. Moreover, Youannis placed a condition that the Pope would pay him 30 denarii yearly as Al Farma was a poor diocese and also ordain his brother to another bishopric. The nominated Pope promised to do so.

The bishops kept proposing other monks for this position, but they finally agreed on Shenouda Al Maqari, so they promoted him to the rank of hegumen, then took him to Alexandria to be ordained.

The elders in Alexandria gathered to discuss the issue, as this person would become their Pope. They made him sign a written document stating that he would pay them 500 denarii yearly to be spent on the needs of the churches in Alexandria. In this document, he also promised not to ordain anyone by taking money from them.

Afterwards, he was not able to pay the annual 500 denarii, so someone said to him: "Are you better than your predecessors who used to ordain priests and bishops in return for a sim of money?" He started doing so, thus breaking his promise. He ordained a bishop for Banha Bishopric and took 600 denarii from him. He continued loving money greatly, to the extent that the 'The History of the Patriarchs' wrote about him: "He loved and collected so much money, and used to give it to his family. He loved the glory of this world."[124]

---

[124] The History of the Patriarchs, Vol. 2, Part 2, p. 153-154

The bishops took the nominated Pope and headed from Alexandria to Cairo to complete the ordination process. He resided in Archangel Michael's Church in Geziret Al Roda. All the elders and congregation came to congratulate him and take his blessing, among them was deacon Boqeira El Rashidi whom we referred to earlier. As soon as he saw Boqeira the nominated Pope addressed him quoting Psalm 99 "The Lord reigns, let the people tremble", so Boqeira answered, "What do you mean my father?" so he answered: "When I asked for the position of a bishop you refused and ordained Philothaous, now the Lord has made me a king without your choice!"

The Pope dealt with the elders with an inappropriate attitude, which represented a poor start for his papacy. Boqeira said: "These words were said by David the Prophet about the Lord Jesus because He reigned over the Jews without having the desire to be a King, as He came only for the salvation of the world. Now you have likened yourself to Christ and us to the Jews." They all left angry because of his words and knew that it was not going to be a successful papacy.[125]

It is written in the 'The History of the Patriarchs': "Truly there was no salvation during his papacy. As mentioned he ordained a bishop for Banha and another for Assiut after taking money. The congregation of Assiut prevented this bishop from entering their city for three years, as he was ordained in a manner contrary to the Lord's commandments, 'Freely you have received, freely give.' The bishop went back

[125] The History of the Patriarchs, Vol. 2, Part 2, p. 153-154

to the Pope and gave him two choices: either to return the money he had taken or to allow him enter Assiut by force, so the Pope gave him back the money. The bishop started acting in a shameful way, finally writing a letter to the bishops of two neighbouring cities adjoining Assiut asking them to allow him to enter into one of the surrounding cities of the diocese."

One incident proving his love of money is as follows: A bishop named Elijah departed, so the Pope came and took his house, along with his money and all his possessions. The deceased bishop's brother pleaded with the Pope just to give them the empty house, but he ignored him. As a result of the Pope's behaviour, this person converted to Islam, raised the matter to a judge who ordered for the house to be returned to the family. This Pope issued a decree stating that all the possessions of bishops should go to the Patriarchate after their departure.[126] This decree was followed until Pope Shenouda III waived it.

One year into his papacy, he stopped paying the annual sum of money promised to the churches and priests of Alexandria. He tried to deceive some of the elders by quietly brushing aside the document requiring him to pay 500 denarii yearly, writing another one with 350 denarii. Boqeira Al Rashidi was attending this reconciliation meeting and advised him not to take money for ordaining priests or bishops, but he answered that he had many expenses he needed to cover. Boqeira promised to organise this matter for him and to

[126] Menassa the Hegumen "The History of the Coptic Church", 1924 Edition, p. 510

pay whatever falls short in his budget saying: "You will be comforted from this sin which upsets the people and God." He pretended to agree and wrote a promise, but when he was assembled with the bishops, one of them started aggravating him and so he withdrew this promise. Finally, he clearly and openly announced "I will lose my position as a Pope if I do not take money for ordinations."

Knowing about this, Boqeira came to discuss the matter, so the Pope regretted what he did and asked Boqeira to bring the written promise for the Pope to read before all the bishops. When Boqeira brought the paper, the Pope tore it into pieces. All the bishops were so angry that he was belittling and deceiving them in this manner. They insisted that he should give up this attitude of taking money for ordinations; they held a meeting from morning till night attended also by Boqeira. Just when they were able to convince him, one of his disciples entered with a note written by a wicked person. After reading the note, he insulted Boqeira and signalled to his disciples who started beating Boqeira severely. The Pope then he left the room before affirming his promise.

In addition to the calamities in the church, the Nile flood decreased for two consecutive years. There were famines everywhere, and because of the corpses the number of mice increased, destroying the crops. People prayed to the Lord to lift the plague of the mice, and so it was that the Nile flood returned and prosperity prevailed once more.

In the year 1027 AD, Al Zaher signed an agreement with the

Byzantine Emperor Constantine VIII that the name of Caliph Al Zaher would be mentioned in all the mosques located in the cities affiliated with the Emperor and that the mosque in Constantinople would be rebuilt. In return, Caliph Al Zaher promised to re-build The Resurrection Church in Jerusalem, which his father Al Hakim had destroyed, and it was so.[127]

The Fatimid Caliph Al Zaher (1020-1035) was different from his father Al Hakim in his dealings with the Christians. He announced freedom of religion; whoever was convinced to convert to Islam was welcomed, and whoever wanted to remain a Christian maintained their free will. In this way, enmity towards Christians started to decrease. He also allowed those who converted to Islam under pressure during the reign of his father to return to Christianity, and permitted the re-building of the churches that had been destroyed.[128]

Pope Shenouda was struck by a severe headache accompanied by a cough; he felt like his head was burning, and experienced pain in his ears. He was sick for three years and on 29th October 1046 he departed, still desiring the lusts of this world.[129]

Pope Christodoulos
66th Patriarch (1046-1077)

His papacy was during the reign of the Fatimid Caliph Al

---

[127] Stanely Lane-Poole; "History of Egypt in the Middle Ages" p. 136

[128] Iris El Masry "Story of the Coptic Church" , Volume 3, p. 78, from Aref Pasha "The History of Jerusalem"

[129] The History of the Patriarchs, Vol. 2, Part 2, p. 158

Mostanser. He is one of the ascetic fathers who performed many miracles and wonders. He was born in the city of Bora and became a monk at a young age in St. Macarius Monastery in the Scetis Wilderness, then he moved to live in solitude in a granary at Netrawa (currently Lake Brolos).[130] He kept the body of St. Tekla, St. Paul's female disciple, in his granary.

The elders of Alexandria chose him to be ordained as the Pope, so ten of them approached him together with Simon the priest of St. Mark's Church. With difficulty, they found and convinced him, then he was ordained on 15th Kiahk 763 AM corresponding 11th December 1046 AD. 'The History of the Patriarchs' witnesses to his papacy: "He made a good start; the Holy Spirit was very close to him and he performed many miracles. He was chosen by God." Then, as was the custom straight after ordination, he headed to St. Macarius Monastery. Deacon Mawhoob Ibn Mansour Ibn Mofarrag from Alexandria, the author of his biography, mentioned that the Pope told him that he had a dream of Sts. Peter and Mark giving him a key ring with lots of keys while he was in the granary.

After his ordination, he consecrated six churches in Alexandria: St. John the Evangelist, St. Mercurius Abu Sefein, Archangel Raphael, St. Mina, St. George and he renovated St. Mark's Church. Pope Christodoulos told the writer of his biography that on the day he consecrated St. John's Church he saw a vision of St. John standing in this church with a

---

[130] On the western bank of Damietta and it is one of the cities which vanished (Geographical Dictionary, Vol. 1, pp. 176-177)

golden censer full of incense. When consecrating Archangel Raphael's Church he ordained one priest and 62 deacons on the condition (which he had informed their parents about) that they do not own anything in this church.

Pope Christodoulos suffered greatly at the hands of Mohamed Al Bazory, the minister of Al Mostanser, whom we mentioned previously in the context of Al Mostanser's strong hatred for the Copts. He also endured much affliction from the members of the Al Tawata tribe who arrested him, having behaved with violence in Alexandria and other nearby cities. They released him after paying 3,000 denarii as mentioned previously.

One of these afflictions is related as follows: Bishop John (known before his ordination as the unjust scribe) of Sakha, Bishop Khael of Qator, Bishop Elijah of Tammuh, Bishop Gerga of Al Khandaq, Bishop Marcos of El Balyana, Bishop Michael of Tinnis together with some priests from Alexandria came to Cairo trying to excommunicate Pope Christodoulos, claiming that some ritual prayers were not prayed during his ordination. The real reason, however, was a dispute between Bishop John of Sakha and the Pope, who was not moved by this storm. A wise elder named Abu Zekry Yehia Ibn Maqara interfered, brought Bishop John and served a Holy Liturgy with him and ended the dispute.

Another incident occurred when a monk named Flotas wanted to be ordained as a bishop but was rejected by the Pope as he was not suitable. He kept complaining to the officials until they arrested the Pope in Damru, where they seized 6,000 denarii and took it to the Ministry of Finance. After a lot of mediations the Pope was released and went back to his seat in Damru.

Pope Christodoulos also suffered because of a monk priest named Yacoub who desired to become the Pope instead of Pope Christodoulos. He thought he could achieve his dream after becoming friends with Naser Al Dawla Ibn Hamdan who promised him to fulfil his wish. This monk walked to Alexandria and waited for Ibn Hamdan but he immediately fell sick, died and was buried. A disciple of this monk, also named Yacoub, said that he suffered a lot as his soul departed from his body; he kept saying: "O my Lord I have sinned, give me one more year to repent, or even six months, or even one month," then he became mute and died, receiving swift punishment.[131]

Another incident occurred when a man named Ali Al Qafty falsely informed the Army General Badr El Gamaly that the Pope had ordained a Metropolitan in Nubia named Boqtor who had destroyed a mosque, and another in Ethiopia named Qoreel who was trying to convert Muslims to Christianity. El Gamaly thus arrested the Pope, simultaneously sending a messenger to investigate in Nubia, but the messenger returned with no evidence whatsoever of the destruction of a mosque. Consequently, El Gamaly saw that the Pope was an honourable man, and the messenger and Al Qafty confessed their lie. He then gathered the judges and scholars asking their opinion about punishing Al Qafty, and they all agreed he should be killed. They asked the Pope his opinion

---

[131] The History of the Patriarchs, vol.2, part 3, pp. 202-203

and he replied, "In our religion we do not reward evil for evil, or a life for a life. You are the Sultan, the matter is between you and God." So he ordered him to be killed, then the Pope also exposed the lie concerning the Metropolitan of Ethiopia, so El Gamaly honoured the Pope even more.[132]

During the era of Pope Christodoulos the Copts were able to keep the head of St. Mark in Egypt although the Romans tried to take it in exchange for 10,000 denarii; we referred to this when talking about Al Mostanser. Many miracles were performed through the head of St. Mark. It is written in 'The History of the Patriarchs' that one person doubted whether it was truly St. Mark's head. That night St. Mark appeared to his brother and said to him: "Your brother is doubting about me." The next morning, he informed his brother and they were both astounded. His brother was terrified, confessed his doubts and headed straight to where the head was kept, crying and asking forgiveness.[133]

It is worth noting Pope Christodoulos' strict adherence to the rites of worship in the churches. He issued ritual canons, a copy of which is kept in the Coptic Museum in Old Cairo. He started issuing these canons on 8th Misra 764 AM, corresponding to 1st August 1048 AD, less than two years after the date of his ordination. The first canon was regarding the Sacrament of Baptism, followed by canons related to the worship in churches and the awe and reverence of the believers while entering the church. There were many other canons concerning the obedience of wives

---

[132] The History of the Patriarchs, vol.2, part 3, pp. 204-205

[133] The History of the Patriarchs, vol.2, part 3, P. 181

to their husbands, the Holy Lent, Pascha Week, Pentecost, the Wednesday and Friday fast, the Apostles' Fast, the Advent Fast and Epiphany.

The monks of St. Macarius Monastery used to reserve the Eucharist from Palm Sunday up until Wednesday, so he explained to them what was wrong with this practice, and he excommunicated whoever would do this again. Some of the bishops were attending this meeting, but the monks rebelled saying to the Pope: "You do not know better than your predecessor Popes". Pope Christodoulos headed to the library of the monastery and produced a book containing some facts about this custom, and so the monks calmed down and ceased this wrong custom.

An example of Pope Christodoulos' strictness in following the Church's rites is as follows: Sheikh Abul Bishr, the Syrian private doctor of the Caliph visited St. Mercurius Church to attend the Holy Liturgy with the Pope. He brought the Syrian holy bread with him (the custom in Syria is to add oil and salt to the bread) and wanted the Pope to use it as the Lamb. When the Pope spoke to him explaining that he could not accept this bread, the doctor was not convinced, so the Pope ordered his disciples to take him out of the church. The doctor complained to the Minister and the Patriarch of Antioch, but Pope Christodoulos did not care about the complaint.

Another incident: Some of the elders came asking him to give an absolution to a relative of Abu Zekry Yehia Ibn Maqara (the person who reconciled the Pope with John

Bishop of Sakha). This relative was excommunicated as a result of a grave matter, and so the Pope refused. When they kept pressing him, he said to them, "One word is richness to the wise man, and many words do not make an ignorant man rich," so they ceased asking him.[134]

Towards the end of his papacy, a new saintly Patriarch was ordained for Antioch named John. As was the custom, Pope Christodoulos sent him a message congratulating him and affirming the unity of faith between the two churches. In his message he also mentioned all the afflictions and suffering he passed through such as his imprisonment and the theft of more than 10,000 denarii etc. Patriarch John of Antioch replied in a message full of love and grace, writing: "We, who are unworthy of this honourable position, do not care about money at all, our real richness is the Lord Jesus Christ. None of the disciples and apostles of whom we are followers were rich. Each one of them had only one robe; even St. John the Beloved of the Lord Christ used to serve a Roman man amidst the remains of pigeons in Ephesus, and ate his food on top of the furnace of the public baths. So how could one in a lowly position such as ours possess money?" He wrote much similar advice in his letter as something of a mix between comfort and reproach.[135] Then the saintly Patriarch John of Antioch departed.

Pope Christodoulos ordained a jeweller from El Balyana as Bimen Bishop of Armant after a rumour was spread that Bishop Basilious had departed. When the new Bishop

[134] The History of the Patriarchs, vol.2, part 3, p. 169

[135] The History of the Patriarchs, vol.2, part 2, p. 206

arrived to Armant he discovered that Bishop Basilious was alive so he stayed in one of the cities for 10 years until the departure of Bishop Basilious of Armant.

As mentioned before, Egypt went through a hard time for 7 years during the reign of the Fatimid Caliph Al Mostanser. Because of the low tide of the River Nile, there was famine and inflation, which led to a civil war. This was definitely a punishment from the Lord for His children who deviated from the straight path and followed the lifestyle of the unbelievers. The author of 'The History of the Patriarchs' wrote: "When the Christians reached high positions and became the majority in government departments, they became puffed up and started to envy and dispute with each other. Being haughty and filled with pride, the Divine wrath of the Lord Jesus Christ came upon them, in order to purify them from their iniquities before the Day they stand in front of the Judgment Throne."[136]

He also wrote concerning this era: "The peoples' sins and iniquities are numerous to the extent that credible Muslim and Christian witnesses saw tears coming down from the eyes of the saints in icons hung in different churches."[137]

A touching story related to the Lord's chastisement of His people:

> *A Christian person whose patron saint was St. Mercurius Abu Sefein once pleaded to the saint regarding an issue, but*

---

[136] The History of the Patriarchs, vol.2, part 2, p. 173

[137] The History of the Patriarchs, vol.2, part 2, p. 182

the saint did not respond as he usually did. So he started doubting about St. Mercurius. While asleep at night the saint appeared to him, took him to an wide empty space and made him stand on the rim of a large pit full of horses and weapons and said: "Do you know me? I am Mercurius. Do not doubt, because together with my fellow martyr saints we have ordered not to intercede on behalf of anyone, because this is the time of chastisement. We have left all our horses and weapons here."' [138]

Pope Christodoulos had a good relationship with the Orthodox Church in Nubia. After the departure of their Metropolitan, Girgis the king of Nubia sent a letter to the Pope asking for the ordination of another Metropolitan for them, so immediately he ordained a pious monk and sent him there. They greatly rejoiced especially because he consecrated the church which his predecessor had just finished building before his departure. The king of Nubia had stopped paying the levy to Egypt, but after the messenger of the Pope convinced him to pay it - to keep the peace between the two countries - he started paying it again. The messenger assured him that he was not interfering in politics between the two countries; this was just advice.[139] This proves that the Church of Alexandria always knew its limits, and focused solely on religious rather than political issues.

---

[138] The History of the Patriarchs, vol.2, part 2, p. 198

[139] Dr. Zaher Riad, "Alexandria Church in Africa" p. 168-169

Important personalities at the time of Pope Christodoulos' papacy

Bishop Basilious of Armant

He was a saintly person, about whom it was said that he used to give all his possessions to the needy during the famine. One night a poor person came to his cell, so Bishop Basilious asked Mina his disciple to give the man some bread. As they only had two loaves, he gave him one, giving the second loaf to another needy person knocking shortly after. The next morning when someone knocked on the door, his disciple was cranky saying that they had nothing to give, but to his astonishment he found someone bringing some bread to the saint and his disciple.[140]

Bishop Elijah of Tammuh

He was an elderly Saint, who performed many wonders some of which were personally witnessed by the author of his biography. Once Bishop Elijah was praying the Holy Liturgy at St. Boqtor Church in Giza when he saw a bright light on St. Mary's icon in the sanctuary. This light remained for a long while and the congregation also saw it.

Bishop Michael of Tinnis[141]

His name was Abu Habib Michael Ibn Bedeir El Damanhoury; he became a monk at St. Macarius Monastery in the Scetis Wilderness. He had an uncle named Mina

---

[140] The History of the Patriarchs, vol.2, part 2, p. 184-185

[141] An ancient city in Egypt not existing any more, situated in an island in Manzala lake. The island is still known as Tinnis Island around 9 km far from south west of Port Said city

who was an employee in the government departments. He introduced Abu Habib to deacon Boqeira Al Rashidy whom we referred to earlier, and they became very close friends. He was ordained as a deacon and he wrote the biography '10 Popes of Alexandria' (56th Pope to 66th Pope). He teamed up with Bishop Severus of Al Ashmonin and translated the lives of the popes from Coptic to Arabic.

Then the 62nd Patriarch, Pope Abraam Ibn Zar'aa chose him to be his scribe so he wrote the Synodica (the message of sharing the One Faith), which Pope Christodoulos sent to the Pope of Antioch. He kept writing the Synodica during the papacy of another 5 Popes. In order to honour him, the Pope ordained him as Bishop Michael of Tinnis, all the while he continued to write the Synodica. He was the one who delivered the Synodica to the Pope of Antioch accompanied by Bishop Gabriel of San Alhagar.

As for his departure, it occurred toward the end of the Pope Christodoulos era.[142] Thus deacon Michael had been a contemporary to six Popes.

Monk Bisos[143]

He was a great saint, and probably one of the hermits because of his many miracles, including his ability to see the future, some of which include:

Eleven people from Alexandria visited him to take his

---

[142] Taken from an article to deacon Saleh Kamel Nakhla, "The Story of the Church" Part 3, p. 106-107 also "The History of the Patriarchs"

[143] From St. John Kame Monastery which was destroyed

blessing. He offered them food then got a small pot of water, prayed on it and they all drank from it, yet it was still half full.

In St. Macarius Monastery, there was an elder named Abul Badr Ibn Mina El Zarady who wanted to have confession with this saint, so Monk Bisos headed to St. Macarius Monastery and took Abul Badr's confession. The monks there insisted that he spend the night there in order to take his blessings, so he accepted. When he asked to be left alone to pray, they locked him in a cell and spent the night outside his cell to hear his prayers and participate with him. When they opened the cell in the morning they did not find him. Contacting St. John Kame Monastery, they found out that he left the monastery and headed to St. Macarius Monastery after sunset, returning to his home monastery before Midnight Prayers. This is much faster than the usual duration of the trip. Moreover, he obviously left the cell while the door was closed and locked.

The author of his biography asked him about this incident, but he answered: "You do not need to know the details."[144]

In the year 978 AM/1082 AD there was a plague of smallpox; around 20,000 people died in one month. At the same time, sweat was dripping off the pillars of St. Moses Monastery and some of the icons at St. Tadros Church in Cairo. The author of the biography of St. Bisos sent him a letter asking for his prayers, and also that he might ask the 700 monks of the Scetis Wilderness to pray for this matter. The carrier

---

[144] The History of the Patriarchs, vol.2, part 3, p. 187-189

of the letter was a pious monk from Nahia Monastery who was close friend of St. Bisos. On the morning of Christmas Day, the monk from Nahia Monastery asked the saint to give him an answer to their request before he goes back to his monastery, so the saint answered: "My answer is that they are already saved by the grace of Lord Jesus Christ." Then he wrote a letter of reply and included this phrase: "The Master Jesus Christ has saved them on this day." It happened that the plague stopped on that day.[145]

Deacon Habib Michael Ibn Bedeir El Damanhoury (who collected the biography of the Patriarchs) recalled this miracle: "Together with some other Christians I was hiding in St. Bisos' cell at St. John Kame Monastery. I saw him putting some oil in the lantern; for 15 days I was there writing down the biography of the Popes and the oil never reduced in the lantern."[146]

Once two monks who had been disputing with one another came to him. He tried to reconcile them; one of them agreed but the other monk refused and left. After three days this monk came back stricken with leprosy and asked the saint to clothe him in one of his garments. The next day the monk came to return St. Bisos his garment after being healed.[147]

A young monk from St. Macarius Monastery was paralysed and could not talk, so they brought him to St. Mary's Church in St. John Kame Monastery where he stayed for three days.

---

[145] The History of the Patriarchs, vol.2, part 3, p. 189-190

[146] The History of the Patriarchs, vol.2, part 3 , p. 191

[147] The History of the Patriarchs, vol.3, part 2, p. 191

This monk mentioned that he saw three people coming out of the sanctuary; two of them addressed the third saying: "Listen to Bisos' request concerning this youth." So this third monk kicked him saying, "Get up" and the monk was healed and stood up. Immediately St. Bisos called him asking him to come downstairs to him and he did, bowing to him and thanking the Lord.

Another miracle: A Christian youth in Ibn Aly village was also paralysed and could not talk, so they took him on a mule to St Bisos. He prayed for him continually for three days and nights, after which he was healed, and returning to his village glorifying the Lord.[148]

St. Bisos' disciple, Youannis the monk, related the following: "St. Bisos went up on the roof to pray, whereupon 18 Sudanese men entered the Monastery, looted it, caught a monk and started torturing him. Bisos came down, grabbed their leader by the neck and took him out of the monastery. He did so with the each of the rest until he had expelled all of them, then closed the monastery's gate. These Sudanese people said that they lost their sight and that Bisos' hands were like heavy rocks on their necks."[149]

During the reign of Caliph Al Mostanser and the papacy of Pope Christodoulos a severe famine took place, and so the Bedouin used to come to St. John Kame's Monastery to collect food. St. Bisos never sent anyone back without fulfilling their needs, until only a one day's supply was left.

[148] The History of the Patriarchs, vol.3, part 2, p. 228

[149] The History of the Patriarchs, vol.3, part 2, p. 192

After this, they would have had to go and look for food outside. A group of people came asking for food, but when St Bisos asked the monks to give them, they grumbled and were very furious. But St Bisos said to them, "Do not be upset; by the end of the day, our Lord Jesus Christ will send us plenty, enough for many days". They gave all the grains of wheat to these people, and when they told the monks that they did not have a grinder, St. Bisos gave them the one owned by the Monastery. Again, the monks blamed him saying: "Concerning the wheat, you said that we will get more by the end of the day. What about the grinder, shall we chew the raw wheat or boil it?! So St. Bisos answered, "Cheer up, for the Lord will never allow us to be in need."

By sunset, two camels arrived at the monastery, one loaded with grains of wheat and the other with a grinder much larger than the one they had given away. The monks thanked and glorified the Lord.[150]

Once he went to pray on the rooftop where there was a basket full of bread. Some people came asking for food, so Bisos asked his disciple Youannis to give them whatever was in the basket. After a while another group came, so he asked his disciple to give them from the basket, so the disciple said "Did not we give the bread to the first group?" So Bisos answered, "Did not I fill it again?" but the disciple - who related this story - answered, "No you did not, you were praying here all the time and never left this spot!" Bisos said, "I have filled it with bread, now go and give food to all the hungry people." Youannis his disciple witnessed

[150] The History of the Patriarchs, vol.3, part 2, p. 192

that St. Bisos never touched the basket after it was emptied; he was praying the Third Hour together with him!¹⁵¹

There was a blind monk named Yustus; St. Bisos prayed for him for a whole month, after which he regained his sight.

After the departure of Pope Christodoulos, the bishops were thinking of ordaining St. Bisos, but he kept beating his chest with a hard stone telling them, "I am not worthy to become a Pope, leave me alone, along with Maqqara El Amnot the porter of St. Macarius Monastery who had fled and hid himself. Do not trouble yourself, your Pope is dwelling here in St. Macarius Monastery."¹⁵²

'The History of the Patriarchs' mentioned many things prophesied by this saint, which were completely fulfilled.

Peter the Solitary in Singar Granary¹⁵³

He performed many miracles. Once while he was praying in the Holy Liturgy, after placing his finger on the rim of the chalice saying, "And this cup also, into the Honoured Blood of His New Covenant", the Chalice was filled and about to overflow. His finger was also stained with the dark red colour of blood. He was greatly terrified and nearly fainted. For 15 years since that day, he never served the

---

¹⁵¹ The History of the Patriarchs, vol.3, part 2, p. 192-193

¹⁵² He is a saint monk contemporary to St. Bisos, when sought to be ordained he disappeared until the ordination of Pope Kyrillos II

¹⁵³ It is called "Kom Singar" located now in an island in Borolos Lake 10km south west of El Borg village on the Mediterranean Sea in Borolos Province, Bebla city north of Delta

Holy Liturgy, always wrapping this finger with a piece of cloth so that no one might see its colour.[154]

Monk Shenouda in Noosa

He was a deaf elderly saintly monk living in a granary in Noosa.[155] The writer of his autobiography in 'The Lives of Popes' sent him a letter requesting prayers for himself and his brother Fahd as they were arrested upon orders of Badr Al Gamaly the Army Chief General. Shenouda sent a reply saying "The Lord Jesus Christ has saved you today." They were released on the same day.

Monk Keel in St. John the Short Monastery

He was a saintly monk named Keel Ibn El Gendy who used to disclose people's thoughts before they said them. Once some people went to him, among them a Christian from Fowah. He rarely opened his door, but when they knocked he opened and immediately addressed this man saying: "O (the name of the man) did not you fear the Lord Christ when you committed adultery in the windmill in Fowah on Sunday night?" Hearing these words, the man fell on the ground, wept and asked forgiveness, so Keel said, "I can guarantee forgiveness for you if you offer repentance right now." The man offered repentance, then Keel said, "Cheer up, the Lord has forgiven you!" Then he was able to address each person by their own names and answered their questions and concern before they said a word about it.

---

[154] The History of the Patriarchs, vol.3, part 2, p. 193-194

[155] Affiliated with Agga Province, Daqahleya Governorate

He was praying before St. Mary's icon on a Sunday eve, so Satan came behind the icon and said, "that's enough Keel you have toiled too much". As usual, Keel rebuked it and immediately it disappeared in a black cloud of smoke.

Keel knew his hour of departure; he had asked the monks to come and farewell him on Friday at the Ninth Hour. When they went, he was whole and very healthy and kept serving them. He then had a bath, wore new clothes, lay on the ground and asked them to pray the Psalms, then he departed in peace.[156]

Martyr Bafam Ibn Baqqora Al Sawwaf

He was the nephew of Bishop Gerga of Misara. When he renounced his Christianity as a 22 year old living in Cairo, his parents rejected him. But God had mercy upon him, he repented and decided to return to Christianity.

He headed to the Church of the Archangel in Geziret El Roda where he spent a few days, and then he accompanied some monks on their to St. Macarius Monastery intending to stay there according to their advice. When it was time to head for the monastery, he changed his mind saying, "What is the point of going with you to the wilderness before confessing Christ in the place where I had denied him?" He left them, wore his cross and started going around the streets and markets in Cairo.

His father had a good relationship with one of the nobles in Cairo named Edat El Dawla Refq. When the Muslims saw

---
[156] The History of the Patriarchs, vol.3, part 2, p. 195-196

him wearing the cross, they took him to the police station where he was arrested. His father asked Edat El Dawla to release his son in return of a big amount of money, but the latter told him that he could do nothing for his son except if he pretended to be insane, then he would take some witnesses to the prison and could release him as a Christian.

An inmate with Bafam was a Syrian monk who kept preaching to him about the honour of martyrdom, to the extent that Bafam wished to become a martyr for the Name of Lord Jesus Christ. When the witnesses entered into his cell, he spoke to them wisely confessing his faith in the Lord Christ. They told him "It was said that you wanted to go back to Christianity because you became insane," yet he answered, "I am sane and believe in my Lord Jesus Christ, Glory be to Him." They took him to the Governor who ordered him to be killed. He insisted on his faith in the face of threats of torture; they escorted him from the prison followed by a large number of people with rods and other instruments of torture. After reaching the place where he was supposed to be killed, the Governor made a last attempt to attract him to deny his faith, but Bafam said, "Even if you offer me all the riches of Egypt, I do not care." The Governor gave him a slap on his face during which a large gold ring on his finger hit his eye and it became swollen. They kept threatening him with the sword, he faced the east and signed himself with the cross, and finally they beheaded him.

Four guards were assigned to guard his body that night, and suddenly they witnessed a very bright light falling on his body and were terrified. Then Caliph El Mostanser ordered for his body to be given to his relatives to be buried, so his father took it and he was buried outside the gate of the Church of the Archangel. On the third day, Pope Christodoulos came to visit this church and he was greatly disappointed when he knew that he was buried outside the gate saying: "A martyr should not be buried outside the church."

He then ordered for the coffin to be taken out, he opened it and kissed his body, taking his blessing. He noticed that there was fresh blood as if it had just been bleeding; he collected some of this blood, signed his garments with the cross, and then he buried him inside the church.[157] He also built an altar in this church after his name.

Pope Christodoulos departed in peace on Saturday 14th Kiahk 794 AM corresponding to 10th December 1077 AD after spending 31 years as Pope. He was buried in St. Mary's Hanging Church in Old Cairo. After a while his holy body was transferred to St. Macarius Monastery in Wadi El Natroun.

Pope Kyrillos II
67th Patriarch (1078-1092)

He was Pope during the reign of Al Mostanser. Three months after the departure of Pope Christodoulos, the Coptic elders, priests and bishops assembled in St. Macarius Monastery in Alexandria to choose the next Pope. They thought of saint Bisos - whom we referred to earlier - but

---
[157] The History of the Patriarchs, vol.3, part 2, p. 170-171

The Fatimid Rule (972-1171)

when they went to inform him, he strongly refused saying: "Your next Pope is in St. Macarius Monastery." Returning to the monastery they chose a pious monk named Gerga, who also refused, yet they ordained him as Pope Kyrillos while he was weeping. What is astonishing is that this monk was nominated previously by Pope Christodoulos.[158] He became the 67th Patriarch, named Pope Kyrillos II, on 18th March 1078 AD corresponding to 22nd Baramhat 974 AM.

Under the leadership of the wise ruler Badr Al Gamaly, peace and prosperity prevailed over the country. He issued a decree to lend the merchants large amounts of money to be repaid in instalments. He also engaged in trade with other countries. He also focused on the agricultural industry, waiving the overdue taxes for farmers for 3 years. As a result of this financial revival, the arts, science and technology, and other aspects of life underwent a renaissance.

The most outstanding feature of this era were the architectural designs; there were huge luxury buildings in Cairo and other cities. Badr Al Gamaly erected fortified walls to surround Cairo, designed and supervised by a Coptic monk named Youannis (John).[159]

Alfred Butler comments in regard to Abul Makaram's writings about this Coptic monk Youannis:

[158] The History of the Patriarchs, vol.3, part 2, p. 207-209

[159] Abul Makarem "Churches and Houses of Egypt" in English, p. 51(a); Stanley Lane-Poole "History of Egypt in the Middle Ages", p. 152; Yacoub Nakhla Rofela "The History of the Coptic Church" , p. 138-139

"There is no greater proof that the Copts were the architectural engineers of Cairo."

Gawhar Al Saqqaly built the old walls surrounding Cairo, and the new walls were built after 100 years, in the year 1087 AD. The new walls were built in a different place from the old ones, giving the city a wider look especially from the north and south. The city walls were made from red bricks while the city gates were made from stones; these gates are Al Nasr Gate, Zeweila Gate and El Fettouh Gate.

Al Gamaly also delegated to the Copts the organisation of the government departments, and so the amount of money collected during this time was double what used to be collected before.

After his ordination, Pope Kyrillos II headed to Archangel Michael Church in Cairo in a place called 'The Chosen'; that was why it was called the 'Chosen Church of Archangel Michael'. Bishop Yacoub of Cairo met the Pope there. He also informed Sheikh Abul Fadl Yehia Ibn Ibrahim, the Police Commissioner, who came with other officers, and sent a white horse for the Pope to ride on; he crossed the Nile and a multitude of people celebrated his arrival.

The Pope walked to Caliph Mostanser's palace, accompanied by the congregation and church servants. The Governor (who was called the Master and was a close friend to the Caliph) came to meet the Pope. He took the Pope alone and went to the Caliph who was sitting with his mother and sister at that time. They were carrying some spices, so they anointed the Pope with the spices asking him to bless them and their palace, and so he did. They rejoiced greatly and kept saying: "May the Lord make you a blessing for us and for our country." The Pope asked Botrous Bishop of Daqmira[160] to read the blessing to the congregation and he did, then the Pope gave his blessing again.[161]

Then the Pope headed to the house of Badr Al Gamaly and was welcomed warmly, giving them his blessing. He asked Bishop Botrous to read the blessing again. Al Gamaly ordered for the Pope to be looked after and taken him wherever he wanted as long as it was in Cairo. The Pope was then taken to St. Mary's Hanging Church in Old Cairo, then a few days later he visited the Church of "The Lady" in Haret Al Room.

During the Great Lent, he went to St. Macarius Monastery where something amazing happened on Maundy Thursday: When he placed the Mayroun pot on the altar, it overflowed onto the altar. Everyone watching this was shocked.

Pope Kyrillos II exchanged the Synodica (declaration of faith) with Dionysius Patriarch of Antioch, and thus their names were mentioned in the prayers of each other's church.

---

[160] There is a mix between "Daqmira" and "Demeira" in some books, but it is another bishopric than "Demeira". It is known now as "Kafr Demria Al Gadid", Talkha Governorate, Munier; Liste Episcopales, pp. 27, 28. Also "The Geographic Dictionary" Muhammed Ramzy, Part Two, p.90

[161] The History of the Patriarchs, vol.3, part 2, p. 209-210

During the second year of his papacy, Salmon King of Nubia retired and delegated his position to his nephew Gawargios. Salmon desired to live in solitude for prayers and meditation; he dwelt in St. Abu Noufer Church, around 10 days walking from Aswan (Upper Egypt). One of the officers of Asaad Al Dawla Shardkin Al Qawasy, the Governor of Aswan, informed the Governor about the presence of Salmon, so they brought him and took him to Cairo where Badr Al Gamaly honoured him greatly. After a year he departed and was buried in Deir Al Khandaq (Anba Reweis), which was located outside of Cairo at the time.

The good religious relationship between the Copts and Nubians was clearly revealed during the time when Salmon King of Nubia was dwelling in Egypt. He exchanged visits with the Pope and noblemen of Egypt who greatly honoured him. Al Gamaly himself approached the Copts to mediate in signing trade agreements between Egypt and Nubia, making use of the good relationship between them. He also granted Pope Kyrillos funds to rebuild the destroyed churches and monasteries.[162]

Pope Kyrillos ordained a Metropolitan for Ethiopia named Severus, who was the nephew of the late Metropolitan, instead of a person named Qoreel who claimed that he was the Metropolitan although he was never ordained. When the ordained Metropolitan arrived in Ethiopia he was greatly resisted by Qoreel who finally collected a large amount of money and tried to flee. He was eventually arrested and brought to Al Gamaly. The latter investigated the issue and

---

[162] Yacoub Nakhla Rofelah, "History of the Coptic Nation", pp.140,141

The Fatimid Rule (972-1171)

finally ordered Qoreel's beheading in the year 860 AM.

Metropolitan Severus explained to the people that custom of having concubines beside their wives was wrong. He asked the Pope to support him by sending a letter to the King of Ethiopia, the ministers and the statesmen, and the Pope did so.

Some bishops revolted against Pope Kyrillos because of some of his associates who used to do shameful things which harmed him. So the Pope signed a document excluding these associates, but the bishops soon began to overrule the Pope, which the latter resented. This development was not only related to the exclusion of his associates, but to various other factors. For example, like the 12th Patriarch Pope Demetrious the vine dresser, this Pope was of lesser education and experience, so the bishops thought it would be easy to constantly overrule him. But to their regret and surprise, this Pope kept studying the holy books and excelled in this field more than many bishops and priests.

When these bishops found that he had changed his mind about excluding his associates, they contacted a person named Yaseeb who was the superintendent of Al Gamaly's gardens. After befriending him, they gave him complaints against the Pope to present to Al Gamaly while the Pope was away in Demeira for a few months. Al Gamaly called the Pope and all the bishops; the Holy Synod was assembled at Al Gamaly's garden on Saturday 23rd Misra 802 AM corresponding to 1086 AD. The number of bishops was 47, 22 from Lower Egypt, 22 from Upper Egypt, bishop Jacob of Babylon Cairo, bishop Gabriel of Khandak and bishop Ezekiel of Giza. This shows that the number of Copts was large at the time

Bishops of Lower Egypt

John Bishop of Sakha and Mark his brother bishop of Samanud - Samuel bishop of Tennis - Misael bishop of Damietta - Tawadros bishop of Telbana - Youannis bishop of Demeira - Khaeil bishop of Abu Seer - Justus bishop of Sahraget - Khaeil bishop of Menouf - Youannis bishop of Tanta - Khaeil bishop of Noosa - Khaeil bishop of Borollos - Gabriel bishop of Nastouh (west of Borollos on the coast between Borollos Lake and Mediterranean Sea) - Maqqara bishop of Sa - Maqqara bishop of Bana - Tawadros bishop of Kherbeta - Gabriel bishop of Damanhour - Marqora bishop of Maseel - Rafael bishop of Sarsaly - Justus bishop of Rashid - Tawadros bishop of Itrib (Banha) - Mina bishop of Banwanin. Bishops from Lower Egypt who were sick and did not attend were: Khaeil bishop of Qattour - Tawadros bishop of Sengar - Peter bishop of Demeira - Bafam and Qozman bishops of the Oasis.

Bishops of Upper Egypt

Jacob bishop of Etfih - Daniel bishop of Tamuh - Samuel Bishop of Wahnas - Mettaous bishop of Fayyoum - Maqqara bishop of Al Kis - Peter bishop of Bahnasa - Babnoudah bishop of Taha - Khaeil bishop of Al Ashmonin - Isaac bishop of Ansena - Marqora bishop of Qusqam - Andona bishop of Assiut - Afraam bishop of Shateb - Mettaous bishop of Kaw - Kleydas bishop of Akhmim - Mark bishop of El Balyana - Qolta bishop of Hoo - Marqora bishop of Al Oqsoreen - Bamon bishop of Armant - Tawadros bishop of Esna - Bafam bishop of Aswan - John bishop of Dandara - Bedeir bishop of Qus.[163]

Badr Al Gamaly addressed the bishops in a harsh tone, which God had put on his lips. He ordered them to write down the Laws of the Religion and present them to him. He had sympathy on the Pope and honoured him before all the attendees. The Assembly was divided into two groups: a group consisting of 5 bishops: John Bishop of Sakha and Mark his brother bishop of Sammanud, Youannis bishop of Demeira, Khaeil bishop of Abu Seer and Maqqara bishop of Al Kis, joined by deacon Abu Ghaleb Bimen Ibn Tayader Ibn Markora El Singary. They started issuing laws mostly from the Old Testament according to their own desires. The other group consisting of the Pope and the rest of the bishops issued simplified laws.

After three weeks they finished the laws and Al Gamaly assembled with the Pope and all the bishops; this time he addressed them kindly saying:

> "Be of one accord and do not disagree, obey your leader and be like him. Do not store silver or gold, carry out Christ's commandments to give alms. I do not need these laws which you had issued, I just asked for them so that you may sit together and re-issue those laws when I noticed how far you were from reading or following them. The meeting has now

---

[163] The History of the Patriarchs", vol.2, part 3, p. 212

concluded, go your way and pray for me."

He ordered his secretary to look after all their needs, and they all left with joy. It was a Saturday and they all headed to St. Mercurius Abu Sefein Church in Old Cairo and celebrated the Holy Liturgy together.[164]

The Lord honoured his servants and took vengeance on Yaseeb, to whom the five rebellious bishops resorted as mentioned before. After the meeting between the bishops and Al Gamaly ended, Peter, one of the Pope's disciples blamed Yaseeb for his attitude, and so the latter spoke to him rudely and aggressively. One of the bishops tried to calm him down, but in vain. The Pope came to intervene but Yaseeb was still out of control. Finally, the Pope said: "Yaseeb, if you have an authority here on earth, I have Christ with me Who has authority on earth and in heaven," then he bowed down with a metania to Yasseb; some Christians who were attending cried, being touched at the Pope's humility.

The next day, Al Gamaly knew about what Yaseeb had done and he was very upset, ordering to behead Yasseb. This took place in the same hour and at the same spot where the Pope had offered Yaseeb a metania. People were amazed and Al Gamaly honoured the Pope exceedingly.

A critical situation later developed between the Pope and Badr Al Gamaly because of a present sent to the Pope by the Metropolitan of Ethiopia through his brother. Al Gamaly

---

[164] The History of the Patriarchs, vol.2, part 3, p. 214-217

did not like this present, and he became very upset because of an unwise word uttered by one of the Bishops. As a result he issued a decree, mandating that every bishop who was meeting with the the Pope at the time (they were 10 bishops) must pay him 2 denarii daily until they could correspond with the king of Ethiopia. Two bishops travelled to Ethiopia with a message for the King. The meeting ended sadly, with an order to arrest the brother of the Metropolitan who brought the present. Al Gamaly was later placated when the King of Ethiopia sent him a present which he liked, so he called the Pope and the 10 bishops and treated them generously.

Before sending him off to Ethiopia, Al Gamaly had asked Metropolitan Severus of Ethiopia to build 4 mosques there. The Metropolitan actually built 7, but the Ethiopians had destroyed them and tried to kill him, even the king of Ethiopia arrested the Metropolitan.[165] Al Gamaly was relieved when he knew the truth about this issue.

'The History of the Patriarchs' mentions that Pope Kyrillos II wrote 34 laws which were to be recited in all the churches. they included warnings regarding taking money for ordaining priests (simony), and to accept the repentant; he said: "Any bishop or priest who refuses to accept a repentant person will be excommunicated." He also addressed the issues of pastorship of the bishop to his priests and his duty towards the poor. Among these laws was a warning to the priests and laymen to depend on any verdict in any cases away from the church. He also spoke about the importance

[165] The History of the Patriarchs, vol.2, part 3, p. 220-222

of fasting, the Sacrament of Matrimony and the respect of clergymen. He prevented laymen from entering the altar.[166]

After completing his struggle, Pope Kyrillos II departed on Sunday 12th Baounah 1092 AD/808 AM after partaking of the Holy Communion and was buried in Archangel Michael Church in Geziret Al Roda. His body was later transferred to St. Macarius Monastery in the Scetis wilderness.

During the last year of his life he did not go to the Scetis wilderness as was his custom, but he used to go to The Wax Monastery west of Tammuh (no longer existing), and to Archangel Michael Church in Geziret Al Roda, and to St. Mary's Hanging Church in Old Cairo. He used to read the four Gospels frequently in the Coptic language.

His biographer stated, "He was a spiritual saint, very humble, meek and simple, and never possessed anything. Anything given to him by the bishops he would either give to the poor, or use it to rebuild the destroyed churches and monasteries or make new utensils for the altars. He also used to pay for the release of arrested Christians. When he passed away, they did not find one denarii in his possession. His deeds were all good and admirable. He had a pleasant demeanous and spoke gently, fasting and praying a lot, and eating only one kind of food, no matter the variety cooked by his disciples."[167]

---

[166] The History of the Patriarchs, vol.2, part 3, p. 118; Iris Al Masry, "Story of the Coptic Church" vol. 3, p. 116-118 from Oswold Pormestor who published these laws in Arabic and English in 1936

[167] The History of the Patriarchs, vol.2, part 3, p. 229-230

The Fatimid Rule (972-1171)

It is worth mentioning that during the papacy of Pope Kyrillos II, in the year 1088 AD/804 AM, the number of monks in the Scetis Wilderness was 700: 400 in St. Macarius Monastery; 165 in St. John the Short Monastery; 25 in St. John Kame Monastery (these two monasteries no longer exist); 20 in Baramous Monastery; 4 in St. Bishoy Monastery; 60 in St. Mary The Syrian Monastery; two in Abu Moses cave, one was Syrian and the other was Egyptian,[168] in addition to the hermits whose number the writer of this biography did not know.

Pope Michael Al Singary
68th Patriarch

After the departure of the 67th Patriarch Pope Kyrillos II, it was the Alexandrians' turn to choose the next Pope, and so the bishops, priests and elders assembled at St. Mercurius Abu Sefein Church in Old Cairo. When they could not decide, they headed to St. Macarius Monastery in the Scetis Wilderness. They knew about a Syrian monk named Samuel the Solitary, but then they changed their minds, as he was not of an upright faith. Then they were informed about an old solitary monk, named Michael of Singar. He had religious knowledge as well as an upright spiritual life and upright faith. When they went to Singar everyone there praised father Michael so they decided to ordain him Pope.

Bishop Sanhout of Cairo, deacon Abu Ghaleb Ibn Marqora Al Singary and other bishops spoke to him, thus confirming his upright faith. They informed him about their decision,

---

[168] The History of the Patriarchs, vol.2, part 3, p. 160

and when he refused, they asked him not to let them take him by force, as this was not appropriate, so finally he agreed. They asked him to write down his sound faith, to ensure the priests of the churches of Alexandria are fulfilling their monetary duties towards the Pope, and to adhere to the rule of ordaining clergymen without taking money (simony). They also asked him to return to some bishops what other Popes had taken from them, whether money or real estate. As an example they informed him that Pope Christodoulos had taken St. Mary's Hanging Church, Abu Sefein Church and St. Mary's Church in Haret El Room from the Diocese of Cairo, Archangel Michael Church in Geziret El Roda from the Diocese of Oseem, and The Wax Monastery and the Pottery Monastery (Abu Sefein) from the Diocese of Tamuh.

Father Michael Al Singary accepted all their requests and wrote down everything, excommunicating whoever should delete or add to his writings.[169] He asked the entire gathering to be witnesses to his promises, whether those attending the meeting or those waiting downstairs.

On 12th Babah 809 AM corresponding to 9th October 1091 AD he was ordained as the 68th Patriarch Pope Michael Al Singary in Alexandria. Then he went to St. Macarius Monastery in the Scetis Wilderness, and then to St. Mary's Hanging Church in Old Cairo. After a few days, Bishop Sanhout of Cairo asked him to fulfil his promises, but he refused. Moreover, he denied that it was his own handwriting and he excommunicated whoever would witness that it

---

[169] The History of the Patriarchs, vol.2, part 3, p. 240-241

The Fatimid Rule (972-1171)

was him who wrote it![170] This attitude was not only towards Bishop Sanhout, but to all the other bishops.

There were 4 copies of his written pledge: one with him, one with the priests of Alexandria, one with Bishop John of Sakha as he was the eldest bishop and one with Bishop Sanhout of Cairo. Refusing to carry out his promise, the Pope threatened the priests of Alexandria with excommunication if they did not send the written pledge back to him, so they did; the same with Bishop John of Sakha.

'The History of the Patriarchs' mentions harsh details about this dictator Pope:

> "When he had established himself in his papacy, he increased in power and ascendancy. All the bishops and people feared him as they did Pope Christodoulos; no one could resist him.[171] He humiliated and disgraced the bishops trampling them under his feet."

When the Pope failed to take the fourth copy from Bishop Sanhout, he prevented the bishop from praying or supervising the churches in his diocese, but the bishop did not care, telling the Pope;

> "You denied that it was your handwriting, so why do you want it back then?"

The Pope ordered all the priests and bishops not to mention

---

[170] The History of the Patriarchs, vol.2, part 3, p. 240-241

[171] The History of the Patriarchs, vol.2, part 3, p. 241

his name in any Liturgy or prayer, but Bishop Sanhout stood strong. Finally, he knew that the Pope was planning to send some of his disciples to take him by force to the Pope to announce his excommunication, so he fled to St. Samuel Monastery in Qalamun.

The elders went to meet the Pope in Archangel Michael's Church in Geziert Al Roda complaining about the absence of their Bishop Sanhout saying: "We want to know the reason for preventing him from praying. If he is guilty we will judge him, if not, then it is not fair to misjudge our bishop, humiliate us and take him away from us. Here we come to you, we offer you a metania, so do not force us to take action against you and go and complain to anybody else".

After many arguments, the Pope gave Bishop Sanhout permission to go back to his diocese and carry on his clerical duties. Everyone rejoiced and when he came back they all went to the Pope and reconciled,[172] thanking the Pope for returning their beloved bishop.

Yet this reconciliation was a fake one from the Pope's side, for he kept seeking a chance to take revenge on Bishop Sanhout and to depose him, sometimes he even fabricated accusations in order to remove him from his diocese. In the tenth year of his papacy, the Pope called the bishops for a trial for Bishop Sanhout, claiming that he prayed two Holy Liturgies in one day: one in St. Mary's Hanging Church and one in St. George Abi Serga Church. Although

---

[172] The History of the Patriarchs, vol.2, part 3, p. 242

The Fatimid Rule (972-1171)

Bishop Sanhout did not attend, all the bishops signed to excommunicate Bishop Sanhout for fear of the Pope. This was accusation was false and the synodical decision void because the bishop was not there to defend himself.

Pope Michael departed while Bishop Sanhout was still excommunicated. When they sent for Bishop Sanhout to read him the decision of excommunication, some priests in Cairo hid him, then he went to St. Severus Monastery in Assiut (not existing now), where he spent some days, during which time the Lord avenged him.[173]

In the second year of Pope Michael's papacy, Badr Al Gamaly was struck by paralysis in his old age, so his son Al Afdal carried out his duties. He was an honest and just person, exceeding all his predecessors in good deeds and returning the possessions of those who had been treated unjustly. Nine months later, Caliph Mostanser Bellah died, so his youngest son Al Mosta'ly Bellah reigned. Initially, his elder brothers Nazar, Abdullah and Ishmael did not pledge their allergiance, but eventually Abdullah and Ishmael did. Nazar the eldest brother went to Alexandria and made an alliance with its governor. As a result, Al Afdal, together with his army headed to Alexandria and besieged it. After a fierce battle, Nazar and the governor yielded, so he took them to Cairo, and there Caliph Mosta'ly Bellah imprisoned them until they died.

During that time, Badr Al Gamaly died and then Al Mosta'ly Bellah also died after falling ill - this was on the tenth year

---

[173] The History of the Patriarchs, vol.2, part 3, p. 247-248

of Pope Michael's papacy. Caliph Al Mansour, the son of Caliph Mosta'ly Bellah, then ruled the country at the age of 6 years old.

Following these incidents, a messenger from the King of Ethiopia came to minister Al Afdal to send them a Metropolitan, and so Al Afdal asked Pope Michael to quickly ordain a Metropolitan for Ethiopia. So he ordained a monk named Girgis, yet he soon regretted this. This Metropolitan failed in shepherding the flock there, it was even said that he committed shameful inappropriate acts. The King of Ethiopia arrested him, seized all the money he had gathered and sent him back to Egypt, writing a letter to Al Afdal explaining all that he had done in Ethiopia.

Al Afdal imprisoned him for many years with a monk named Farag. This monk used to falsely accuse the bishops during the reign of Badr Al Gamaly and the papacy of Pope Kyrillos II, in order to blackmail them for money.[174]

As mentioned before, Bishop Sanhout had fled to a monastery in Assiut. The Pope wanted to append the diocese of Cairo and its churches to his own diocese of Alexandria, so he went and stayed at St. Mary's Hanging Church and kept looking for the bishop but in vain. On Friday 28th Bashans, three days before his departure, he informed all the priests that he will pray the Sunday Holy Liturgy at St. George Church Abi Serga, announcing that this church will be his papacy headquarters, thus ending the bishopric of Cairo. But on Saturday, he mounted his mule, and together with

---

[174] The History of the Patriarchs, vol.2, part 3, p. 246-247

some Coptic noblemen they went to meet Al Afdal coming back from Tinnis, so they met at Damanhour and greeted each other. On his way back, the Pope was struck by an illness and became dumb; they carried him to St. Mary's Hanging Church and he departed on Sunday 30th Bashans 818 AM corresponding to 25th May 1102.[175] Bishop Sanhout returned to his seat amidst the joy of his congregation glorifying the Lord.

Bishop Sanhout departed in the year 833 AM/1117 AD. It is written in 'The History of the Patriarchs':

> "He was a righteous pious bishop, knowledgeable, humble, temperate, simple, of clear intentions, pure, abounding in good deeds.[176] Everyone mourned him as they knew they would not find anyone who would combine all his lovely characteristics. The 69th Patriarch, Pope Macarius II, called him 'the beloved spiritual saintly brother Bishop Sanhout.'"[177]

It is worth mentioning that during the era of Pope Michael the Crusade wars started in Syria, where the Franks regained Antioch, most of the northern regions in Asia, and also Jerusalem. For this reason, the Copts refrained from going to Jerusalem. The Franks hated the Copts because of the dispute at the Council of Chalcedon. Accordingly, there was a break in communion between the Catholic Church and the Coptic Church.

---

[175] The History of the Patriarchs, vol.2, part 3, p. 248

[176] The History of the Patriarchs, vol.3, part 1, p. 7

[177] The History of the Patriarchs, vol.3, part 1, p. 13

Pope Macarius II
69th Patriarch (1102-1128)

He was a monk at St. Macarius Monastery. Two major issues are worth mentioning during the 26 years of his papacy:

First: This issue concerning what happened between him and the elders of Cairo when they wanted him to ordain a bishop after the departure of Bishop Sanhout. This story is important revealing the right of the congregation to choose their own bishop, and the importance of the Pope recognising this right.

It seemed as if Pope Macarius wanted to affiliate the bishopric of Cairo to himself, for this reason avoiding ordaining a bishop. Despite of the clarity of the church laws,[178] he kept arguing and manoeuvring, writing a letter to the elders of Cairo saying:

> *"The bishop should be chosen by his congregation, approved by all, corresponding with the qualities they specify, not chosen by another diocese or the Pope. Now, adhere to the law; choose whoever you agree on and I will ordain him for you. God knows,[179] that even if angels were to come from heaven, I will ordain no-one except the one they choose from among themselves."*

When they discovered that these were mere words from the Pope, with no real intention of ordaining a bishop, they said, "As a Christian husband cannot have two wives, it is

---

[178] The History of the Patriarchs, vol.3, part 1, p. 15

[179] The History of the Patriarchs, vol.3, part 1, p. 14

The Fatimid Rule (972-1171)

the same with the bishop. He should not have two seats. Pope Macarius II is the Bishop of Alexandria, so he cannot also be the Bishop of Cairo."

They kept looking for an appropriate person to become the Bishop of Cairo. They considered 12 people, among whom was Markoura the Solitary in Ebiar, then they chose four and Markoura was one of them. When they casted the lot to choose one of the four, it came out to be Youannis Ibn Sanhout, so they ordained him as Bishop of Cairo, they issued a record and sent it to the Pope with a letter from the congregation.

<u>Second:</u> During the era of this Pope was the Crusaders' attack on Egypt. Baldwin the King of Latin Jerusalem came to invade Egypt in 1117 AD. He landed at Al Farma, burning the city and killing both Christians and Muslims. He kept advancing slowly until he reached Tinnis, yet he was forced to withdraw after falling sick and coming close to death. The Egyptians did not try to avenge this attack, but rather remained neutral until the end of the Fatimid rule.[180]

Minister Al Afdal was killed at the orders of Caliph Al A'mer at the end of 1121. There is no doubt that Al Afdal was a wise ruler who treated the Copts generously, but because he experienced jealousy from his minister, the Caliph committed this horrible crime.

Caliph Al A'mer Be'Ahkam Allah used to go to Nahia Monastery (next to Giza) and spent some days there, giving

---

[180] Stanley Lane-Poole, "History of Egypt in the Middle Ages", p.165

the monks 1000 dirham during each visit. In his first visit, he granted them 30 acres. The total amount granted to this Monastery by Al A'mer was 30,000 dirham.

Pope Gabriel Ibn Turek
70th Patriarch (1131-1145)

He was born Abul Ela Said Ibn Turek from Cairo, from a pious wealthy Coptic family. His father was a rich widowed priest, a righteous man, very knowledgeable in church matters, living an ascetic pure life. Abul Ela was raised up in the fear of God, close to the church, a gifted scribe and very eloquent in both the Arabic and Coptic languages.

Despite his high position in the government, he used to go to church regularly, sacrificing himself for the service of the needy, strangers and the sick, caring for the widows, orphans and visiting the prisoners. Ahmad Ibn Al Afdal, the grandson of Badr Al Gamaly, was his close friend. For this reason, he was allowed to be a consecrated deacon at St. Mercurius Abu Sefein Church in Old Cairo while keeping his job in the government. Of course, this was because of his honesty, righteousness and wisdom in dealing with various issues.

After the departure of Pope Kyrillos II there was no Pope for two years because of the instability of the country, with various allegations and accusations being thrown around. We can summarise the reasons for taking so long to ordain a Pope:

First: The Copts during this period were very poor, so they were not able to pay the amount of 3000-6000 denarii to the Treasury Department to issue the document for ordination. Taxes at that time were very high as a result of the war with the Europeans.

Second: The Coptic elders had fears that the Minister would refuse to approve of their choice of patriarch given the instability at the time. Making matters worse, two ministers, one a Muslim named Ibn Abi Qirat and the other a Samaritan, named Ibrahim, hated the Christians greatly. They falsely informed the Caliph that the Copts had collect a large amount of money and sent it to help the Franks. Consequently, the Caliph ordered for any money owned by Coptic individuals or churches to be confiscated. Later both of these evil ministers were murdered during a riot. A Melkite Christian afterwards occupied their position; during his time Ahmad, Badr Al Gamaly's grandson, reversed this decision. He also allowed the ordination of the Pope.[181]

Many saints prophesied about that Pope Gabriel would be chosen as Pope without previously knowing him. Among them were Pope Macarius II, the solitary monk in Ibiar, and a saintly monk named Youssef from The Syrian Monastery. It was said that in his childhood while playing with neighbourhood friends he used to tell them, "I am your Patriarch", while wearing clothes similar to Patriarchal garments.

---

[181] Aziz S. Atiya, History of Eastern Christianity, p.93; "The History of the Patriarchs" vol.3, part 1, p. 52, 53

He was ordained as Pope Gabriel II on the 5th of April 1131 AD corresponding to 9th Amsheer 847 AM, but was known as Pope Gabriel Ibn Turek.

During the Confession at the end of his first Holy Liturgy which he prayed, he said: "He made it one with His Divinity." The monks were not happy with this sentence, so he explained to them that it was traditioned to him this way by the fathers the bishops while he was practising the Holy Liturgy. After much discussion, they all agreed to change it to "He made it one with His Divinity without mingling, without confusion and without alteration." The Pope approved and sent messages to all the churches to recite the Confession in this way. This incident proved two things: firstly, the deep theological awareness of the monks and their courage in confronting the Pope; secondly, the humility of the Pope and his resolve to maintain the true faith.

At the beginning of his papacy, Bishop Youannis Ibn Sanhot of Cairo departed, so he did not ordain a new bishop but rather affiliated these churches to his own bishopric. This was a response to a plea presented by the congregation of the churches in Cairo.

During his papacy, he witnessed unsettled circumstances in the country, during which many ministers and noblemen were killed. His papacy was also marked by a great conflict between the Muslim Egyptians and the huge Armenian community which had been brought by the Armenian Badr El Gamaly. As a result, the Patriarch of the Armenians

The Fatimid Rule (972-1171)

was killed, their monastery was set on fire and its monks were killed. Many Christian churches were also looted. A minister named Radwan Ibn Walahshi ordered that no Christians should be appointed in government positions, that they should always wear belts around their waists, and that they should not mount horses. He also doubled the taxes on them and the Jews, in addition to many other forms of humiliation.

During the era of these Ministers, the Muslims attacked St. George Church in Menyet Zefta and converted it into a mosque, but this church was affiliated with the diocese of Bishop Mikhail of Sahragt. He contacted Minister Ibn Walahshi and convinced him that it was just an old ancient church, so he regained it.

Pope Gabriel Ibn Turek maintained the rites, traditions and laws of the Coptic Orthodox Church. He issued a decree forbidding burial in churches. When the congregation of a church at Haret El Rom disobeyed his orders and buried their priest there, the church to be closed, but he reopened it after the elders interceded. He transferred the body of his predecessor Pope Macarius - who was buried in St. Mary's Hanging Church - to St. Macarius Monastery. He also ordered that no sacrifices should be offered in the name of Archangel Michael, as sacrifices should only be offered in the name of God. He banned the priests from drinking wine and resisted sorcery and witchcraft. It was said that some wealthy people disobeyed his orders concerning this matter, and after a very short while they all perished. He resisted simony and during his era he ordained 53 bishops on Coptic dioceses. He never laid his hands on any of the churches' real estate or the money for the poor and needy.

One of the his most important achievements in regard to the rites of the church was his organisation of the prayers of Passion Week. According to the apostolic practice up to the era of this Pope, the church used to read both the Old and New Testaments during Passion Week without a set order. So most of the people were reading them on their own in an unorganised fashion, i.e. this was not recited or heard by the whole congregation. Pope Gabriel called for a meeting including all the elders, scientists, chief priests and monks from St. Macarius Monastery, then he organised the readings and issued the Book of the Holy Pascha. He was encouraged to do so because most of the people working in government departments were not able to attend the prayers during this week. It is worth mentioning that the Book of the Holy Pascha was later organised in a more accurate way by the honourable Bishop Botros of Al Bahnasa (next to Beni Mazar).[182]

He was also the first Pope to order the reading of the Gospel and the sermons in the Arabic language after doing so in Coptic. After he noticed that the Copts were speaking Arabic, he reasoned that it was not fair for a member of the congregation not to understand the language of prayers.[183] In doing so, the Copts were able to follow the prayers and sermons and understand them.

---

[182] Kamel Saleh Nakhla, "Biography of Pope Gabriel Ibn Treik p.30-32

[183] Soliman Nassim "History of Coptic Literature" p. 97

Three books were issued setting out the church rules by Pope Gabriel Ibn Turek:

First Book: 38 rules concerning the Church and its relationship with the congregation in religious and civil matters and the duties of bishops and priests towards their congregation. He banned monks from living in the cities; they had to go back to their monasteries. He also ordered that only one of the three liturgies is to be used: St. Basil, St. Gregory and St. Cyril. He also decided to hold the Meeting of the Holy Synod with the bishops twice a year; to make sure the meetings are not overloaded, he asked every bishop to come separately once a year to discuss issues specific to his diocese.

Second Book: Concerning the organisation of matters related to priesthood.

Third Book: Concerning issues related to inheritances.

It was said that this Pope also published other books, one of them called 'The Science of the Church', a copy of which is kept in the Vatican Library, in addition to many other books including interpretations and explanations.[184]

It happened on the third Sunday of the Great Lent in 1144 AD/860 AM that Pope Gabriel fell sick because of his strict ascetical fasts. All the churches were praying for his cure, then he saw St. Mary in a dream telling him, "The Lord has granted you more days for my sake," and he was healed.

---

[184] Kamel Saleh Nakhla, "Biography of Pope Gabriel Ibn Treik" p.35

It was also said that in his dream he saw a group of priests and monks carrying candles, censors and bibles saying: "We came to visit you now, but next year we will come back to take you with us," then he was healed.

After falling sick for a short while, Pope Gabriel Ibn Turek departed the following year (1145 AD/861 AM) after he completed his struggle. The funeral was held in St. Mercurius Abu Sefein Church, he was buried next to the church, and then his body was later transferred to St. Macarius Monastery.

Pope Michael II
71st Patriarch (1145-1146)[185]

He was a simple monk from St. Macarius Monastery characterised by his holiness and chastity. Although he was not a scholar or a reader of the books, he maintained his canon of monasticism without reading Arabic or Coptic. They cast lots after writing two other names along with his, and a fourth one for the Lord Jesus Christ The Good Shepherd. They put their names on the altar and prayed three Holy Liturgies for three consecutive days, then a little boy picked one paper with the name of Michael. Everyone was a witness to his good conduct and chastity.

In St. Mary's Hanging Church, Old Cairo, he was ordained

---

[185] Known as Michael Ibn Dinshitry; a Coptic word which means 'the big cell', one of St. Macarius cells (Evelyn White book), the English translation for "The History of the Patriarchs" Vol.3 Part1, p.26 in Arabic edition and p.59 in English edition

as a deacon, then a priest, and a hegumen on the third day, then he was ordained as a Pope in Alexandria. It is written in 'The History of the Patriarchs' that they hardly managed to teach him the Liturgy of St. Basil to pray on the day of his ordination.

His papacy was for short but blessed. No-one renounced the Lord Jesus Christ in his days. He ordained 8 bishops, among them a bishop for Shubra El Kheima, a bishop for Shubra Damanhour, a bishop for Meinet Beni Khasib, a bishop for Akhmim and a bishop for El Balyana.

His papacy lasted for 8 months and 4 days; three of these months he was in good health, then he fell sick for the other 5 months which he spent in St. Macarius Monastery.

Pope Youannis V
72nd Patriarch (1147-1166)

The duration of his papacy was around 19 years, he was a contemporary of the Fatimid Caliphs Al Hafez, Al Zafer, Al Fa'ez, and the last of the Fatimid Caliphs Al A'aded.

He was a monk from St. John the Short Monastery named Youannis Ibn Abi El Fateh. He was one of the three nominated for the papacy the previous time, but when they chose the paper it was Michael II's name. This time they all agreed on ordaining him as the 72nd Pope, so they brought him from the monastery to Cairo. He was ordained a priest then a hegumen in St. Mary's Hanging Church, Old Cairo.

Since the ordination of Pope Michael II, there was a monk in St. Macarius Monastery named Youannis Ibn Kadran who was fighting for this position. He tried again this time around by making a complaint to the government; the Caliph ordered for the issue to be referred to a committee consisting of some bishops, judges and noblemen. It is very important to record here the opinion the bishops proclaimed in the meeting:[186]

> "The bishops and priests who attended said that their Pope is the only one whom they wanted. They did not want to ordain this person. It has been the rule of Christians since the beginning, that whoever is ordained Pope should have the qualities of being religious, knowledgeable, kind, pure... they would often cuff him with chains and take him to be ordained lest he should flee to the inner wilderness. Although all are our fathers and our brethren, very few clergy have these qualities. You can find just one of these people in every 1000 monks. For example, one who lives in solitude, isolated from the whole world, living with beasts and wild animals, whose ferocious nature the Lord had tamed for them. The lions would come and sit under his feet without harming him. This is such a person whom the Christians should ordain as their Pope. If they cannot find him, then they should choose someone who is humble, religious, knowledgeable, and pure. It is not acceptable to ordain a Pope who is asking for this position."

The Caliph was a level-headed and just man, so he sent an order with one his guards to Alexandria, that the bishops,

---
[186] The History of the Patriarchs, vol.3, Part1, p.41

priests and elders should assemble and choose either Youannis Ibn Abi El Fateh or Youannis Ibn Kadran as Pope. It was an important meeting which included many bishops and members of the congregation from Alexandria and Cairo. The judge asked the attendees to choose and they all shouted the name of Youannis Ibn Abi El Fateh.

It is worth mentioning a story proving the holiness of Youannis Ibn Abi El Fateh. A Muslim person attending the meeting asked him, "What is your opinion about Youannis Ibn Kadran, do you think he deserves this position better than yourself?" He answered, "Yes he is better than myself and more educated," and this was a proof of his virtue.

He was ordained as the Pope in Alexandria, then he headed to Cairo where he was welcomed warmly by the congregation who escorted him to Abu Sefein Church which were his headquarters.

A proof of his kindness: He wanted to cheer Youannis Ibn Kadran up so he offered him to become the bishop of Samanoud, but he refused, and he kept moving between the monastery and the countryside until the day of his departure.

This period witnessed much national instability, with many riots and assassinations of ministers and Caliphs. Copts were also killed, some being sold as slaves at a very cheap price. Among the martyrs was a monk from St. Macarius Monastery named Shenouda. After arresting him, they asked him to convert to Islam and when he refused they killed him. They then tried to burn his body but it did not burn. The Christians took his body and buried him in Abi Serga Church, Old Cairo on 24th Bashans. Many churches were looted and burnt, among which was Al Hamra Church in Haret El Room and Al Zahry Church. In addition, the situation became worse after the invasion of the Crusaders under the leadership of Amalric, and the defeat of the Egyptians at Belbeis.[187]

Despite all the difficult circumstances, there was a righteous man named Sheikh Al Ass'ad Saleeb in the government offices who renovated Al Hamra Church and Al Zahry Church.

During the era of this Pope a rich, scholarly Jewish man named Abul Fakhr Ibn Azhar became Christian, having studied the Christian books thoroughly and learnt the Coptic Language. He used to debate with the Jews in Hebrew Language, and explain to the Christians in Coptic. This person suffered much from both the Muslims and the Jews. They tried to kill him several times, yet he kept firm in his Christian faith for 40 years until he departed.[188]

Also during his era an intruder exiled the Emperor of Ethiopia and proclaimed himself ruler. Pope Youannis reprimanded him; as a result the intruder sent a message to Egypt's minister Al Adel Ibn Silar asking him to ordain a Metropolitan for Ethiopia. He also sent a copy to the Pope claiming that the current Metropolitan had gone

---

[187] Stanley Lane-Poole, History of Egypt in the Middle Ages, p.177

[188] The History of the Patriarchs, vol.3, p.53

insane. When the minister asked the Pope to ordain another Metropolitan for Ethiopia, he answered: "In our tradition, we cannot strip someone of his priesthood rank; only if he departs can we appoint another one because priesthood is a heavenly, not an earthly, rank."

Minister Al Adel was furious and the Pope insisted on his refusal, so he imprisoned him. The Pope suffered a lot due to the poor conditions and rotten odour of the prison. He was kept in jail until minister Al Adel was assassinated, then he was released.[189]

Pope Youannis went through a great tribulation because of some words in the Holy Liturgy: In Samanoud there were some monks from the Beshbish cell (next to Al Mahalla) who were originally from St. Macarius Monastery. They added the word "the Life Giving" to the final confession in the Holy Liturgy as an adjective to the Body of Lord Christ - "This is the Life Giving Body." When the bishop of Samanoud - who was against this addition - informed the Pope, he called for a meeting with some bishops, who, after researching could not find anything wrong with this addition. However, the priests of St. Macarius monastery opposed the Pope. They escalated the matter, writing a complaint against the Pope to Minister Al Saleh Ibn Rezeik who was unjust and loved money. The minister held a meeting with the Pope and the monks and started discussing the dogma of Christianity. Then the Pope asked the minister "Who is Moses in your religion?" He answered "A prophet." Then he asked him, "And who is Christ?" The minister answered, "He is the

[189] The History of the Patriarchs, vol.3, Part1, p.53-54

Spirit of God and His Word." So the Pope asked him, "Could you say that the Spirit of God and His Word is a prophet?" He answered, "No." The Pope explained that the Spirit of God and His Word are more honourable and noble than the prophets because They are the Creator of everything.

The minister kept silent while the Pope and the monks were arguing. Then the Pope rebuked them and lifted up his metal cane as if to hit some of them, so they complained to the minister about the attitude of the Pope towards them. The minister dismissed the Pope who left telling the minister "As you made the little ones dare to rebel against us, may the Lord do the same with you." The minister ordered the Pope's arrest, then started gathering high taxes from the bishops of the regions of Lower Egypt.

In prison, the Pope was praying and fasting as usual. Once after he saw a dream he said to the prisoners with him, "Be strong and of good spirits, after few days the Lord will release us all." 14 days after his dream, this unjust minister was killed by one of the least of his attendants.[190]

Pope Youannis departed in peace on 4th Bashans 882 AM/29th April 1166 AD and was buried in Abu Sefein Church, Old Cairo with Pope Gabriel Ibn Turek. Their bodies were transferred to St. Macarius Monastery during the era of Pope Marcus Ibn Zar'a.

---

[190] The History of the Patriarchs, vol.3, Part 1, p.54-56

Pope Marcus III
73rd Patriarch (1166-1189)

He was a contemporary of the last of the Fatimid Caliphs Al'Aded and the end of the Fatimid rule in Egypt. He was also a contemporary of Salah El Din El Ayyoubi and the beginning of the Ayyubid rule. Similarly to the 62nd Patriarch, Pope Abram Ibn Zar'a, he was a noble Syrian layman known as Abi El Farag Ibn Abi Ass'ad. He had a good reputation among both Christians and Muslims. He was a pious and chaste person who practised much charity, living single and studying the church's books with depth and contemplation.

It was said that the late Pope Youannis V prophesied that he would be his successor. After the departure of Pope Youannis everyone agreed to ordain him and the Seat of St. Mark was empty for just one month and 14 days. His headquarters was at St. Mary's Hanging Church, Old Cairo.

This era was marked by chaos because of the struggle between the military and the ministers, as well as the invasions of the Crusaders. The minister of the Fatimid Caliph Al 'Aded was Talaa'e Ibn Rozeik, known as Al Malek Al Saleh. He was a strong man who killed any ministers trying to foment division in the country. Soon a disagreement took place between him and Caliph Al'Aded who killed his minister. Then he appointed his son Abu Shogaa Al Adel as minister, who was also killed after two years and was followed by Shawer. Then appeared a person named Dergham appeared on the scene. He was the leader of a Legion from Barqa,

Morocco. Dergham took over so Shawer fled to Syria in 1164 AD seeking help from Nour El Din the governor of Halab and Damascus to return him to his previous position in Egypt. At the same time minister Dergham sought help from Amalric the Latin King of Jerusalem. Nour El Din and Amalric invaded Egypt three times.[191]

Nour El Din and Amalric answered Shawer and Dergham's pleas. Nour El Din sent troops under the leadership of Assad El Din Shirkoh and his young nephew Salah El Din El Ayyoubi. The Crusades also came headed by Amarlic himself. There was a battle between Shirkoh's soldiers and the Egyptians for many days, where Shawer was able to kill his rival Dergham. Shawer ordered his soldiers to process through the streets showing his head to everyone in celebration. He was sure that he would be the minister; but soon Shawer disagreed with Shirkoh and refused to pay one third of the expenses of the invasion which they had agreed upon earlier, and he also refused to pay the levy which he had promised. Shirkoh went back to Syria after witnessing the chaos prevalent in Egypt, and together with Nour El Din he started preparing for the next campaign to invade Egypt.[192]

The invasion of Egypt took place in 1166 AD headed by Shirkoh and his nephew Salah El Din El Ayyoubi at the

---

[191] Dr. Ali Ibrahim Hasan, "Egypt in the Middle Ages", p. 250-251; Dr. Gamal El Din Serour, "Fatimid Country in Egypt", p.127-129

[192] Dr. Ali Ibrahim Hasan, "Egypt in the Middle Ages", p. 250-251; Dr. Gamal El Din Serour, "Fatimid Country in Egypt", p.127-129

The Fatimid Rule (972-1171)

same time as the Crusaders. Both armies walked parallel to the River Nile until they reached Cairo. Shawer and the Egyptians united with the Crusaders who camped close to Al Fustat, while Shirkoh camped in Giza as he had some soldiers who were already heading to Upper Egypt. So the Crusaders and the Cairenes followed him and the two groups met at Al Babin (a county approximately 10 miles south of El Minya). A fierce battle took place where Shirkoh won victory. Wisely, he decided not to go through the desert to invade Cairo, but rather headed to Alexandria and overtook it very easily. He appointed his nephew Salah El Din as its governor, while he went back to Upper Egypt to collect money from the residents.

As for the Crusaders and the Cairenes, they went back to Cairo after their defeat in Al Babin, then headed to Alexandria and besieged it from the land, while the Crusaders sieged from the sea. As Salah Al Din did not have enough soldiers to raise the siege, Shirkoh came to help him. Soon, the Crusaders and the Cairenes sent messengers for reconciliation; Salah Al Din agreed on condition the Crusaders should depart Egypt and go back to Damascus. Yet, not all of the Crusade troops departed Cairo as had been agreed with Shirkoh. Rather they signed an agreement with Shawer to have their own garrison; they also agreed for the Crusaders to receive 100,000 denarii every year from Cairo's income.

Shawer believed that after the return of Shirkoh and the Crusaders to Damascus his position in Cairo would be secure. Yet soon Shirkoh invaded Egypt for the third time in 1168 AD; Nour El Din realised that the Crusaders had launched a new invasion on Egypt with even more troops, thus breaking their previous promise to the Cairo. This time, Shawer allied himself with the forces of Nour El Din, not with the Crusaders like last time. When the Crusaders reached Al Fustat, Shawer ordered it to be burnt to prevent them from proceeding further. They poured a 20,000 barrels of petrol and used 10,000 torches to ignite it. This huge fire lasted for 54 days, and of course the citizens, mostly Christians, fled. Only six churches in the Babylon Fort were saved from this fire including St. Mary's Hanging Church in Old Cairo.[193]

The citizens hurried to Cairo to face the Crusader army and defeated them. Shirkoh entered Cairo as a victorious warrior, and was highly honoured by Fatimid Khalif Al'Aded, considering him to be the one who saved them from the rule of the Crusaders.

Despite the unity between Shawer and Shirkoh in facing the Crusaders, Shirkoh knew that he had to get rid of Shawer in order to rule Egypt; he arrested him and ordered Salah El Din to kill him, thus he became the minister for around two months after which he died. Salah El Din succeeded Shirkoh and the fall of the Fatimid rule in Egypt commenced as the Sunni Nour El Din began making moves to end the Shia Fatimid rule.[194]

Salah El Din started lobbying people to attract them to

---

[193] Aziz S. Atiya, History of Eastern Christianity, p.93, 94

[194] Dr. Ali Ibrahim Hasan, "Egypt in the Middle Ages", p.252

The Fatimid Rule (972-1171)

his regime. Al 'Aded's authority thus became weaker, so Al'Aded's entourage tried to remove Salah El Din. They communicated with the Crusaders to come and kill him, and there was a battle between the Caliph's soldiers and Salah El Din's which ended with the latter's victory. At the same time, a Crusader army came to Damietta assisted by a fleet in 1169 AD and besieged the city. They were forced to depart back to their country after a short while, and so they failed in invading Damietta and taking over Egypt.[195]

Salah El Din's victory made him more secure in his position and he started concentrating on completely destroying the Shia rule in Egypt. They began to mention the name of the Abbasid Caliph instead of Al'Aded's name in the Friday sermons in mosques. At that time Al'Aded was sick and he did not know about this change; the Shia Fatimid rule ended with his death in 1171 AD.[196]

It is worth mentioning that Salah El Din started his era opposed to the Christians as we will explain later; yet this attitude did not last long. Because of the prayers of Pope Marcus III, the Lord softened his heart and he appointed Christians in his government departments, gaining higher positions than before.[197] Pope Marcus III departed on 1st January 1189 AD.

---

[195] Dr. Gamal El Din Serour, "The Fatimid Country in Egypt" p.134-136
[196] Dr. Gamal El Din Serour, "The Fatimid Country in Egypt" p.134-136
[197] The History of the Patriarchs vol. 3 part 2, p. 97

The Copts During the Fatimid Administration[198]

Many Christians held high positions in government departments during the Fatimid era, mostly financial positions which they dominated. They were characterised by issuing very accurate accounts which nobody else was able to achieve. By that time they had mastered the Arabic language and issued many publications showcasing their great knowledge and eloquence. They also translated many Greek and Coptic books into Arabic. They were highly honoured by the government and given very high positions and titles such as: the President, the gift of God, the great, the honourable, the sheikh, crown of the country, the honour of the country, etc.

Pedant Serrour Al Galal

He worked as a guarantor during the era of Caliph Mostanser. He was very rich, charitable, knowledgeable and an honest person. He thus found favour in the eyes of the Caliph; he never rejected a plea from Serrour. It is also mentioned that he was very humble, generous, polite, serving both Christians and Muslims, and so he was beloved by everyone.

Sheikh Al Said Abul Fakhr

He was known as Ibn Sa'ed and was responsible for the Human Resources Department during the reign of Al Hafez (1130-1149 AD), then he was promoted as the President of the Department. When he departed, his son Sheikh Al

---

[198] Yacoub Saleh Nakhla Rofeilah, "History of the Coptic Nation", p. 142, 163-168

Said Shedid Al Malek was appointed to his father's initial position; he also had another son named Al Said Ibn Al Barakat.

Sheikh Al Wagih Abul Hasan Al Ammah

He was scribe for the biographies of Khalif Al Hafez.

Al Ass'ad Abul Kheir Gerga Ibn Abi Wahab

He was known as Ibn Al Miqat: he was one of the nobles and one of the richest people during the era of Caliph Al'Aded (1160-1171 AD) the last of the Fatimid Caliphs. Minister Shawer claimed that he was secretly conspiring with the Crusaders, so he arrested him and kept torturing him until he passed away. He was a descendant of a famous family, known later as the Al Nashw family; one of them was Aboul Fetouh Ibn Al Miqat who was the Army Commander during the era of Al Malek Al Adel Al Ayyoubi.

Mrs. Terfa

She was a very rich honourable lady in Old Cairo known for her generosity and charitable deeds. She built a Church for St. Abu Noufer and a convent for nuns on top of the Church. She transcribed many books and manuscripts as endowments for the convent.

Abul Yemen Youssef Makraw Ibn Zanbour

He was known as The Secretary of Trustees, he was the Caliph's treasurer. He was the one who built St. Abu Sefein

Monastery in Tamuh overlooking the River Nile south of Giza. He decorated it with beautiful wide gardens so it was considered one of the best places for recreation. Even minister Al Afdal, the son of Badr Al Gamaly, used to go there for relaxation. Abul Yemen was a descendant of a noble rich charitable family; its last member was Ibn Al Qasis Ibn Zanbour who converted to Islam during the Mamluk era and changed his name to Alam Eldin.

Abu Saad Mansour Ibn Abi Al Yaman

He was an erudite scribe and a courageous hero. He was the minister during the era of Caliph Al Mostanser. He resigned after finding himself in a critical situation; he was asked by the Turkish soldiers to give them their salaries while the government treasury was empty.

Sheikh Safi Eldawla Ibn Abi Yaser Ibn Elwan the scribe

He built a church for St. Agia Sophia close to the Giza Pyramids, which was later demolished. Most probably he was a Melkite from the Roman Church.

Sheikh Abul Fadel known as Ibn Al Osqof

He was the scribe of Al Afdal, son of Badr Al Gamaly.

Pedant Zowein

He lived during the reign of Caliph Al Hafez.

Abul Tayyeb

He was the scribe of Naser Al Dawla the Turkish leader during the era of Caliph Al Mostanser. During his time the followers of Naser Al Dawla were causing havoc in Lower Egypt, attacking and looting the monasteries; they also arrested Pope Christodoulos while he was visiting one of the monasteries. They asked the Christians to pay a large ransom to release him, but Abul Tayyeb succeeded in releasing him.

Sheikh Al Ahzam

He was responsible for auditing finances at the clerk's office. Whoever occupied this position had the authority to appoint or dismiss employees.

Abul Barakat Ibn Abi El Layth

He was the head of the Parliament. Some people envied him so they complained to the Khalif that he was stealing the country's money, as well as favouring his relatives in promoting them to high positions. The Caliph ignored their complaint as he knew it was untrue.

Abul Melig known as Mamati

He lived during the era of Al Mostanser and minister Al Gamaly. He was a rich man known for his charitable deeds to both Christians and Muslims, especially during periods of inflation and famine. He was the grandfather of Asaad Ibn Al Mohazab Ibn Zachariah who converted to Islam during the era of Al 'Aded and minister Shirkoh.

Many others were given honourable titles such as: Sheikh Al Akram Abi Al Fada'el Ibn Abi Said, Abu Ghaleb Ibn Abil Makarem Al Belbisy, Sheikh Abu Zikry Al Sirfy, Sheikh Abil Barakat Ibn Abi Said Hilan the great scribe, Sheikh Ibn Amin Al Malek Ibn Al Mohazzab, Sheikh Abil Yaman Albazaz, Sheikh Al Mohazzab Abi Isaac Ibrahim Ibn Abi Sahel Al Fayyoumy known as Al Zaqzouq, Fakhr Al Dawla Abul Makarem Ibn Al Fateh the Alexandrian etc. and many others who were very honourable and performed many good deeds for the country, the churches and the monasteries.

One of the honourable Copts during the era of Al A'ded was Al Asaad Saleeb Ibn Mikhail, known as the Son of the Hegumen. He was a respectable scholar and scientist. When minister Shawer burnt Al Fustat, Al Asaad renovated the Church of St. Mina there and established a school and a scientific club, which became a meeting centre for the professors of science and literature. There is a handwritten epistle by him about the Mysteries of the Church kept in Leningrad Library in Russia.[199]

Although the Christians enjoyed a peaceful time during the era of the Fatimid and were held many high positions, many of them converted to Islam. Among them was Sheikh Abul Nagah Ibn Al Raheb, who kept acquiring high positions until he became the head of most of the government departments, persecuting the Christians with all his might. He doubled their levy and bullied all the Christian heads of department. They complained about him to the Caliph, who, after investigating the issue, ordered him to be imprisoned

---

[199] Ramzy Tadros, Coptic Encyclopaedia, p. 17

and beaten with shoes until his death. He also took all of his numerous possessions.[200]

There were two Coptic Christians in the 12th Century whom Yacoub Nakhla Rofaila[201] called 'the reformers', whereas priest Manasseh Al Qummus[202] referred to them as 'the innovators'. Here is a brief summary about them and their views.

Priest Yaser Ibn Al Qastal

He was a monk who was well-acquainted with the situation of the Copts. He believed that they needed to stop practising some foreign customs. He insisted on the right of the fiancée to see his bride before marriage, and rejected of forced, arranged marriages. He focused on these issues because of the many marital problems in his day. All of these foreign customs led to problems with inheritance and polygamy.

An infamously bad custom that the Christians started to practise since the Arab invasion was shaving the head bald and circumcision, to the extent that they postponed baptism if the child is not circumcised! He explained to them that circumcision was not a religious rule, but just a custom. There was nothing wrong with this, but the clergymen objected claiming that Ibn Al Qastal was spreading a fad. He issued many letters concerning this issue, but they insisted on their opinion. Then they excommunicated him and dismissed him from his monastery which was located in Al

---

[200] Yacoub Nakhla Rofeilah, "History of the Coptic Nation", p.66
[201] Yacoub Nakhla Rofaila "History of the Coptic Nation"
[202] Manasseh Al Qummus "History of the Coptic Church"

Adaweya, between Old Cairo and Turah. This monastery was luxurious; many of Coptic noblemen used to go there. It was surrounded by a beautiful garden established by Ibn Al Qastal's own money. After they dismissed him, the Pope laid his hands on the garden; priest Yaser lived in grief and poverty for a little while and then departed. The Pope did not enjoy the garden for long, as Prince Gabriel son of Caliph Al Hafez (1130-1149 AD) seized and expanded it. He then turned it into a permanent retreat for the Fatimid Caliphs, instead of just visiting for the day and returning back.

After the fall of the Fatimids, Taftakin, Salah El Din El Ayyoubi's brother, seized it and added the surrounding gardens and all the area known as Al Adaweya and the seacoast. The Copts had owned this area; there was also a church there called 'The Church of Sudan' which he destroyed.

One of the exploits of this priest: because he was so educated he succeeded in convincing a Jewish nobleman named Al Fakhr Ibn Zaher to convert to Christianity, after many discussions and arguments. This Jew was both fanatical and erudite. After becoming a Christian he joined the Coptic Church, mastered the Coptic Language and served as a deacon in Haret Zeweila Church until his departure.

Marcos Ibn Al Qonbur

He lived after the era of Ibn Al Qastal and was also very well educated, mastering both the Arabic, Coptic and Greek languages. He translated some books from Greek to Arabic. It was said that he issued some books opposed to the

Church teachings. Before he issued those books, the Bishop of Damietta ordained him as a priest in one of the churches in Upper Egypt. Then the bishops and laymen asked Pope Youannis V to excommunicate him. The Pope tried to give him a chance to change his mind, he knew that the priest had left his wife and became a monk as he desired to become a bishop. Hence, the Pope was sure of his bad intentions, so he excommunicated him and prevented him from entering the church. He did not really care and kept promoting his ideas, which attracted many others.

When Pope Ibn Zar'a was ordained, the bishops and elders of Upper Egypt asked him to act quickly to save the church because of the troublesome teachings which Ibn Al Qonbur was spreading. When the Pope sent messengers to advise him of this. he acted as if he had repented and confessed his wrongdoing. The Pope therefore waived his excommunication and sent him back to his city. However, he returned to his old heresies, so the Pope held a meeting with 60 bishops who all agreed on excommunicating him and deposing him from the priesthood.

Marcos Ibn Al Qonbur appealed this to the government officials who attempted to interfere. The Pope and the bishops refused to bow to pressure, asking the Patriarch of Antioch lend them his support. He tried to reconcile them in vain, so Marcos joined the Roman church. The Roman church was very weak at the time, so he left it and came back to the Pope asking forgiveness. With this, his followers abandoned him and returned back to the mother church, and so he went back to the Roman church, but they refused to accept him. Thus, he spent the rest of his life as a vagante.[203]

---

[203] Menassah Al Qummus "History of the Coptic Church" First Edition, p.551

THE CRUSADERS
(1096-1292)

The year 1096 marked the beginning the Crusader wars in the Middle East, which ended in the year 1292, i.e. they lasted for two centuries. The beginning was when a European crusade from the Vatican, England, France and Germany attacked the Syrian coast. They succeeded in establishing four Crusader states: Jerusalem, Antioch, Tripoli and Al Raha. What also helped these Crusaders in establishing those states was the war between the Suni Seljuks in Iraq and the Shia Fatimids in Egypt, in addition to the divisions between the Islamic states in this area.

At that time a strong Islamic power aiming at uniting the Muslims under its leadership appeared in the area. It expanded its land by seizing it from the Crusaders, until they completely annhilated them. An example of this process in action is when Emad Eldin Zenki seized the Crusader state Al Raha and the Europeans failed to regain it. After the fall of Al Raha at the hands of the Muslims, the states of Jerusalem, Antioch and Tripoli served as the Crusaders' base for launching attacks.[204]

Egypt and The Crusaders

During the Crusaders' invasions of the Middle East (1096-1099) and the establishment of the Latin state of Jerusalem, the Fatimids were the official rulers of Egypt, but the actual leaders were the ministers headed by Badr Al Gamaly, followed by his son Al Afdal Shahen Shah, then others as mentioned before.

It was naturally expected that the Muslim leaders would doubt the Copts' loyalty to them in the face of these Christian Crusaders coming to liberate the Holy Land. They did not know about the discordance in doctrine between the Egyptian Copts and the Western church, as a result of the Council of Chalcedon in 451 (concerning the nature of Christ, whether he has one or two natures). They thought that all Christians were the same. Thus, the Muslim leaders in Egypt watched the Copts closely and even increased their taxes. This was the attitude of the official leaders during this period of the Crusades.

The Crusades were the worst calamity for the Copts and the Eastern Christians; it was true that they never enjoyed rest during the Islamic eras, neither did they expect to be treated

---

[204] Dr. Aly Ibrahim Hasan, "Egypt in the Middle Ages" p. 258

equally with their Muslim neighbours. The Copts realised that they had to give up many material luxuries in order to preserve their spiritual heritage. Even before the Crusades, they had to adapt to living with under Islamic rule without losing their faith. The Muslim Caliphs honoured and trusted them greatly, they granted them high positions such as head of government departments, tax collectors, treasurers of the Caliph, etc.

The Crusades - as they were supposed to be the holy wars of the cross - made the Muslims the enemies of all Christians, whether they were Latin, Greek or Egyptian; thus a new era of persecution and torture of Christians started. On the other hand, it was a double calamity for the Eastern Christians; the Muslims persecuted them as mentioned before, and the Western Latins, considered the Eastern Christians - especially the Copts - as dissidents, heretics and infidels, even worse than the pagans because they followed the doctrine of One Nature of Christ.

During the reign of Al Amer Ibn Al Mosta'ly, the Fatimid Caliph (1101-1130 AD), the Crusaders tried to seize Egypt, but they failed. Infuriated that the Copts did not help them, they prevented the Copts from visiting the Holy Land.

A Coptic historian expressed his great pain and distress at this treatment, writing: "The grief of the Jacobites (Copts) was not less than the Muslims - who has the right to prevent the Copts from visiting Jerusalem? The Crusaders hate us, as if we had strayed from the true faith."[205]

---

[205] Jack Tager "Copts and Muslims" p. 162 from Rithodo "History of the

There is no doubt that the Crusades placed the Copts in a difficult situation. Ignorance and fanaticism led to some Muslims accusing some of the Copts of cooperating with the Crusaders and being their spies. It is very important here to record the witness of a Muslim historian in the modern age, Dr. Ahmad Zaki Pasha, who wrote an article in 'The Egyptian Scientific Gleaner' magazine in 1916, "The Jacobites [Copts] in Egypt spied on Salah El Din."[206]

Dr. Aly Ibrahim Hasan wrote, "In the middle ages the Copts were neutral, especially during the wars which took place between the Muslims and Crusaders. It was proven that they never helped either of the two parties."[207]

Salah Al Din and the Copts

Salah Al Din was a devout Muslim. He immediately dismissed the Copts from government positions as soon as he became the leader, once the situation had settled down in the country. He openly humiliated the Copts by imposing a special costume for them to wear, forbidding them from riding horses, which is a form of moral humiliation, in addition to high levies which forced them to sell their possessions to pay the levies. Many Copts gave their lands and their freedom over to the Arabs to protect themselves, others converted to Islam to save themselves. Some of them occupied high positions in the country, they only cared about keeping their jobs and positions. An example was a

Jacobite Popes of Alexandria"
[206] Jack Tager "Copts and Muslims" p. 163
[207] Dr. Aly Ibrahim Hasan, "Egypt in the Middle Ages", p.497

The Crusaders (1096-1292)

noble Coptic family in Assiut. The head of this family was named Zachariah Ibn Abi El Mallih Ibn Mamaty, who tried to waive the high taxes and the moral humiliation but in vain. He changed his first name and converted to Islam together with jos whole family; thus he kept his position as the head of Treasury and Defence and his son followed him in the same position. This man was a contemporary of the latter Fatimid Caliphs and Sultan Salah Al Din. He was a poet and an author; he died in Halab in 1209, and we have referred to him before.

In Alexandria, the Ayyubids decided to demolish St. Mark's Cathedral overlooking both harbours of Alexandria, claiming it was in a strategically significant location which the Crusaders could leverage if they were to attack Alexandria. The Copts tried to stop them by paying 2,000 denarii, yet they completely destroyed the Church.

Salah Al Din also sent troops to chastise the Christian Kingdom of Nubia and to destroy the strong Coptic congregation in Upper Egypt. In 1172 was the first Islamic invasion of the Christian Kingdom of Nubia, in which the old monastery of Simon in Aswan was destroyed and another monastery in the area of Ibrim. Many Copts were arrested as well as the bishop; they were jailed and then sold as slaves. The Ayyubids also destroyed the splendid Coptic city of Qaft, with all its houses and buildings; afterwards it just became a small poor village.

Salah Al Din's numerous victorious wars against the Crusaders ended with the fall of Jerusalem in 1187 AD. For this reason, the Ayyubids became more tolerant with the Copts. Sultan Salah Al Din granted them a monastery next to the Holy Sepulchre in Jerusalem, known as Al Sultan Monastery; it is the only Coptic monastery which does not bear the name of one of the saints.

Salah Al Din also allowed many Copts to go back to their high positions in the government departments. Others regained their possessions and treasures which they had lost. Salah Al Din also chose a Coptic person named Safi El Dawla Ibn Abi Al Maali, known as Ibn Sherki, to be his personal secretary.

We do not know exactly whether Salah Al Din's persecution of the Copts was out of hatred and fanaticism or just for political reasons. The prevalent atmosphere at the time was not at all sympathetic towards the Christians. The arrival of the Crusaders in the Middle East worsened the situation, to the extent that Nour El Din the ruler of Halab and Damascus wrote to the Abbassid Caliph, "The Muslims ruled for 500 years and never hurt the Christians, but now, after all those years, no Christians should remain in the Islamic Empire. he who would not convert to Islam should be killed."

But the Caliph was a devout Muslim knowledgeable in his religion, and so he replied to him: "You do not understand the words of the Prophet properly. God does not order us to kill him who has not commited a sin."[208]

---

[208] Jack Tager "Copts and Muslims" p. 163 from "History of Michael of Syria"

After seizing Jerusalem, Salah Al Din behaved moderately with the Christians of Jerusalem. The agreement made when taking over Jerusalem contained a clause stating that the European Christians would be taken as hostages of war, if they do not pay a war ransom. As for the Christian citizens of Jerusalem, they requested to pay a ransom in exchange for staying in their houses and Salah Al Din agreed. And so they were settled in the land and bought from the Europeans whatever they could not take back to their countries with them.[209]

It is worth mentioning that the famous Salah Al Din Citadel in Cairo was built by two Coptic engineers: Abu Mansour and Abu Mashkour.

Successors of Salah Al Din and the Copts

After the death of Salah Al Din, Egypt faced two dangerous Crusader invasions: one by Jean De Brienne and one by King Louis IX. Jean De Brienne landed on the shore of Damietta and occupied the city. The Muslims reacted against the Christians; they were wondering whether the Christians would welcome the Europeans like what the Armenian and Syrian Christians did outside Egypt? They were wondering what would happen if the Christians were to cooperate with them, as this would have very poor consequences for the Muslims. Moreover, there was a large number of Melkite Christians in Damietta. All these worries and thoughts were enough to create disturbances especially in Cairo.

---

[209] Jack Tager "Copts and Muslims" p. 164, 165 from "The Complete in History" for Ibn Al Atheer

All the citizens were frightened and shocked; they started to have doubts towards the Christians and many turned against them.

The Sultan gave his orders to conscript half of the citizens of Cairo and Egypt to fight the Crusaders; a tax was imposed on all the Christians living in Cairo, both rich and poor.[210] In this way, the government leveraged the state of panic prevailing over the country and filled its coffers which had already been depleted by the war.

It happened that while the soldiers of Cairo were on their way to Damietta they looted the churches. It seems as if this persecution was very harsh as the historians who wrote about the history of Ethiopia mentioned that Negus Lalibela announced in 1218 AD that 10,000 Copts had escaped to Ethiopia. There was no justification for this persecution as there was not a single Arabic document confirming that the Christians had helped the Crusaders. It was the mere presence of the Crusaders which was enough to make the Muslims doubt the Christians; this was the case in all the Middle Eastern countries where the Crusaders were present.[211]

As for the crusade by King Louis IX of France during the reign of King Al Saleh Ayyoub (1240-1249 AD), who was the husband of the Armenian Shagaret Al Dorr, the French were completely annhilated. Louis IX sent a letter to King Al Saleh which was full of insolence and arrogance, so

---

[210] Jack Tager "Copts and Muslims" p. 116, from "Al Antaky" p. 227

[211] Jack Tager "Copts and Muslims" p. 167-168

The Crusaders (1096-1292)

King Al Saleh replied with a letter in kind. This affected the circumstances of the Copts negatively; here is a story which took place in Damietta proving this.

While Louis was preparing to blockade Damietta, the Muslims mercilessly killed all the Christians there. The next day, the Crusaders found the city of Damietta empty, the armies of Louis IX were utterly defeated, even Louis was taken captive in Mansoura.

Some Crusaders were confused, afraid and started doubting their faith; so when asked to choose between converting to Islam or getting killed, they chose to convert without any hesitation.

THE POPES DURING THE AYYUBID ERA

Two Popes were contemporary to the Ayyubid reign (1171-1250 AD). Firstly, the 74th Patriarch, Pope Youannis VI (1189-1216 AD), the Papal seat remaining empty for 20 years after his reign, then the 75th Patriarch, Pope Kyrillos III, known as Ibn Luqluq (1235-1243 AD), the Papal seat again empty after him for 7 and a half years until the end of the Ayyubid rule.

Pope Youannis VI
74th Patriarch (1189-1216)

He was ordained as the Pope 35 days after the departure of Pope Marcos Ibn Zar'aa. His name as a layman was Abul

Magd Ibn Abu Ghaleb Ibn Soros. Hailing from a rich family, he was a merchant who had many shops in Egypt, as well as a sugar factory, mills and other possessions.

The book 'The History of the Patriarchs' mentions a lot about his piety: "He was a celibate, erudite, perfect in body and stature, jovial, polite and spoke gently... he never neglected any of the morning or night prayers of the hours, he loved everyone and hosted the strangers, visiting the sick and the imprisoned, and was kind and beneficent to everyone."

As the Muslims loved him very much, Judge Al Maridy and Al Reda his brother, the sons of Al Gabab, pleaded for his ordination. This was consistent with the conditions set by St. Paul in choosing a bishop, that he should have a good witness from those who are outside, i.e. the non believers. 'The History of the Patriarchs' wrote about the church during his era: "When Lord Jesus knew that this father loved Him, He handed him His sheep to pastor them. He did so with purity of his heart, and by the gentleness of his hands he guided them. The church was safe during his days and the people lived happily." His ordination was during the era of Sultan Salah Al Din El Ayyubi.

During the era of this Pope the Coptic Metropolitan of Ethiopia departed, so the Emperor asked the Pope to ordain another Metropolitan for Ethiopia. He also sent a valuable gift to the Sultan of Egypt with a letter asking for the Pope to ordain a Metropolitan for them. The Pope kept searching for someone suitable among the monks for three months, so that messengers of the Emperor became tired of waiting

The Crusaders (1096-1292)

for so long. This was during the reign of King Al Adel (1200-1218 AD). Finally, he decided to promote Kayeel the bishop of Fowah to metropolitan and send him to Ethiopia. The Crusaders had already exterminated all the citizens of Fowah, whether Christians or Muslims, so the bishop was residing in the monastery anyway.

The Pope thought that Bishop Kayeel had had enough experience during the years he spent as a bishop. Metropolitan Kylous (Kayeel) was heartily welcomed in Ethiopia. Even the Emperor received him a three days' walking distance outside the capital, and gave him many gifts. He had 10 priests as his disciples for service. The Ethiopians had great hopes in him as it was drought there, and indeed when this father prayed, it rained.

Four years later, and in the fifth year of his papacy, a golden sceptre was lost from the safe deposit of the Metropolitan, so he accused the head of the 10 priests of stealing it and ordered his slaves to hit him. They kept hitting the priest mercilessly in front of the Metropolitan, who kept asking them to hit him all the more fiercely until he died. The family of the killed priest tried to avenge the Metropolitan, so he fled carrying much treasure with him. Yet it was all taken from him by force during his long trip to Egypt, and so he arrived there with nothing.

When he met the Pope, he told him a different story. He told him that the Queen of Ethiopia kept pushing him until he ordained her brother Khiron as a bishop for the king's city. After his ordination, he started stirring the citizens up against the Coptic Metropolitan, and plotted to kill him. The Pope did not believe this story and made him live in Haret Zeweila Church in Cairo. He also sent a letter to the Ethiopian Emperor with a priest named Moses asking for the truth of this matter. The Emperor explained to the Pope in a letter that Metropolitan Kayeel was living a luxurious lifestyle, even building a lavish castle for himself to live in. Here we notice that the Pope did not rush into conclusions.

The Pope called for a meeting in the Hanging Church concerning Metropolitan Kayeel and he excommunicated Kayeel, stripping him of all his orders, after he confessed his misdeeds. Kayeel was standing before the members of the council wearing his clergy attire and after the decision to excommunicate him, they tore off his clothes. The Pope then ordained another Metropolitan for Ethiopia named Isaac who was a monk in St. Anthony's Monastery. His eldest brother was also a monk and the Pope ordained him priest and sent both of them to Ethiopia. Metropolitan Isaac served the Ethiopian Church with honesty. The Lord gave him grace in the eyes of the Ethiopians and they considered him a saint. He brought Coptic workers from Egypt to engrave the churches in Ethiopia with drawings. This Metropolitan served the Ethiopians for 40 years.

During the era of this Pope it happened that the wife of a priest from Al Bashmour died, so he married another woman. When the Pope dismissed him from his city he headed to Alexandria and served in its churches. When the Pope knew about it, he was very disappointed and rebuked the priests in Alexandria. He issued a decree stating that no church should accept any unknown priest to serve unless he had a written permission from his previous bishop.

Finally, this pure father departed after spending 27 years on the Papal throne. Both Copts and Muslims lamented his departure.

It is worth mentioning that, since the time of this Pope, the Coptic church stopped sending bishops to the five western cities because their citizens converted to Islam, after being severely tortured by the Melkite Byzantine kings then the Muslim rulers.

Pope Kyrillos III (Ibn Luqluq)
75th Patriarch (1235-1243)

After the departure of Pope Youannis VI, the papal seat was empty for around 20 years because of the circumstances surrounding the Crusader invasion, as well as the factions among the Copts trying to choose an appropriate person for the honourable papacy. Before his departure, Pope Youannis had prophesied concerning the long period without a Pope.

The author of 'The History of the Patriarchs' wrote about Pope Youannis: "One day before his departure he lost consciousness for around three hours. Then he opened his eyes and spoke to those around him, asking them about his disciple Mansour as he was sick. They told him that he had died, so he said to them, "Shroud and bury him for tomorrow I will join him." Then he lost consciousness for few seconds, after which he said: "There will be a great division among you in choosing my successor; the seat will remain without a Pope for a long time until Christ should bring someone from out of nowhere." He departed the next day."[212]

There were three nominees for the Patriarchate, each supported by a group of elders. Unfortunately, the means they used to achieve their goals were miles away from not only the church's laws, but even the basic principles of Christian piety! The three nominees were priest Boulos El Boshy, David Ibn Luqluq Al Fayyoumy and Archdeacon Abu Shaker Botrous, the superintendant of Abi Serga Church in Old Cairo (said to be the Hanging Church). The supporters of these three nominees did their best for the success of their man, fighting one another and resorting to worldly means for a long period of time, but in vain.

The group of Abu Shaker Botrous tried to achieve the papacy illegally by giving large amounts of money to the Treasury and the Sultan personally but they failed. As for priest Boulos El Boshy and David Ibn Luqluq, they kept working together in issuing religious books defending Christianity. Priest David Ibn Luqluq was trying to use any chance available to reach the Patriarchal seat, while priest Boulos El Boshy and Archdeacon Abu Shaker Botrous, seeing that the competition was contrary to Christian ethics, withdrew. Thus, priest David Ibn Luqluq Al Fayyoumy was the one nominated.

---

[212] The History of the Patriarchs, vol.3, part 1, p.122

Here, we need to pause and learn some background about monk priest David Ibn Luqluq Al Fayyoumy: During the 13th century there were many monasteries full of monks in Al Fayyoum. David joined one of them, probably St. Victor Monastery; monk Boulos Al Boshy was his colleague in the same monastery. David was ordained as a priest and served in a church in Al Fayyoum. Soon a dispute happened between him and the priests of that church. Some noble Muslims arrested him so that peace might prevail once more, but after a short while he was released because of the mediation of Abul Fettouh Ibn Nashi Al Khelafa. He was a senior Coptic nobleman known as Ibn Al Miqat. He hosted him in his own house in Cairo during the time of Pope Youannis VI. Since then, there was a strong relationship between monk David Ibn Luqluq and Nashi Al Khelafa Abul Fettouh. It seems as if monk David, rather than being a scholarly genius, had some teachings contrary to those of the church.

During this time, the Metropolitan of Ethiopia passed away, and so monk David tried to be ordained in that position. He offered 200 denarii to King Al Adel in order that he might instruct the Pope to ordain him. The king sent a messenger to the Pope with such an order, but the Pope apologised diplomatically, based on the fact that monk David was not suitable for this position due to his deviated faith as he was following the Roman Melkite doctrine. He also added that sending him to Ethiopia may cause many troubles; thus the king withdrew his order and the Pope ordained another monk as Metropolitan of Ethiopia. It seems that monk David shared with the Melkites in their doctrine, imitating them even in their attire.

The biggest supporter of monk David was Sheikh Abul Fettouh Ibn Nashi Al Khelafa, and those against monk David used to complain against Abul Fettouh to Sultan Al Kamel the son of King Al Adel. All of Abul Fetouh's attempts to ordain monk David failed, so he resorted to another means: he sent his messengers to the bishops of Lower Egypt and to the Bishop of Tanbady in Upper Egypt. He hosted 7 bishops very generously, and then asked then to nominate monk David as the Patriarch.

It happened one day that King Al Kamel left Cairo for Alexandria for a retreat. On his way, he passed through the diocese of Ibiar and saw the hermitage of a solitary monk. He stopped and spoke to him; the King complained to him about his illness. The monk prayed on some oil, and then said "Rub the sick part of your body with the oil and God will heal you." When the King did so, he was immediately healed and he offered something to the monk, and they became friends since then.[213]

In the face of the many controversies and arguments surrounding Ibn Luqluq, the King remembered the monk of Ibiar, and he said to the bishops who were asked for a patriarch, "I order you to ordain the monk of Ibiar as your Pope and I am pleased with this decision." Immediately he wrote a letter to the Governor of Al Gharbeyah and Judge Shams El Din to go to Ibiar and bring the monk from his hermitage to Cairo.

---

[213] The History of the Patriarchs, vol.3, part 1, p.123

When Nashi Al Khelafa Abul Fettouh heard about it, he colluded with Prince Fakhr El Din Osman Prime Minister of King Al Kamel to tell the Sultan that the monk of Ibiar said that he was "asking His Majesty not to bother him or take him out of his hermitage." They sent messengers taking him back to Ibiar after he had already reached Qalyoub.

A senior Coptic nobleman named Al Assaad Ibn Sadaqa heard about this. With holy zeal, he took some people and went to the Sultan, in order to resist Nashi Al Khelafa Abul Fettouh's plot to ordain monk David Ibn Luqluq saying to King Al Kamel: "He is using bribes to reach his aim, he paid a lot to King Al Adel to push the Pope to ordain him as a Metropolitan but failed. Are you permitting him to become Patriarch to spoil our religion, converting all the Copts in Egypt to Romans, thus releasing them the hands of Muslims?" Thus King Al Kamel sent a message to the Governor of Egypt saying: "If you allow Abul Fettouh and his followers to ordain a Patriarch without my orders I will hang you."[214]

Abul Fettouh tried one last time to ordain monk David. One day King Al Adel was going to Alexandria, so he met him and spoke to him about ordaining David. The King told him: "Ordain him as the Pope; go to Alexandria and do not linger." David actually prepared his clerical attire and went with the bishops and Abul Fettouh to the Hanging Church to be ordained. However, some people contacted the Governor of Egypt who immediately came to the Hanging

---

[214] Kamel Saleh Nakhla "Pope Kyrillos III" Al Syrian Monastery edition, p.15

Church with his soldiers and dispersed them. Monk David fled and the bishops went back to their dioceses. Since then, Nashi Al Khelafa Abul Fettouh never discussed the issue of ordaining monk David.[215]

David gave up about his ordination as the Pope, so he lived in St. Philothaous Monastery known as Al Nastur Monastery, which was a monastery close to Cairo supervised by one of his followers. A long time passed without a Pope; there were no bishops except for two bishops in Lower Egypt and two bishops in Upper Egypt. Many churches were without priests, to the extent that there was only one priest serving the Alexandria and Scetis wilderness. They ran out of the Myroun so most churches had to take the leftovers and put it into the baptismal font. Other churches in the villages had to use the oil of Ghalylaoun instead of the Myroun.

Finally, a monk named Emad agreed with monk David to give him 3,000 gold denarii. He would give this money to the Treasury Office to secure his ordination. This took place while King Al Kamel was in Alexandria and thus he agreed to ordain monk David in Alexandria away from those who were opposing him in Cairo. Finally, monk priest David was ordained in Alexandria as Pope Kyrillos III Ibn Luqluq by the laying of hands of the bishop of Ashmoun Tannah (Eastern Ashmoun) and bishop Marcos of Melig on 16th June 1235 outside the city in St. Shenouda Church. The ordination was completed on the next Sunday in the

---

[215] Kamel Saleh Nakhla "Pope Kyrillos III" Al Syrian Monastery edition, p.16-17

Church of the Saviour.[216]

One of Kyrillos III's many mistakes was resorting to simony in clergy ordinations, as he was supposed to pay 3,000 denarii to the Treasury Office but he did not have that amount. It was said that he never ordained a bishop, priest or deacon without taking money. He ordained a large number of bishops because at that time most of the dioceses were without bishops. It was said that he had ordained more than 40 bishops in one year, and a great number of priests and deacons.[217] His only excuse for those who objected to his simony was that he had to pay a large amount of money to the Sultan. Because of his attitude, most of his close friends such as Nashi Al Khelafa Abul Fettouh, his greatest supporter for his ordination as a Pope, turned against him; he was insulted and imprisoned numerous times because of his behaviour.

Some friction occurred because of a mosque adjacent to the church. The Imam of this mosque tried to annoy the Patriarch. They even broke into his cell and stole some silver utensils.

Pope Kyrillos III kept practising simony until people were fed up with this behaviour. Some of the elders gathered and headed to the Patriarchal residence to speak to the Pope about it. They said to him, "How long will you behave in such a manner, which is making us a worldwide laughing

---

[216] Kamel Saleh Nakhla "Pope Kyrillos III" Al Syrian Monastery edition, p.17, 18

[217] Kamel Saleh Nakhla "Pope Kyrillos III" Al Syrian Monastery edition, p.28, 29

stock?" He asked them, "Which deeds are hurting you?" They answered, "Taking money for ordination." He gave his usual excuse of giving money to the Sultan, so they said: "You should not have promised to give anything to the Sultan. You were not forced to become the Pope, you offered bribes to reach this position. You have spent 29 months now as a Pope and our church is facing destruction because of you." He answered, "On the contrary, I have done many good things for the church, it only had 2 bishops, now there are 50 and numerous priests." They said, "the bishops are also taking money for ordinations." He answered, "I do not agree, if I have known that a bishop was taking money for an ordination, I would have suspended him." They ended the meeting by an agreement that he would write a message to the bishops prohibiting them from taking money for ordinations.[218]

In order to collect more money, Pope Kyrillos III also made put the monasteries under the supervision of the Patriarchate, after it had been the responsibility of the bishops of the dioceses. He established a Coptic Diocese for Jerusalem and Syria and ordained Bishop Basilious to look after the Copts living there. He was the first Pope to ordain a Metropolitan for Jerusalem.

Due to the above mentioned situation and behaviour, several reforms were proposed, including maintaining the faith of the Copts and putting the simony to an end. However, the Pope just ignored them and never changed anything. They

[218] Kamel Saleh Nakhla "Pope Kyrillos III" Al Syrian Monastery edition, p.30, 31

asked him to call for a meeting of the Holy Synod. Fed up with the Pope's behaviour, 14 bishops, mostly from Lower Egypt came and met the Pope at Haret Zeweila Church in 3rd September 1238 AD. They signed some decisions and decided to excommunicate whoever disobeyed them; they are known as the 'Canons of Kyrillos Ibn Luqluq'.

The preface of these laws was about the ratification of the Orthodox faith represented in the first Three Ecumenical Councils in Nicaea, Constantinople and Ephesus, the Church fathers, the Apostolic Canons and the local councils. The laws were published in 4 books: the first book about the structure and management of the Patriarchate; the second book regulated the customs, rites and organisation of the Church; the third was about real estate and donations, and the fourth book dealt with doctrinal issues. These canons and books were written between 1238-1239 AD, and in 1240 AD a fifth book was added including what was agreed upon in the council of Zeweila, it was known as 'The Hanging Agreement'.

The bishops then headed back to their dioceses, yet Pope Kyrillos did not follow the rules for church management which he had agreed upon with the bishops in the council of Zeweila; so on 8th September 1240 AD they assembled in Salah El Din Citadel, with the attendance of Minister Moein El Din Ibn El Sheikh, the bishops, the elder monks and Christian noblemen and some Muslim personalities who attended with the Minister.

In the presence of Pope Kyrillos this council decided that the church should follow the same canons previously suggested in the council of Zeweila, in addition to the following rules:

a) Two erudite bishops should dwell in the Patriarchate, one being Hegumen Boulos El Boshy who was ordained as Bishop of Cairo; and the other was one of the erudite Bishops in Lower Egypt and they mentioned his name. The Pope would work with them concerning any church management issues.

b) Each church in Egypt, Cairo and Alexandria, should manage its own real estate.

c) To abridge the canons issued in 1238 and 1239 with the agreement of the Pope and the attending Bishops.

d) Concerning the monks serving in churches in the cities: whoever was there at the departure of Pope Youannis VI would continue his service, without giving Holy Communion to the ladies.

Towards the end of the era of Pope Kyrillos Ibn Luqluq some disputes occurred because of the mosque adjacent to The Hanging Church. The Muslims demolished the church's wall that was adjacent to the mosque; they used to go onto the roof of the Pope's cell to pray. Although the governor of Cairo struck and imprisoned a large number of them, yet they did not cease creating trouble.[219]

---

[219] Kamel Saleh Nakhla "Pope Kyrillos III" Al Syrian Monastery edition, p.125, 126

The Crusaders (1096-1292)

The honourable Bishop Boulos El Boshy of Cairo advised the Pope to have a spiritual retreat, live in solitude, look deeply at his behaviour, and have a break from dealing with people so that he might act wisely during the final days of his life. In this way, his good deeds would square with his great talents, as referred to by Abu Shaker Botrous, known as Ibn Al Raheb, in his book 'The History' saying: "He was a gifted man, with many talents, yet he loved collecting money through simony, that was why people rebelled against him."

Bishop Boulos El Boshy succeeded in convincing the Pope, so he lived in solitude in El Shame' Monastery in Giza until his departure on 10th March 1243 and was buried there. He was a contemporary of the following Ayyubid kings: Al Adel, Al Kamel, Al Saleh and Al Mo'azzam. One of his publications was the book of 'The Teacher and The Student'. When he departed the Sultan seized all his possessions and the Papal Seat was empty for 7 and a half years.

FAMOUS COPTS DURING THE AYYUBID ERA

The Ayyubid era lasted for 80 years (1171-1250 AD), during which many Copts were renowned for their high education. They occupied important positions in the government departments, which proves the good treatment of the Christians by the Ayyubids. We will mention some of their names, then we will speak in detail about other personalities:[220]

+ Sheikh Al Raeis Safi El Dawla Ibn Abul Ma'aly known as Ibn Sharafi was the Scribe of Sultan Salah El Din. The Sultan loved him very much and he served the Sultan until his departure.

+ Sheikh Nashi Al Khelafa Abul Fettouh, known as Ibn El Miqat, was the Army Commander during the reign of King Al Adel. As mentioned before, he played an important role in the ordination of Pope Kyrillos III.

+ Al Assaad Ibn Sadqa, the scribe of Dar El Toffah, was the leader of the group who resisted the ordination of Pope David Ibn Luqluq.

+ Sheikh Abul Said Ibn Andona who held a high position in the private entourage of King Al Adel.

+ Sheikh Al Theqa Gabriel was a great Coptic nobleman during the reign of the Ayyubids. He became known for renovating the churches that had been destroyed.

+ Sheikh Sharaf El Re'asa, the Army Scribe.

+ Sheikh Al Assaad Abul Farag Saleeb Ibn Michael, who was the head of King Al Saleh's Office.

+ Sheikh Al Sadeed Abul Fada'el, known as Ibn Sotome'ah, who was the Scribe of Prince Aly Ibn Ahmad E Kordy and

[220] Yacoub Nakhla Rofeila, "History of the Coptic Nation", p. 183, 184

his Treasurer. He renovated St. Abu Sefein Church in Old Cairo and made it the headquarters of the Patriarchate.

+ Sheikh Ibn Amin El Malek Ibn Al Mohazzab Abu Said Youhanna from Alexandria who was a great author and honourable poet.

+ Sheikh Al Makin Abul Barakat, known as Ibn Katamya.

+ Amin El Dawla Ibn Al Mossawaf who was the government Treasurer during Sultan Salah El Din's era.

+ Sheikh Abul Makarem Ibn Hanna, Sheikh Saniaat Al Malek Abul Farag Ibn Al Wazir, Sheikh Alam Al So'adaa Abul Yaman, and Sheikh Abul Farag; they were all from the family of Abul Yaman Ibn Zanbour who was very famous during the Fatimid era.

+ Sheikh Al Safy Boutros Ibn Mehanna.

+ Al Assaad Saleeb Ibn Michael, known as The Son of the Hegumen, who was an honourable scholar. As mentioned before, when Shawer burnt Old Cairo he renovated St. Mina's Church and built a school and a scientific club.

+ Abu Said Ibn Al Zayyat who was a rich Copt, Sheikh Yehia Ibn Hebat Allah known as Sniaat Al Khilafa, Sheikh Mustafa Al Malek Ibn Abi Youssef, Sheikh Alam Al Re'assa Ibn Al Sefr and Sheikh Fakhr Al Saad Ibn Zaytoun.

+ Sheikh Abul Makarem, who was a scribe. When his wife died, he resigned and became a monk in one of the monasteries, and then was ordained a bishop.[221]

+ Botrous Ibn Al Ta'ban the monk, known as the Senny Sheikh who was the teacher of El-Assal's children. He was a scribe, then resigned and became a monk. He resided in the monastery of the Hanging Church in Old Cairo until he departed at an old age (it seems that he was married, and after the departure of his wife he became a monk).

Here are some of the famous Coptic personalities in detail:

Awlaad El-Assal (Children of El-Assal)[222]

The three children of El Assal are famous figures in Coptic history and were the descendants of a noble Coptic family. Abi Beshr Youhanna the Scribe was the father of Aba Sahel Girgis, who was the father of Isaac Ibrahim, the father of Sheikh Al Aggall Fakhr El Dawla Abul Fada'el Assaad, who was the father of the three famous scientists, Awlaad El-Assal: Sheikh Al Safi Abul Fada'el Al Amgad, Sheikh Mo'taman Al Dawla Abu Isaac and Sheikh Abul Farag Hebat Allah. The most important one of these three was probably Sheikh Al Safi Abul Fada'el Al Amgad.

We actually do not have many sources for the lives of Awlaad El-Assal. All we know is that they studied in the

---

[221] Yacoub Nakhla Rofeila, "History of the Coptic Nation", p. 185

[222] Kamel Saleh Nakhla "Pope Kyrillos III" El Syrian Monastery Publication, p.109-117

various Coptic libraries, coming into contact with the great Coptic thinkers and clergymen of their time. Their honourable teacher was Al Sunni Abul Magd known as Sheikh Al Sunni Botrous Ibn Al Tho'ban after becoming a monk. He was considered one of the great characters of the 13th century; he was famous for being the parish priest of Abi Serga Church in Old Cairo. Awlaad El-Assal mastered the Arabic language and its grammar, in addition to the Coptic, Greek and Syrian languages.

Here, we will focus on the most famous one of the Awlaad El-Assal, Sheikh Al Safi Abul Fada'el Al Amgad:

The Copts used to resort to him for legal support and advice, including Pope Kyrillos III. The Council of the Citadel mentioned earlier delegated Sheikh Al Safi Ibn Al-Assal to collect and organise the canons, as he was appointed to record the minutes of the Council. He organised the canons, adjusting them to match the original Greek. He then added some canons that were needed at the time; these are now known as 'The Canons of Ibn El-Assal' (Al Magmoo' Al Safawi).

It was distributed to all dioceses to serve as their constitution in order to aid the resolution of any problems. This put to an end the conflicts taking place between the Copts, their bishops and the Pope.

Sheikh Al Safi Abul Fada'el published many books, of which we are aware of 14, but unfortunately we know nothing about his life and the date of his departure. Generally speaking,

Awlaad El-Assal concentrated on defending the Christian faith, the Coptic language and the Epact calculation.

As for Sheikh Mo'taman Al Dawla Abu Isaac Ibn El-Assal, he was became widowed and subsequently lived in complete asceticism and isolation. He became a disciple of the Coptic monk Botrous the solitary. He was ordained priest, and then hegumen. He lived in the Patriarchal headquarters as he was helping Pope Kyrillos III with his correspondence. He published around 10 books. One of them was about the Coptic language entitled, 'The Ladder and Pure Gold in the literature of Coptic Language'; it is a Coptic-Arabic dictionary.

The third son of Awlaad El-Assal was Sheikh Al Assaad Abul Farag Hebat Allah, he published 8 important books, among them the Holy Bible in Coptic, Syrian and Greek languages.

Bishop Boulos El Boshy of Cairo

He was a monk in one of the monasteries in Al Fayyoum and was a close colleague to monk David Ibn Luqluq (Pope Kyrillos III). He was the thinker of his time, combining piety and knowledge. According to the decisions of the Council of the Citadel concerning the behaviour of Pope Kyrillos III, after being ordained as Bishop of Cairo, he was appointed to dwell in the Patriarchal residence, together with another bishop from Lower Egypt in order to share in the management of the Patriarchate with Pope Kyrillos III.

Bishop Boulos El Boshy published many books, some of them were theological such as rational proofs concerning the incarnation. He also co-authored 'The Known Confession' with Pope Kyrillos III, and published a book known as 'The Teacher and the Student.'

Bishop Boulos was a genius in explaining the Holy Bible. He had a very valuable interpretation of the Book of Revelation; unfortunately, most of his writings are still in manuscript form, none being published until this day! It is worth mentioning that he was the one who convinced Pope Kyrillos III, after his disastrous mismangement of the Patriarchate, to live in solitude in order to settle down towards the end of his life. We know nothing about Bishop Boulos' departure.

Bishop Yousab of Foah

Before being ordained a bishop, he was the deputy abbot of St. John the Short's Monastery, known for his wisdom and problem solving skills. Renowned for his righteousness and great knowledge, he was ordained Bishop of Foah in 1225 AD. Some of his great achievements were his uprightness during the scandals of the era of Pope Kyrillos III, and his role in choosing his successor Pope Athanasius III. Bishop Yousab lived to an old age, yet we know nothing about his departure.

Girgis Ibn Al Amid

Known as Ibn Al Makeen, he was the scribe of the army of Al Mansoura and an honourable scholar. One of his most famous books was a two-part volume with his name as the title, dealing with the history of Al Tabary. However, his most important religious book was Al Hawy which provided answers to some of the objections against Christianity; he also explained some of the hard verses in the Holy Bible. He died in Damascus in 1272 AD.

Ma'any Abul Makarem Ibn Barakat

He was a Coptic scribe from Al Mahallah Al Kobra. He may have been of Syrian origin, becoming a Copt through marriage when his parents settled in Egypt. There was a large Syrian community in Al Mahallah Al Kobra and Sunbat who mixed with and married Copts. He lived to an old age, and he was the one who wrote the biography of the 73rd Patriarch, Pope Abraam Ibn Zar'a, and the 74th Patriarch, Pope Youannis. In 'The History of the Patriarchs' he recounted the wars of the Ayyubids in detail.

Botrous Abu Shaker Ibn Al Raheb

He was a deacon in The Hanging Church and Abi Serga. When the 74th Patriarch, Pope Youannis, departed he nominated himself to become Pope. His supporters utilised illegal means such as paying large sums of money to the Treasury. He was one of the three persons nominated to the papacy, together with monk David Ibn Luqluq and monk Boulos El Boshy. Despite the best efforts done of his honourable father Al Sunni Al Raheb Ibn Al Tho'ban, the parish priest of Abi Serga church, he did not succeed to fulfil his aim of achieving the papacy.

After failing to become the Pope, he concentrated on becoming an author, so he published an important book on the Divinity of Christ called 'Healing in Discovering the Mystery of the Divinity of Christ'. He also wrote an introduction on the Trinity and another book about the calculations of Epact with a preface in Coptic and Arabic languages, also a book called 'The Seven Malachite Councils' and many others.

Alam Al Re'asa Ibn Salem Qaysar

He was the scribe of Prince Alam El Din Qaysar. His most important publications were a book explaining the Book of Revelation, an introduction to the grammar of the Coptic language called 'Insight in the Coptic Language', and explanations of the Gospel of St. Matthew, the Book of Acts, St. Paul's Epistles and the Catholic Epistles. He also published a full translation of the four Gospels in Arabic.

Priest Peter of Sedment

He was one of the writers who enriched the Coptic library with many valuable publications. He was a monk at St. George Monastery in Sedment Mountain in Beni Sweif Governorate. He has 14 publications scattered between

Paris, the Vatican and the libraries of some monasteries. His most famous published work is 'The Truth of the Passions of the Master Christ', which is a great book examining the passion and crucifixion of Christ in detail. He also has another book called 'Spiritual Meditations'.

Al Makeen Samaan Ibn Kalil

He was a Coptic monk in St. John the Short's Monastery in the Scetis Wilderness. After serving in the army offices during the era of Al Nasser Salah El Din Youssef, he published a book entitled 'Retreat and Solitude'.

Bishop Youhanna Ne'mat Allah of Al Borollos

He published an article about the Lord Christ's resurrection and the resurrection of the body in 1218 AD, and he made a translation of the biography of martyr St. Demiana.

Bishop Michael Al Atriby of Melig known as Al Gamil

He was known as Michael Al Gamil of Melig in Menoufiah Governorate. He had many publications; the most famous among them was the Coptic Synaxarium, a book entitled 'The Spiritual Medicine', and many other letters.

Youhanna Ibn Zakareya Ibn Sebaa'

One of the important characters of the 13th century, his most important book was 'The Precious Gem in the Sciences of the Church'. Comprising 113 chapters, it was printed a long time ago, but was reprinted recently by the Franciscan monks in Cairo. Unfortunately, we know nothing about his life.

www.ingramcontent.com/pod-product-compliance
Lightning Source LLC
Chambersburg PA
CBHW032034150426
43194CB00006B/267